Murder and the Making of English CSI

MURDER

and the
Making of English CSI

IAN BURNEY

AND

NEIL PEMBERTON

Johns Hopkins University Press
Baltimore

© 2016 Johns Hopkins University Press
All rights reserved. Published 2016
Printed in the United States of America on acid-free paper

2   4   6   8   9   7   5   3   1

Johns Hopkins University Press
2715 North Charles Street
Baltimore, Maryland 21218-4363
www.press.jhu.edu

Library of Congress Cataloging-in-Publication Data

Names: Burney, Ian, author. | Pemberton, Neil, author.
Title: Murder and the making of English CSI / Ian Burney and
Neil Pemberton.
Description: Baltimore : Johns Hopkins University Press, 2016. | Includes
bibliographical references and index.
Identifiers: LCCN 2015041796| ISBN 9781421420400 (hardcover :
alk. paper) | ISBN 1421420406 (hardcover : alk. paper) | ISBN
9781421420417 (electronic) | ISBN 1421420414 (electronic)
Subjects: | MESH: Forensic Sciences—history—England. | Forensic
Sciences—methods—England. | Forensic Pathology—history—
England. | History, 20th Century—England. | Homicide—history—
England. | Mass Media—history—England.
Classification: LCC RA1051 | NLM W 611 FE5 | DDC 614/.10942—dc23
LC record available at http://lccn.loc.gov/2015041796

A catalog record for this book is available from the British Library.

Special discounts are available for bulk purchases of this book.
For more information, please contact Special Sales at 410-516-6936
or specialsales@press.jhu.edu.

Johns Hopkins University Press uses environmentally friendly book
materials, including recycled text paper that is composed of at least
30 percent post-consumer waste, whenever possible.

For Cailin, Rohin, and Janice

Contents

Murder and the Making of English CSI

Introduction

Though they may have never physically encountered one themselves, readers of this book will have an idea about what a crime scene looks like, what takes place within it, and why. This familiarity derives in large part from a seemingly inexhaustible fascination with the forensic investigation of crime that, on our television screens and in our newspapers, has made it almost impossible to be unaware of the revelatory possibilities of this world of latent traces. The practices that cluster around the crime scene and shape its evidentiary and symbolic meaning—collectively shorthanded as "crime scene investigation," or CSI—frame it as a place of wonderment, where transgressive secrets are revealed by investigators who identify and harvest hidden matter that promises to anchor a narrative reconstruction of the crimes that had occurred within it.

This process of revelation involves meticulous work and exacting levels of self-discipline on the part of its protagonists. Their physical discipline is linked to an understanding of the crime scene as a fragile space, one prone to contamination by unguarded activity within it and to inescapable forces of degradation that mitigate against an ideal of perfect and perpetual preservation. Thus, we appreciate a strict choreography of movement within crime scenes, in which gestural restraint minimizes disturbance and enables a regime of systematic observation and scrupulous recording designed to capture the exact positions of trace matter prior to their removal. This physical discipline has a recognized cognitive counterpart. Investigators patiently and dispassionately harvest the scene in a way that foreswears both preconception and emotionality: like other intrepid heroes of horror zones, they are unmoved by the often disturbing detritus left behind by acts of criminality, deploying routine and method as both shield and tool.

We are also primed to regard CSI as the opening act of a multistage drama, one that proceeds in an ordered fashion, first to forensic laboratories, in which crime scene objects are analyzed, and ultimately to the courtroom, where their evidentiary status is decided. This process depends on another layer of work that, though perhaps not so prominent in imaginative renderings of CSI, would on reflection be recognized as integral to its operation: the mundane protocols that underwrite what is known either as "continuity of evidence" or a "chain of custody," designed to secure scene objects, materially and bureaucratically, as they make their way along the various staging points of the investigative process.

If this is our shared understanding of contemporary CSI, where did it come from? This is the central question posed in this book. The search for an answer proceeds from the founding premise that the crime scene is an artifice, something that has been built. The objective of this study, accordingly, is to explore its origins, conditions of production, and historical development as a novel space of forensic interrogation. This is done with reference to one national context—England—and with respect to one crime—homicide. Our national focus stems from our professional identity as historians of modern England, and in particular of the history of medical and scientific knowledge-making practices. The rationale for focusing on homicide is more strategic: murder investigations, past and present, are the best documented of all forensic interventions, as they capture both professional and public attention and provide an intense and circumscribed stage for the performance and evaluation of forensic expertise.

Murder's capacity to distill and project historically specific conceptual and operational regimes of investigation, and the broader expectations that surround them, is of particular benefit to this project, given the paucity of scholarly work that has been devoted to twentieth-century forensic investigation. Historians have shed considerable light on the development and deployment of specific techniques—fingerprinting, anthropometry, and, most recently, DNA profiling[1]—but, with a few exceptions, they have not attempted to provide an integrated outline of forensic investigation as a system grounded in a network of institutions, concepts, and practices.[2] In the absence of such studies, the story of modern English forensic activity is dominated by practitioner accounts and by biographical studies of celebrated twentieth-century figures in the true crime genre.[3]

As a consequence, our understanding of twentieth-century English forensic practice is fragmented at best. In exploring this territory with the intent to bring (partial) illumination to a darkened landscape, murder investigations serve as "flash moments" casting bright light on discrete moments in this story. We have selected two such moments as anchoring points for our analysis, both iconic investigations, separated by roughly three decades, which bring into view distinct configurations of practice. The detailed rationale for selecting these investigations—the 1924 case of *R v. Mahon* and the 1953 case of *R v. Christie*—is best left to the substantive discussion that follows. The overall objective in devoting three chapters and the epilogue to capturing these moments in time and analyzing them, both on their own terms and in relationship to one another, is to produce a provisional map of a hitherto unknown forensic terrain and to demonstrate how this terrain was transformed through the conceptual, technical, and institutional processes charted in the four chapters that surround and contextualize these two moments of illumination.

Why is a history of CSI worth doing? There are two main (and related) answers. The first is that it opens up a window upon a past forensic world, one that generated and sustained the crime scene as an object of intense practitioner and public interest. The claim that crime scenes have a history is not in itself evident, for, in some sense, they have always been there: crimes, after all, have to occur somewhere. But it was only over the course of the last hundred years or so that the crime scene came to be understood as a new substantive entity—that is, as a distinct space, bounded conceptually and operationally by explicit rules of practice and recognized as such by forensic investigators and the broader public alike. This is a story worth telling on its own merits. But, in doing so, this text also engages in a history of the present. By directing critical attention to the historical construction and architecture of CSI, it invites reflection upon the forensic world we inhabit today.

From what we take to be the founding moment of our forensic present—the introduction of what was then called DNA fingerprinting in the mid-1980s—the practices and rationales of forensic investigation have tended to be read through genomic spectacles. Over the past three decades, a vast academic literature has developed around the forensics of DNA, some historically inflected but most driven by the disciplinary interests of sociologists of scientific knowledge and legal scholars. This literature has focused on two main questions. The first relates to what has become known as "the DNA wars"—that is, the debates and contestations over the reliability of DNA typing arising primarily from its early deployment in the Anglo-American courtroom. Covering debates ranging from probability theory and population genetics to the processes of standardizing crime scene and laboratory protocols and agreeing universal thresholds of tolerance for accepting DNA matches as courtroom evidence, this literature has made DNA profiling the most thoroughly conceptualized forensic technique in history.[4]

Though the much-heralded cessation of hostilities in the DNA wars is recognized by some as only partial and provisional, the gradual stabilization of genomic forensic profiling has generated a second line of scholarly analysis, one that, with varying degrees of conceptual self-reflexivity, take this victorious and unarguably powerful technique as a benchmark against which prior regimes of forensic truth making are judged.[5] This critique has thus far focused on the questionable evidence base for forensic identification sciences—the analysis of finger- and footprints; bite, tire, and tool marks; and bullet striations, for example. Long the mainstay of expert contributions to criminal investigation, these practices have come under sustained attack in the post-DNA era precisely because of their dissimilarities to the grounds upon which DNA claims to individuation are made. While DNA profiling adopts a probabilistic model of identity based on large data sets that also enable the calculation of random match probabilities, traditional identification sciences are now cast as "ancient" practices reliant on "unspecified, unsystematic 'experience' coupled with plausible-sounding arguments."[6]

The general effect of this kind of retrospective critical judgment is to generate a caricatured past that is then used as the basis for insisting upon the exceptionality of our forensic present, and it is this reading of the past that has dominated contemporary discussion. However, very recently, an alternative present-day use of the past has been emerging, in which history is being enrolled in a diametrically opposed manner—to serve as the ground for challenging the triumphalist account of forensic modernity. This revised version was prominent at a February 2015 meeting of forensic and legal practitioners at the Royal Society in London to discuss the future of forensic science in the UK and global context. The future was not painted brightly: the field was, in the conveners' words, "heading for a crisis on an international scale" and on a path "destined for disaster."[7] A detailed analysis of the reasons for this catastrophic vision lies beyond the scope of this study, but in broad terms for many of the delegates—who were almost exclusively drawn from nongenomic forensic fields—the DNA-based norms and expectations of what should count as useful and reliable forensic evidence had resulted in a dangerous narrowing of a prior world of "holistic" forensic activity. By narrowing the locus of forensic legitimacy to the laboratory and privileging evidence relevant to establishing individual identity over all other forms, DNA has, in the words of one set of participants, "submerged the holistic perspective in a single trace view of solving cases, based solely on identification, tending to 'squeeze others out.' "[8]

At the heart of this vision of an "unsqueezed" forensic holism sits the subject of this book—the crime scene laden with multiple traces. For its proponents, an embrace of the multilayered and dynamic crime scene serves as a means of escaping the constraints of the lab, and the profusion of different forms of trace evidence that it contains equally suggests a way to break free of the reductionist search for biomatter. In seeking to assert the centrality of this world of traces in space, moreover, history is explicitly enrolled as a strategy of legitimation: "Part of the solution to addressing the forensic science crisis," the University of Technology Sydney trace analyst Claude Roux and his coauthors suggest, "is to look back at the first part of the twentieth century in order to revisit and better understand how the fundamental principles of forensic science have been ignored since then and how these could be adapted in the twenty-first century." A more "general concept of 'trace,' " they argue, one found in the writings of forensic founding fathers, might serve as a means to "[re]define forensic science as a discipline."[9]

The forensic past, then, is currently organized around two polar stories, a dominant one in which the past stands as a primitive other to genomic-centered modernity, and another in which it serves as a resource for reimagining an enriched forensic landscape liberated from the normative shackles of that self-same modernity. Our account of the making of English CSI sits precisely at the intersection of these two uses of history. On the one hand, it challenges the simplistic characterization of prior forensic regimes as, in the words of one particularly trenchant assessment, founded upon "untested assumptions and semi-informed guesswork."[10] The crime scene emerged over the course of the first half of the twentieth century as a novel space of discipline enabling rigorous knowledge practices founded upon innovative processes, procedures, and protocols of evidence collection and management from which new ways of association, knowing and behaving, and institution building emerged. These were complex enterprises that cannot be summarily dismissed as relics of a forensic dark age from which we have been rescued by recent advances in forensic techniques, no matter how compelling or powerful these advances might be.

On the other hand, by providing a textured analysis of the historically contingent processes through which CSI and its pursuit of trace evidence emerged over the course of the previous century, this study serves as a reminder that the past is a messy place. If this world is going to be used as a proxy for a twenty-first-century rethinking of what forensic science could be, historians can encourage those who seek it to resist a nostalgic vision of "holism" lost and instead to recognize it as itself a product of past processes that are equally complex and contingent as those that have produced the two versions of forensic modernity that preoccupy the present-day forensic discourses of reform.[11]

At this point a few explanatory disclaimers are in order about the way this account is framed and what has been left out. First, an observation on terminology: it will not escape the reader's notice that the book's historical focus is consistently referred to as "CSI." This decision might seem odd, perhaps even inappropriate, encouraging a mode of reading that verges on historical anachronism. According to the *Oxford English Dictionary*—which added "crime scene investigation" as an entry only in its 2010 edition—CSI's etymological roots are shallow, extending only as far back as 1946.[12] Our use of this modern term, however, is deliberate and strategic. Though the actual historical actors did not designate the ensemble of techniques, practices, and concepts as such, they worked within, and upon, the complex terrain that is now claimed for CSI. This anchoring point of our modern forensic imagination, in other words, is the product of the historical work that is at the center of our study, and our use of the term "CSI" throughout is designed to serve as a reflexive tool for our readers, at once a description of what is coming into being and a constant reminder that our present-day construct is not the exclusive preserve of the present.

Second, the forensic pathologist is a significant actor in our analysis not merely in its two core murder investigations but as a continuous presence throughout. This book, however, does not attempt to provide an analysis of the development of forensic pathology that is symmetrical to its treatment of the crime scene. This is a history that deserves telling, but one that is not attempted here. Instead, we limit ourselves to a consideration of forensic pathology's relationship to an emergent and characteristically English model of CSI—specifically, how expertise in bodies and expertise in traces intertwined over the course of the period in question.

The relationship between bodies and traces in space is worth further consideration. In broad overview, this account explores two main strands of the emergence of CSI in twentieth-century England: first, developments in techniques and working practices of forensic pathological investigation and, second, developments in "crime scene" investigation driven by forensic science. It charts the shifting landscape of twentieth-century forensic homicide investigation in England by following the historical interplay between these two investigative paradigms, seeking to understand their developing relationship as they interacted over the course of the century at four principal sites: the crime scene, the mortuary, the laboratory, and the courtroom. Over the course of the century, the latter model of trace-oriented and team-driven investigation made inroads into the historically preeminent status of the pathologist, but this did not amount to a straightforward takeover. Instead, forensic pathology could draw on considerable resources to integrate and accommodate the methodological and organizational innovations associated with scene- and lab-based forensic science, both conceptually and practically. This is therefore not a linear story, in which a forensics of *bodies* was ultimately eclipsed by a forensics of *things*. Instead, the relationship is better characterized as a dynamic interplay between two sets of practices, personnel, and institutional locations, through which forensic pathology was ultimately resituated in a new and explicit regime of CSI.

A further caveat on what might be considered another omission is in order. The history of forensics as an applied science connects with a far broader historiography than simply that of the subject itself, and there are elements of our account that clearly map onto a number of thematic concerns—especially in the history of science and medicine. The pages that follow feature networks of fields and labs, regimes of expertise and objectivity, incommunicable knowledge, matter out of place, boundary objects, and spatial production.[13] Readers from different disciplinary positions will recognize the potential for a more explicit engagement with these, and no doubt other, well-established and productive analytical frameworks. But we have chosen not to do this for a number of reasons. One reason is that, though we seek to interest a variety of specialist audiences, this book is designed to be as ecumenical as possible, so that it might be appreciated across a range of readerships. Another is that, though it profits from the analytical insights offered by scholars who have probed the processes through which expert knowledge is generated, stabilized, and enacted, none has taken a determinant role in shaping the analysis presented here.

One final note of caution: the material presented in the following pages deals with troubling subject matter and features graphic images and descriptions of homicidal violence.[14] Though we have taken care in our choice of materials, and in their presentation, many are disturbing nonetheless. They are, however, essential for assembling a practice-centered account of homicide investigation, as the close examination of the full range of material gathered for forensic scrutiny elucidates the methodologies, processes, and variety of labor enacted at scenes of murder. It will also be evident that the cases selected as the anchor points of this historical narrative feature the brutalization of women by men. This selection reflects the historical record: in terms of violent homicide, men are disproportionately the perpetrators, and women are disproportionately the victims. This said, the crime scene, as a space that in some respects retains and reproduces gender identity, stereotypes, and knowledge, could be a prime candidate for a sophisticated analysis of gender relations.[15]

We have not attempted this here. Rather than focusing on crimes (and their various gendered, classed, racialized, and other cultural dimensions), this book is about changing forensics cultures and practices that developed to solve those crimes. The objective, then, is to present a history of CSI in twentieth-century England by placing forensic knowledge and practice at the heart of its analysis. This has entailed drawing on a diverse range of sources, from detective fiction to sensational newspaper stories, the curricula of detective schools and pocket guidebooks designed for police officers, legal and medical case studies, the contents of crime scene bags, laboratory protocols, autobiographical and biographical narratives, and the transcripts of murder trials, in order to trace the changing ways in which homicide investigations were operationalized and how investigators, reporters, and others, behaved at the crime scene. This history unfolds in seven chapters and an epilogue, which, broadly speaking, follow the story chronologically, beginning with the publication of a groundbreaking textbook laying out the principles and ideals of CSI at the turn of the century and ending with the crime scene inquiries carried out half a decade later at the site one of the most notorious homicide investigations in English history—Number 10 Rillington Place, "the House of Murder."

Let's start, then, at an Austrian beer garden, where an intemperate argument ended in a death that required scrupulous investigation. . . .

CHAPTER ONE

The Origins of Crime Scene Investigation

This account of the making of English CSI begins in an Austrian garrison town, where a clash between an inebriated civilian and an irritated dragoon ended in the former's violent death. The details of the confrontation are sketchy: the victim, drunk and swearing, entered the garden of a café, argued with the dragoon, and had his skull split with a blow from his antagonist's saber. The local investigating officer was summoned, and he swiftly confiscated the sabers of every soldier who had been granted leave from the barracks on the evening of the fatal attack. Microscopic examination found that none had any trace of blood but that one had a fragment of a fresh blade of grass, "hardly visible in spite of considerable enlargement under the microscope," attached to a tiny notch in its cutting edge.[1] This discovery led ultimately to the assailant's confession: following the affray, he had first cleaned his blade upon the wet grass and then wiped it with a cloth. In so doing, he had successfully removed all traces of blood, but the telltale fragment of grass had remained in the notch.

For the author of this tale of blood-free mayhem, the event was instructive on several grounds. First, it showed the need for expeditious investigation. The evidential value of the grass blade was dependent on it having been found in a fresh state, thereby fixing it, and the sabre blade to which it clung, within a defined temporal frame. Second, it underscored the importance of looking beyond obvious indicators of a criminal act and the expected places where these might be found: a search "should not be restricted to the search for a single object (as in this case traces of blood) but it ought to be extended to all the isolated or extraordinary peculiarities which the object may possess." Finally, it demonstrated that the contribution of scientific experts to resolving such crimes was dependent on the quality of instruction that they were given by the responsible investigating officer: "If in the above case the expert had received an order only to look for traces of blood upon the sabre, he would have fulfilled his task by merely giving a reply in the negative. But here he knew the case in detail and he was able at the first sight of the blade of grass to make up his mind as to how it came there and say that it was of the greatest importance."[2]

The source of this account of the evidential promise of obscure and ostensibly insignificant trace matter is the 1906 English translation of Hans Gross's *Criminal Investigation: A Practical Handbook*, first published in 1893. Gross was an Austrian criminal jurist and examining magistrate, and professor of criminal law at the Universities of Czernowitz (1897–1902), Prague (1902–5), and finally Graz (1905–15). At Graz he established the university's Institute of Criminology and founded the journal *Archiv für Kriminalanthropologie und Kriminalistik* (Archives for criminal anthropology and criminalistics). Gross's *Handbook* derived from his work as a professional crime fighter, which preceded his academic career. Having completed his law studies in 1870, he was appointed as an examining magistrate for Upper Styria. It was in this capacity that he accrued two decades of practical experience of engaging in the investigation of specific crimes and the pursuit of their perpetrators, experience that would form the basis of his monumental treatise on criminal investigation.[3]

Gross's *Handbook*, supplemented to a lesser extent by the work of the French criminalist Edmond Locard, will dominate this opening chapter. There are two principal reasons for starting in this way. First, Gross and Locard laid the conceptual cornerstones of modern crime scene investigation. This is not a novel insight: contemporary practitioner accounts of the rise of forensic science in general, and of scientific approaches to criminal investigation and policing in particular, routinely pay tribute to these "founding fathers."[4] Second, as will become evident in subsequent chapters, for the architects of English crime scene investigation, Gross and Locard occupied a privileged place: to the virtual exclusion of all others, it was this pair of theorists who were cited by those seeking to bring the rigors of CSI to bear on English forensic practice.

Gross's *Handbook* articulates a new set of tools, protocols, and behaviors that combine to transform the scene where a crime was committed into a new substantive entity—a "crime scene." This transformation is more than a matter of mere semantics. Over the course of nine hundred pages Gross lays out in unprecedented detail a set of interconnected disciplines that he considered essential for effective criminal investigation. The main features are

(1) the suspension of the scene in time and space, so that evidentiary objects and their physical context could be subjected to a sequential and differentiated set of practices, undisturbed by decay, degradation, or contamination; (2) its dispassionate, systematic excavation for material evidence—especially seemingly unimportant bio- and other physical trace matter; and (3) the protocol-driven processes through which crime scene objects retained their integrity as they passed through different hands and across different spaces—from scene to subsequent sites of analysis and ultimately to the courtroom.

Gross devolves responsibility for these actions upon a single actor: his eponymous *Untersuchungsrichter* (examining magistrate, or, following the English translations, investigating officer, hereafter IO). In doing so he develops a role that in many respects will be recognizable to a modern reader familiar with the broad visual and instrumental features of a crime scene. Yet this familiarity is worth probing for two reasons. First, close attention to the manner in which he assembles a specifically "Grossian" regime of CSI enables us to appreciate that crime scenes are constructs, not natural kinds, products of specific (and historically contingent) configurations of knowledge and practice. Second, there is a key feature of Gross's text that does not so easily map onto present-day expectations: the multilayered, synoptic role assigned to the IO as the enterprise's central character. Gross's description of this figure involves a strikingly self-reflexive account of the combined physical, physiological, and psychological considerations that underpin—and equally threaten to undermine—even the seemingly most simple act of crime scene perception.

We start with a systematic analysis of how Gross's text constructs the crime scene as a site of disciplined investigation and the IO as its equally disciplined interlocutor. Broadly following the sequence of the text, we begin with his reflections on the psychological and emotional determinants of successful crime scene investigation. We then turn to his discussion of the crime scene as a physical space—characterized by minute, evanescent trace evidence that required adherence to a set of gestural and bureaucratic protocols in order to be of significance. We review several exemplary traces—blood, hair, fiber—before focusing in some further detail on the evidentiary status of "dust." Dust enables us to introduce our second crucial figure, the French police scientist Edmond Locard, and to suggest linkages of fin de siècle CSI with cognate models of scientific trace hunting.

PREPARING THE INVESTIGATOR: GROSS AND THE PSYCHOPHYSIOLOGY OF PERCEPTION

The first line of Gross's *Handbook* makes its author's objective crystal clear:

> The aim of this book is to be as practical as possible. It is not a law book, though we confidently hope that it will be of the greatest interest to lawyers. It is not a work on medical jurisprudence, though we trust that medical men will find it useful and suggestive. It is a Manual of Instruction for all engaged in investigating crime, its aim being, not only to deal in detail with subjects coming directly within the province of a criminal investigator, but also to inform that official in what cases and in what manner specialists may or must be resorted to.[5]

Yet its sheer scale signals that this was no straightforward set of commonsense guidelines. For Gross, "practical" action, effectively executed, was anything but straightforward. An individual's most basic perceptual judgments were deeply mediated, and these levels of mediation, and their potential to mislead, needed to be systematically analyzed for effective criminal investigation to take place.

Still in the introduction, Gross begins to unpack this world of complex mediation. He starts with what seems like a secure and, in his day, increasingly commonplace opposition between the testimony of human witnesses and the testimony of physical things. Human testimony, even that of the most well-intentioned witness, is in his view "much over-rated," because it is subject to a myriad of distorting influences—the physical and emotional status of the witness or the physical conditions that frame an event, for example. He then, and again at first glance entirely conventionally, turns to the comparative value of material proof:

> The trace of a crime discovered and turned to good account, a correct sketch be it ever so simple, a microscopic slide, a deciphered correspondence, a photograph of a person or object, a tattooing, a restored piece of burnt paper, a careful survey, a thousand more material things are all examples of incorruptible, disinterested, and enduring testimony from which mistaken, inaccurate, and biased perceptions, as well as evil intention, perjury, and unlawful co-operation, are excluded.[6]

So far, so simple. But Gross's more challenging notion of the "practical"—into which the reader will soon be drawn—is signaled by the immediately preceding sentence: if psychology teaches us to be attentive to the sources of distortion in human testimony, he wrote, "so the other parts of the subject show us the value of facts, where they can be obtained, how they can be held fast and appraised—these things are just as important as to show what can be done with the facts when obtained."[7] In other words, the identification, retention and evaluation of *physical* evidence are acts of perception and cognition that equally require self-scrutiny to be effective. It is important to note at the outset, then, that Gross's text does not operate on a preestablished privileging of things over humans (though it does operationalize this as a legitimate hierarchy once properly justified). Instead, it is treated as the outcome of a way of seeing and acting that creates the conditions for things to speak for themselves.[8]

In the context of criminal investigation, the lynchpin of "incorruptible, disinterested, and enduring testimony" is the IO. It comes as no surprise, therefore, that the first part of the *Handbook* is entirely devoted to sketching out this crucial figure. His heroic general attributes (possession of "the vigour of youth, energy ever on the alert, robust health . . . liveliness and vigilance") are supplemented by a formidable intellectual capacity, an ability "to solve problems relating to every conceivable branch of human knowledge," and mastery of topics ranging from boiler explosions and account books to slang and ciphers.[9] In outlining these essential characteristics, Gross emphasizes their broad and practically engaged nature—anything and everything may be of use in his line of work, so from the moment of taking up the role the IO becomes a student of the world and everything in it. Importantly, this omnivorous attitude is an on-going matter of disposition enacted prior to any specific investigative engagement: "He who seeks to learn only when some notable crime turns up," Gross warns, "will have great difficulty in learning anything at all. His knowledge should be acquired beforehand by constant application in his ordinary life. Every day, nay every moment," he continues,

> he must be picking up something in touch with his work. Thus the zealous Investigating Officer will note on his walks the footprints found on the dust of the highway; he will observe the tracks of animals, of the wheels of carriages, the marks of pressure on the grass where someone has sat or lain down, or perhaps deposited a burden. He will examine little pieces of paper that have been thrown away, marks or injuries on trees, displaced stones, broken glass or pottery, doors and windows open or shut in an unusual

manner. Everything will afford an opportunity for drawing conclusions and explaining what must have previously taken place. [10]

By engaging in this routine observation and the causal inferences that ordinary phenomena suggest to the attentive observer, the IO trains for the moment when these background skills are called upon in the face of the extraordinary—the "crime scene."

In this discussion, the theme of "preparation" recurs. A mental preparation is accompanied by a physical and spatial one, through which the IO embeds himself within a known context from which information and resources, once required, can be readily called upon. Thus, in his everyday ramblings he will have, as ever-present companions, instruments (e.g., an ordnance survey map, a watch, a compass) enabling him to establish objective coordinates such as distance and travel time between fixed points. Indeed, Gross includes a named subsection on "orientation," in which he instructs the IO on methods for assembling a "base of operations"—including a team of subordinates and auxiliaries (from police officers and grave diggers to local medical men and university-based experts) on which he could draw with confidence in the event of an occurrence requiring investigation.

There are obvious practical dimensions to this preparatory attitude, but underneath it lies a more fundamental consideration: preparation aids the IO to be an effective observer by helping shield him from the vicissitudes of perceptual and cognitive error. In this way, Gross presents the translation of the place in which a crime occurred into a "crime scene" as dependent on, and interactive with, a *prior* set of labors undertaken by his IO. The scene and IO are coextensive products, called into being by the thoroughness of Gross's advice and dependent not merely on material requirements but their human correlatives as well.

Attention to this interplay between observer and observed, investigator and material trace, results in a collapsing in his text of the seemingly straightforward opposition mentioned above between the testimony of things and of human beings, an opposition that figures both in the writings of Gross's contemporaries and in modern histories of fin-de-siècle forensics. The point of departure for both is the significance attributed to research into the psychophysiology of perception from the mid-nineteenth century, initially in the German laboratories of investigators like Hermann von Helmholtz and Carl Ludwig and then by a second generation of researchers, most notably Hugo Münsterberg in the United States.[11] The core insight of this work—that the dynamics of memory, cognition, experience, and the like may lead even the most honest human witness to provide false testimony—had two linked results. First, it led to the recognition that everyone involved in the investigation and prosecution of crime needed to be aware of the causes and implications of witnesses' perceptual fallibility and to adjust their strategies for eliciting and interpreting witness statements accordingly. Second, commentators elevated material over human testimony, seeking out "mute witnesses" wherever possible to short-circuit the evident dangers of relying on the human alternative.

But, in developing his manual, Gross adds a complication to this simple reversal in the evidentiary hierarchy. Yes, the IO needed to be instructed in the vicissitudes of human testimony, and, yes, physical evidence was invaluable and often more reliable than its human counterpart. Yet making matter testify accurately was itself a complex task fraught with possibilities for error. This is because research into the contingencies of cognition and perception applied as much to the IO as it did to any other testifier. For the crime scene to speak in a secure language of material fact, its examiner needed to be prepared in advance to receive and appreciate its meaning. It is in this sense that the Grossian vision of CSI entails interdependent human and material work. The protocols of CSI that at first glance appear to merely secure the material objects at the scene (the careful delineation of a space of investigation, the physical restraint in approaching and handling objects in that space, the meticulous graphic recording of those objects in their spatial and temporal dimensions) at the same time serve to secure the IO as a reliable harvester of trace evidence.

This background work prepares the IO to confront, and conquer, what Gross identifies as "the most deadly enemy of all inquiries"—preconceived theories. These, Gross advises his reader, will be shown throughout his *Handbook* to be numerous in origin, astonishingly easy to take root, and exceptionally difficult to extirpate. As a rule, preconceived theories result from examining an issue "from a false point of view." This can happen, Gross explains, for physical reasons—objects can appear different from what they really are, for example, either by virtue of a faulty sensory apparatus (e.g., physical pressure on the eyeball) or by the conditions in which the perception took place. But there were more subtle, and dangerous, "moral" sources of error. By way of illustration Gross offers a hypothetical case in which an IO is informed of a case of arson in a distant locality:

Immediately in spite of one's self the scene is imagined; for example, one pictures the house, which one has never seen, as being on the left-hand side of the road. . . . In imagination the whole scene and its secondary details are presented, but everything is always placed on the left of the road; this idea ends by taking such a hold on the mind that one is convinced that the house is on the left, and all questions are asked as if one had seen the house in that position. But suppose the house to be really on the right of the road and that by chance the error is never rectified; suppose further that the situation of the house has some importance for the bringing out of the facts or in forming a theory of the crime, then this false idea may, in spite of its apparent insignificance, considerably confuse the investigation.[12]

At its root, Gross continues, this error of the imagination follows from a "psychical imperfection" inherent to humans, who at a general level are interpreters rather than recorders, interpreters who bring their own predispositions to bear on any given act of observation. They tend to complete stories, to fill in gaps with a bank of prestored data that supplement what is registered via direct experience.

There are several consequences to this, none more important than the ordinary observer's penchant for noticing, and prioritizing, that which appears striking and vivid:

It is only in conformity with human nature to stop the more willingly at what is more interesting than at what belongs to everyday life. We like to discover romantic features where they do not exist and we even prefer the recital of monstrosities and horrors to that of common every-day facts. . . . A hundred proofs, exemplified by what we read most, by what we listen to most willingly, by what sort of news spreads the fastest, show that the majority of men have received at birth a tendency to exaggeration.[13]

In itself, Gross observes, this is no great evil—indeed, it is the wellspring of the creative imagination. But the IO ought, by definition, to be a class apart: "In the profession of the criminal expert everything bearing the least trace of exaggeration must be removed in the most energetic and conscientious manner."[14] Here the IO's background habituation to noticing the ordinary comes into its own—he knows that what appears the most striking is not necessarily the most significant. But adhering to this attitude requires constant work: "The only remedy is to watch oneself most carefully, always work with reflection, and prune out everything having the least suspicion of exaggeration."[15] The IO's acts of perception, then, are subject to the same sources of error as those of any other witness. Information given to or unearthed by him is registered through his own perceptual apparatus and is thus subject to the very distortions that threaten any act of witnessing. As a necessary consequence, the objectivity of material traces is an outcome, rather than a prior condition, of the procedures Gross is delineating.

This outcome ultimately depends on the IO's "submission to severe discipline," one that that comes into its own at the crime scene.[16] It is to this novel space that we now turn. It is important to emphasize that in doing so our aim is to both describe the making of the crime scene and show how its constitutive elements (its gestures, sensibilities, and routines of investigation, recording, and preserving) reinforce Gross's characterization of the IO. The instructions he provides on the proper way of effecting CSI thus serve a double function: they can be considered generic (and often banal) homilies on the importance of methodical investigation, but the constant self-monitoring is also essential to the practice of CSI. Gross's engagement with the problems of perception, then, is a logical and operational prerequisite for the crime scene's epistemic status as a field of latent, objective material traces that can be utilized as such for the purposes of investigation. The crime scene as a space of hidden but objectively apprehensible traces is not merely the site for the deployment of a highly structured way of seeing but is in fact *produced* by it.

CSI: SUSPENDING SPACE AND TIME

Gross's preliminary strictures on the dynamics of perception, the mediations of the imagination, and the need for submission to forms of physical and mental rigor are all put into action in the subsequent sections of the *Handbook*. The first of these focuses on witness testimony. In it he provides a comprehensive outline of what the IO needs to consider when gathering and evaluating evidence based on human perception other than his own. But it is his next section, "Inspection of Localities," that most interests us, for it is here that Gross at once calls into being a new space—the crime scene—and aligns his earlier observations to it as a necessary precondition for its successful management.

There are several interlocking elements of Grossian CSI that this chapter will outline generally and then subject to further critical scrutiny. First, the crime scene is a space of record: the IO's report, Gross stipulates in the opening line of this discussion, "is a real touchstone."[17] Second, despite its often alarming elements (e.g., blood, corpses), the crime scene is a space of emotional and physical equilibrium. Third, it is a space of mental and physical restraint: mentally, it has no place for preconceptions as to what transpired within it, which of its material traces are significant, or what they might signify; physically, it demands suspension of any impulse to engage (and thus potentially disturb) that which appears to be of interest and value. As he develops these three virtues of CSI, they interlace to simultaneously construct a space of investigation and align its investigator to it, and in so doing call into play the preparations and self-understanding that have gone into the making of an effective IO.

The opening lines of the section "What to Do at the Scene of Offence" capture the essential relationship between investigative space and investigator affect: "On arrival at the scene of the crime certain things must be attended to which are common to all cases, be they of simple theft, robbery, murder, arson, or misdemeanour. The first duty is to preserve an absolute calm. With it everything is won, without it everything is compromised." This calm serves several functions. First, it enables the IO to efficiently activate his team of auxiliaries, thereby preserving a key feature of his prior orienting work:

> An Investigating Officer who fusses about, sets to work aimlessly, starts a plan only to drop it, asks everybody useless questions, and gives orders only to cancel them, makes a most painful impression on those engaged with him in the inquiry and destroys any confidence they may have had in his successful management. . . . But if the Investigating Officer shows perfect confidence with no trace of excitement, and acts as with a sure prevision of the results, everyone willingly submits to his orders and each does his very best and the result of the enquiry is assured.[18]

Calm also affords the IO with an initial opportunity for self-scrutiny. Echoing his earlier discussion of the tendency to project and fix an image of phenomena in advance, Gross warns that the very act of being called to the scene itself represents a possible layer of mediation: as soon as he is informed about a case,

> he immediately makes a mental picture of the case itself and all connected with it, in a definite form, with precise outlines; when travelling to the spot he bases upon this idea his conjectures as to how the offence has been commit-

ted, and builds, upon his mental picture of the spot, the plan of inquiry to be pursued. The idea may take root in his mind to such an extent that he cannot rid himself of it either in part or in whole even when the scene is actually displayed before his eyes.

Calm at the start of his physical engagement with the scene enables the IO to realign these preconceptions—or, in Gross's words, to "find his bearings."[19]

Having thus oriented himself, the IO is ready to shift from background to foreground work, but again this work is informed by his prior submission to Gross's strictures. His first task is to secure the crime scene by fixing it as a spatiotemporal entity: "The exclusion of everything happening after the moment when the crime was committed," he explains, "is a very special task for the Investigating Officer." This had several components that have since become CSI staples: marking off a perimeter zone to prevent unauthorized access and shielding "vestiges of the crime" within it from contact with forces that might degrade or contaminate them, for example.[20] In doing this the IO enacts his suspension of ordinary standards of distinguishing between, and reacting to, what seems noteworthy and what trivial:

> Everything may be of importance and nothing too small or insignificant to have a decisive bearing upon the case. The situation of an object an inch or two to left or right, to front or back, a little dust, a splash of dirt easy to efface, may all turn out to be of the first importance.[21]

This realization enforces a set of gestural disciplines that secures the crime scene as a space of latent meaning, meaning inherent, moreover, not merely in the things lying within it but, crucially, in their relationship to one another. The crime scene thus requires protection against the "natural impulse" of those who engage it, that is,

> to immediately touch any object of apparent significance, as e.g., an object left on the scene of the crime by the criminal. It is laid hold of and moved about, and only afterwards is it recognised that the object in itself signifies very little but that everything depends on its position—which can no longer be fixed.[22]

Gross illustrates this with an appropriately striking example, one that underscores his concern to contain the destabilizing effects of the emotive dynamics of perception and cognition. When confronted with a murder victim, he writes, the "involuntary impulse" is to seize the hands and search them for signs of a struggle (hair, torn clothing, etc.). But by thus indulging the desire to assemble narrative out of obviously compelling elements, the undisciplined investigator sacrifices a world of more subtle clues and thus projects himself into the crime scene not as its protector but as a prime source of its degradation and contamination.

By contrast, his properly prepared counterpart follows the investigator's "golden and inviolable rule": "*Never alter the position of, pick up, or even touch any object before it has been minutely described in the report.*"[23] This dictum draws attention to the critical importance of the crime scene report as a means of capturing a moment in time and space, a moment that, despite the IO's best efforts, can only ever be temporarily preserved. Gross lavishes elaborate (and tedious) detail on how to record in order to preserve and suggests a series of aids to this end. In the classic case of hair found clasped in a murder victim's lifeless hand, it was not enough "to state: 'hair found in the right hand of N. N.,' the situation of the hair must be expressly indicated, e.g., 'between the thumb and first finger,' or 'lying obliquely across the root of the first finger and the ball of the thumb.'" Providing a series of "intentionally primitive" illustrations for registering such relational details beyond the mere fact of presence (fig. 1.1), he laments that this approach was all too often ignored in practice:

> It is often irritating to see how the first constable who arrives or the doctor who first inspects the corpse, examines the hand of the dead person carelessly and imperfectly: they sometimes even wipe it or seize it briskly; they notice the hair perhaps if it is in tufts in the hands, but they most certainly miss isolated hair when they act in this manner.[24]

Elsewhere he furnishes more sophisticated instruction on how to capture the crime scene as a matter of visual record, insisting on conformity to a "technical formula" and the utilization of objective reference points secured instrumentally (by compass points, spirit level readings, plumb-line angles). Thus, for example, in sketching a room in which a murder had been committed, Gross instructs the IO as follows:

> The door should be taken as a starting point and the same direction followed as the hands of a clock, i.e., standing in the entrance and facing into the room, start from the left hand and go round the room towards the right hand; in this way one will be certain that nothing has been forgotten. First describe the

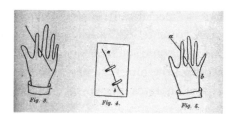

Figure 1.1. Sketching traces in space.
Hans Gross, *Criminal Investigation:
A Practical Handbook*, 1906, 196.

Figure 1.2. Sketching traces in space. Hans Gross,
Criminal Investigation: A Practical Handbook, 1906, 468.

Figure 1.3. Securing crime scene objects. Hans Gross,
Criminal Investigation: A Practical Handbook, 1906, 579.

Figure 1.4. Securing crime scene objects. Hans Gross,
Criminal Investigation: A Practical Handbook, 1906, 590.

size, shape, height, and other peculiarities of the space in question. Then go
from the entrance towards the nearest left corner, then the left-hand wall,
then the wall facing the entrance, then the right-hand wall, then the remainder of the wall to the right of the doorway, and finally the objects in the middle
of the room. . . . Next describe any alterations in the state of the moveables in
the room consequent upon the crime in question, damage done by blows,
bloodstains, changes in the situation or position of objects, damage to win-
dows, doors, etc.; and finally a minute description of the subject-matter of
the crime (e.g., a broken safe, a dead body, etc.) with all the particulars necessary to a detailed description.[25]

A later chapter on drawing (as one of the IO's "special crafts") recommends a further technique for securing objective "orientation," advising the re-plotting of the physical space of the crime scene onto squared paper and the reproduction in the paper's squared units of "everything that may be seen in nature in the large squares" (fig. 1.2). Gross illustrates this with the following explanation:

> Suppose that a certain number of drops of blood which have dried upon a plank have to be depicted. The large sketch represents the actual subject-matter and the small one the finished drawing. First examine the portion of the plank to be drawn and its dimensions. This is then delimited by means of a set-square, setting down the lines A A' & I I' at right angles. These are then divided into a certain number of equal parts, the more there are of them the more accurate the result will be; parallels are then drawn so as to obtain a certain number of squares of equal size.[26]

These instructions at once reinforce and encode in practice Gross's general strictures against rushing to examine what initially strikes the IO as the most interesting or significant element of the scene. Translating the natural space of the crime scene onto a paper grid effects a regime of total recording: it is only at the end of an exhaustive description of the scene as a whole that crime's "subject-matter" is considered.[27] The investigator who systematically records rather than touches thus secures the crime scene for future analysis at a distance. But in addition he confirms his self-restraint, his capacity to defer engagement with the world of immediate appearance in order to preserve one of as yet unseen, fragile traces and interrelationships. It is this set of practices that brings into being a modern regime of CSI, with its imperatives of preservation of matter, of guarding against physical and conceptual contamination, of ensuring the future use value of harvested material. Crime scene recording, then, is at once the outcome of rigorous investigation and its guarantor.

Thus far we have shown how Gross's conception of CSI depended on a new expert imbued with a specific set of cognitive and behavioral qualities. But his capacity to preserve the crime scene in space and time were merely a preliminary requirement. Once identified and captured in record, the "vestiges" of crime had to retain their identity and authenticity as crime scene objects as they moved physically from site of origin to other spaces of interrogation and evaluation, most notably the police science laboratory and the courtroom. To achieve this, the discipline first deployed at the scene needed to be maintained through a subsequent series of transactions amounting to what modern-day practitioners call a "chain of custody" that secures "continuity of evidence": protocols for labeling, packaging, storage, transportation, and reception.[28]

Gross provides a characteristically detailed outline of the work involved in forging a secure chain. This starts with an extension of crime scene recording from spatial description to administrative ordering so as to preserve the utility and integrity of crime scene objects as potentially meaningful units of evidence. Accurate pagination, numbering, and marking of exhibits was crucial, Gross observes, for if materials were "not described accurately or are not placed in their proper position in the record, endless confusion will perhaps result and certainly great loss of time. The best descriptions of objects are good for nothing if they cannot be referred to at need."[29]

A travel box that Gross advises his IO to carry at all times underscores the importance of this bureaucratic labor. It contained roughly thirty items of equipment, including a supply of paper; envelopes of various sizes; sheets of blotting paper; a good map; pens of the best quality and an ink bottle; a tape measure, pair of compasses, and pedometer; tracing paper and cloth; plaster of Paris for preserving footprints and other impressions and a brush for taking impressions of solid objects and surfaces in relief; sealing wax and gum arabic; glass tubes; a magnifying glass; a camel-hair brush; a good watch; and a piece of soap. Of the items listed, only one—the soap— was included for purposes other than recovering crime scene traces: "It is a great comfort to have a wash after a search, handling dirty clothes, perhaps dirty bodies, etc." But even this item had a characteristically Grossian secondary purpose: soap, he explained, "is also useful to take small impressions, as of keys, teeth (in case of bites), etc."[30]

To better appreciate the level of practical detail that Gross devotes to the interlinked processes of trace identification, recording, harvesting, and transportation—detail that, in our analysis, constitutes the hallmark of his transformative approach to crime scene investigation—we turn to his meticulous treatment of that most evocative of traces, blood. This form of trace object, "frequently, especially in big crimes, the most important element to the case," posed a host of challenges to the IO, first in its identification and initial protection from degradation, and then in its subsequent physical handling. Difficulties in identification and protection stemmed in part from blood's particular emotive connotations as a crime scene trace. Blood-soaked scenes were subject to "the curiosity of intruders, and the awkwardness of the local police" who, "time without number . . . make new traces by walking in already existing pools of blood and then tramping all over the place, so that subsequently no one can tell whether the traces of blood have any connection with the crime scene or have been made afterwards by chance or owing to awkwardness and carelessness."[31] To counter this, the IO needed first to establish a "protecting circle" that physically sequestered the scene, one that for Gross "cannot be sufficiently enlarged, for at the outset no one knows in what direction blood traces must be looked for or how far they may extend."[32] Within this circle blood traces should be covered with pots, baskets, boxes, or "bridges" forged from planks supported by bricks. Outdoor stains required extra measures to protect them from the effects of weather and temperature. Against the ravages of rain, for example, simple covering was ineffective, as water may flow underneath. Thus, "pieces of board, sheets of tin, or slips of glass, must be planted in the ground to form a sort of rampart against the filtration of the water."[33]

Blood's public resonance posed a further set of problems. Blood stains, Gross warns, "are not always of the dark red colour of popular imagination." Their age, the surface on which they were deposited, or the ambient temperature at the scene might "make them assume all imaginable tints: reddish brown, greenish brown, light olive green, light rose; sometimes they are almost colourless . . . , so that they may be taken for anything else but blood."[34] The popular resonance of crime scene blood, furthermore, extended to the criminal consciousness, with the result that of all traces it was most in danger of being effaced by the efforts of perpetrators. This meant that special care was required in examining both the bodies and clothing of suspects. Despite the fact that criminals "invariably" wash their hands, these should not be neglected, as even the most careful ablution may leave traces under nails or upon or under the skin where the nails are embedded in the fingers. Faces and hair may prove more promising, however, as these were more commonly neglected by perpetrators. Similar care was required in investigating items of clothing. Though thorough washing might expunge blood from obvious surfaces, traces may be deposited in hems and seams, and thus the IO should take care "not to be content with a mere examination of the suspected parts, but also to unstitch the hems and seams in order to more carefully observe them."[35] In general, the vulnerability of crime scene blood to criminal efforts to remove them forced the IO to engage the scene with a restrained reconstructive imagination, first asking himself, in the absence of visible traces, where under the circumstances traces *might* be and then proceeding "as if they really existed, describing, measuring, and sketching the places that have been washed, scraped, or planed down."[36]

Once identified and secured, the blood traces had to be recorded and removed by the IO. It was imperative that recording came first, following a "scientific scheme" that attended to scale, angle, and coordinate position in order to preserve each stain's original orientation.[37] Even here the ever-present danger of destruction lurked: recourse to tracing paper to capture the dimensions of blood might cause its erosion, and thus before attempting this it was essential to create a written record—without this precaution, the investigator risked having "neither the drawing nor the description."[38]

The next, and arguably most exacting, task facing the IO was the attempt to remove blood stains from their location at the scene. This process of retrieval varied according to the substance upon which the blood was deposited. Ideally, the IO would carry the blood-stained article away whole. When this was not possible, Gross advises detaching it along with a portion of the surface on which it rested. In the case of blood found on wooden floorboards, he proposed the following procedure to ensure the integrity of the stain:

> Cut out the planks above and below the blood with a cold chisel. It is sometimes better to use a horizontal saw instead of the chisel as, by an accidental rebound of the latter, the marks may be injured. In this way the object may be obtained *in natura*. While this work is progressing great care must be taken to protect the blood-stains and prevent them from being damaged by the splinters and shavings which fly about.

Further care was required to preserve the stain's precise location: once removed, pieces of wood should be marked by arrows and compass points to denote their original orientation (fig. 1.3): "These indications must never be forgotten," Gross warns, "even on very small pieces of wood, for these may, in spite of their great importance, prove quite valueless if their true position be unknown."[39]

Threats to the integrity of crime scene blood extended beyond the physical act of detachment. In removing plants stained with blood, for example, it was essential to preserve their freshness, as when they dried they changed shape "and the drops of blood, drying more quickly, often become detached from the plant, not leaving the slightest trace of their presence."[40] Animal life feeding upon the earth's organic substances posed a further threat: "An earth-worm would absorb for example, the portion of the ground impregnated with the blood, which later it would digest, evacuating the inorganic substances, so that in a short time there would be nothing in the box but the earth and the worm, the blood having disappeared." An obvious solution was to deter or destroy the subterranean violators by chemical means, but as this would result in denaturing the specimen and thus vitiating its value as evidence, Gross recommends a simpler mechanical one: "Before raising the clod of earth in question, the ground all round the blood is struck twenty or thirty times with a strong pole or a large stone, etc.; this striking is excessively disagreeable to worms, which if they are within the space in question, immediately come to the surface."[41]

Gross's battle with trace-eating creatures points to a final level of procedural labor required of his IO: that of preparing bloodied objects for transportation from the crime scene to the crime lab, and ultimately the courtroom, so that they arrive "as intact as possible and in a state of integrity which cannot be questioned. All who understand the significance of the expression 'to work with accuracy,'" he continues, "understand that the work of the expert will be much surer, more valuable, and at the same time easier, when the corpus delicti is handed over to him in all its integrity."[42]

To fulfil this crucial objective, Gross identifies two general principles: "avoid all confusion, and pack solidly." To satisfy the first, each object must be "denoted both inside and out by words, figures, or letters, and . . . plenty packing material must be employed." The second objective was achieved by fixing each article "so firmly that no shock can detach it." Blood-stained clothing, for example, should be packed in trunks, "carefully fixed so that the blood marks are uppermost; holes are pierced in the trunk through which are passed cords with which the clothes are securely tied, being very careful meanwhile not to damage the blood in any way." Providing as further illustration a graphic of a properly secured hatchet (fig. 1.4), Gross adds that "it is hardly necessary to state that the cords should neither touch nor rub the blood-stains."[43] To underscore the importance of this procedure, Gross presents an example of poor practice—one that left him "involuntarily seized with a slight shiver"—in which local authorities had handed a bloodied crime scene object to an ordinary delivery man:

[It] arrives at its destination unpacked and unprotected, perhaps in the midst of a cartload of oxen or pigs, just slaughtered; then it is handed over to the expert. What a ridiculous spectacle it is to see the expert proceeding conscientiously and minutely, following all the rules of his science and his art, to the examination of an article which has been treated with so much negligence. He measures it, weighs it, examines it in the most scrupulous manner for traces of blood, some of which have been knocked off by the shaking of the cart, while others have only come into existence since the article started on its journey. Action of this description is in the first place to make a fool of the expert and further shows a marked want of professional conscientiousness.

The lesson was simple and crystal clear: when packing blood-stained objects for transit "neither trouble, time, nor money may be spared."[44]

BODIES AND TRACES: EXPERTS OF THE MORTUARY AND THE MICROSCOPE

Once captured in record, carefully excavated, and suitably packaged, the vestiges of crime could yield their secrets only in a further domain: the crime laboratory. Chapter 5 discusses the development in the English context of this space as an annex of the crime scene. Here we limit ourselves to the observation that its status as a new domain of expertise and experts existed alongside—and in potential tension with—the figure of the skilled medical witness at the post-mortem table.

Medical experts occupy an equivocal place in Gross's text. On the one hand, he observes that they are "the most important and the most frequently questioned," and accordingly this role is the first to be described in his chapter entitled "Experts and How to Make Use of Them."[45] However, in his substantive discussion the range of topics and attributed powers of medical experts are noticeably limited, and there is a persistent theme of containing the medical remit rather than expanding it. He devotes little space to the core medico-legal duties in cases of suspected homicide: namely post-mortem examinations, interpretation of external and internal signs of violence, cause and time of death. Gross dispenses with these in two pages, after which he moves on to a sequence of ad hoc topics—a "regeneration process" for restoring decomposed flesh, tattooing, mental affections, hypnotism, and color blindness—before concluding with a section on the evidentiary value of teeth. Moreover, in discussing the remit of medical evidence Gross tends to a limited description. In terms of its declarative powers, for example, modern medical experts were (justifiably) more aware than before of their limits and thus less inclined to make categorical statements on the basis of their examinations:

> With what certainty did they not use to distinguish *ante mortem* from *post mortem* wounds? And yet every medical jurisprudent of to-day points out most convincingly that the so-called distinctive signs are not always infallible. Again medical jurisprudents used to determine very accurately the beginning and the end of a gash or cut, a point perhaps very important in a case of murder or suicide; modern medical men dare not in most instances form an opinion from the mere sight of the wound.[46]

Gross also exhorts his IO to reach beyond the traditionally narrow circle of expertise centered on "doctors, analysts and gunsmiths" and to seize control of the course of investigations by taking an active role in deciding which expert to call in and when.[47] In his introduction Gross calls attention to this discriminating function that places the IO as a gatekeeper with respect to a differentiated chain of potential experts who might be activated at his call, acknowledging that this may rankle traditionalists:

> We of course foresee and meet on the threshold the charge of encroaching upon the province, and thereby attempting to dispense with the help, of specialists. Nothing could be more harmful than such advice, nothing could so expose the investigator to mistakes as such fancied independence. But there is a vast gulf between permitting an Investigating Officer to undertake work beyond his sphere and instructing him how to recognise when he ought to resort to experts, what experts should be chosen, and what questions must be submitted to them.[48]

In Gross's account, medico-legal expertise—and pathology in particular—is displaced, literally, in the sense that it occupies a tiny fragment of his text, but also figuratively, in that the corpse is relegated to the realm of the immediate and obvious gross appearance, a distraction from the core work of crime scene investigation—trace analysis. This stands in stark contrast to the treatment accorded to his next category of expertise—microscopy. Rather than being overutilized, as suggested in the case of medicine, the microscopist is for Gross underexploited, largely confined to cases involving the identification of biofluids (blood and semen) and morphological identification of hair: "other examinations are the exception, although there are innumerable cases where the microscope expert might be able to give the most interesting information and even clear up more than one dark mystery."[49]

Gross devotes the next thirty pages to illustrating the microscopist's range of powers to bring light to dark mysteries, and in the process he positions him as the exemplary adherent to his vision of CSI. For one thing, he starts at the point at which the medical expert reaches his limits: the IO will "only be in possession of the best information on interrogating an observer at the microscope in cases where medical men are incapable of enlightening him."[50] The microscopist's relationship to the world of minute traces also converges with the pursuit and preservation of unseen traces: "Speaking quite generally it may be said that the microscope expert is useful in all cases where it is desirable to see anything more clearly than with the naked eye, also where it is necessary to establish the composition of an object without destroying or deteriorating it."[51]

Gross then rehearses the range of material traces that falls within the scope of the microscopist: blood, excrement, hair, fiber, and a variety of "stains." In these discussions Gross treats traces as significant not principally in their own materiality but rather in their contextuality. His discussion of the microscopy of hair, for example, is driven not by questions of morphology and its role in identification and comparison but rather by its evidentiary significance within the crime scene as a distinct environment.[52] Gross thus introduces the topic of hair analysis by noting its capacity to testify to its surroundings:

> We should in the first place not lose sight of the faculty of absorption possessed by human hair; it is capable of absorbing gases, odours, etc., with extreme facility and retains them for a relatively long time. This detail is of importance when it is desired to determine whether a man, be he alive or dead at the moment of examination, has been in a place impregnated with a gas or smell, a point upon which the whole case may turn.[53]

This evidentiary potential enfolds the microscopist within the wider regimen of CSI. Capturing absorbed gases from crime scene hair, he explains, necessitated its protection by "placing the hair in a perfectly clean receptacle of small size and hermetically closed."

> The hair should be taken with absolutely clean hands and placed in a bottle having a wide neck and fitted with a close fitting cork, or better still, in a

receptacle of white metal, or in case of need in an ordinary bottle. The stopper or cork and the inside of the lid of the metal receptacle, as the case may be, should be slighted [*sic*] rubbed over with absolutely pure fat; this fat will render the closing more secure, will attract and absorb the escaping gases, and may itself be an object for examination.[54]

—⌒ ⌒—

Gross sought to differentiate his text from traditional medico-legal treatises whose main focus was the relationship between the medical expert and the corpse. To better appreciate this distinction, we turn briefly to a standard contemporary German-language text that appears with some regularity in Gross's endnotes. Johann Ludwig Casper's comprehensive and canonical *Practical Handbook of Forensic Medicine*, published in 1856 and running through seven editions by the end of the century, was aimed at instructing would-be medical experts in the practical tasks of medico-legal witnessing. As such, it is not surprising that the text is dominated by the medical encounter with bodies—sometimes alive, more often dead. Casper's text features the medical expert as the pivotal actor in investigations into murders, attempted murder, wounding, violent assault, and other crimes involving death or injury, but these investigations are dominated by his encounter with the body. Therefore, there is virtually no discussion of what Gross develops as crime scene investigation. In the 1861 English translation, Casper quotes an 1858 Prussian Royal Science Commission report on medico-legal practice that provides some insight into the hierarchy between bodies and scenes:

> It may *sometimes* be necessary for the medical inspectors to examine in the first place, and from a medical point of view, the exact spot and the locality in which the body has been found, to ascertain the position in which it was discovered, and to inspect the clothing. In general, before doing this, the medical inspectors will wait until they are required by the legal authorities.[55]

The medical expert's tangential and occasional relationship to the crime scene was reinforced in Casper's discussion of his duties—or more properly his lack of duties—in relation to the inspection of material found on bodies and at crime scenes: "The medical jurist is not generally required to inspect clothing, shirts, boots, stockings, etc.," Casper observes, further noting with approval the "immemorial custom" in Berlin of delivering bodies naked for medical inspection, a custom which dispensed with the "improper and vexatious" practice of physicians "describing coats, trousers, stockings, etc.," which only "very rarely" informs the investigation.[56]

OUR ENVIRONMENT IN MINIATURE:
DUST AS EXEMPLARY CSI TRACE

The microscope thus emerged as the instrumental counterpart to the heroics of the IO, as an instrument that enabled what appears as ordinary and insignificant to displace the corpse as the modern investigator's core object. Microscopy takes pride of place in Gross's text, with discussions of its uses in analyzing hair, fibers, blood, and other trace matter supplemented by examples drawn from his extensive case file. We have already detailed his engagement with blood, the most obvious species of trace evidence. We now turn to what is arguably blood's polar opposite, what would at first glance seem to be the least promising of all crime scene traces—dust. Dust stands as the exemplary illustration of the care and attention that Gross insists is required of even the smallest and ostensibly least significant objects found at crime scenes; Gross's discussion of dust provided inspiration for Edmond Locard, whom we identify as a second crucial figure in the Continental origins of modern CSI; and, when English commentators turned their thoughts to the theoretical and practical challenges of forging a domestic version of the scientific investigation of crime, it was dust that most captured their forensic imagination.

To the uninitiated, dust is at best meaningless, at worst a barrier to meaning, an interfering layer to be wiped away in order to reveal the desired object lying beneath. But, to the properly trained analyst, dust is every bit as significant as the things it covers. This, Gross explains, is because dust is the eroded vestige of the more easily apprehended world of normal-scaled matter—"our environment or surroundings in miniature."[57] By identifying the qualitative features of any particle of dust found on crime scene objects, the investigator generated potentially vital evidence of the physical interaction between it and the object on which it had come to rest.[58] This capacity of dust to bear witness to the environment from which it derived opened up a new world of trace linkages:

> The dust of the desert will contain little besides pulverised earth, sand, and small particles of plants; the dust of a ball-room, crowded with people, will in great measure proceed from the fibres from which the clothes of the dancers

are woven; the dust of a smith's shop will be for the most part composed of pulverised metal; and that upon the books of a study nothing but the reunion of the particles of earth carried in on the boots of the master of the house and the servants with very tiny particles of paper. Examining more closely, we find that the coat of a locksmith contains a different kind of dust to that on the coat of a miller: that accumulated in the pocket of a school-boy is essentially different from that in the pocket of a chemist.[59]

The rich harvest reaped from dust, moreover, reconfirmed Gross's exhortation for a set of practices and sensibilities that looked beyond the obvious places where evidence might be found. Instead, the investigator would do better to consider the lowly pocket, which "tells us from its composition the whole history of a person during the time he has worn the garment."[60]

If Gross can be considered the founder of what we now think of as CSI, it was Edmond Locard who put dust at its center. Best known for his "exchange principle" with its much-cited (though, in strict terms, apocryphal) aphorism, "every contact leaves a trace," Locard was also a pioneer in the application of lab techniques to criminal investigation. In 1910, after studying medicine and law at the University of Lyon, and working with the criminologist Alexandre Lacassagne, he persuaded the local authorities to establish an innovative police laboratory, with him in charge. This was to be the base for Locard's pathbreaking forensic work, which spanned a full half century and included heralded breakthroughs in such diverse fields as graphology, serology, and poroscopy. His first substantial treatise on criminalistic practice, *L'enquête criminelle et les méthods scientifiques*, was published in 1920.[61] Here and in subsequent texts Locard established modern, lab-based police investigation as dependent on a combination of observational virtuosity and analytical precision rooted in a disciplined deployment of the imagination. Nowhere was this more apparent than in his approach to dust.

Locard's initial English-language reflections on dust's evidential promise appeared in the London-based *Police Journal* in 1928. These were extended two years later in a series of three articles entitled "The Analysis of Dust Traces" published in the *American Journal of Police Science*. In the first of these Locard begins with an expression of surprise that it was only recently that investigators had conceived the simple idea of collecting dust from crime scene objects as "evidence of the objects rubbed against, and the contacts which a suspected person may have undergone. For the microscopic debris that cover our clothes and bodies," he continues, "are the mute witnesses, sure and faithful, of all our movements and of all our encounters."[62] Locard names two inspirations for his recognition of the forensic potential of dust: one was Hans Gross, whom Locard credits as the first author to provide substantive accounts of dust analysis in actual police investigations. "Next to this master," he continues,

> one should not be surprised to find the name of a popular novelist. . . . I hold
> that a police expert, or an examining magistrate, would not find it a waste of
> his time to read Doyle's novels. For, in the adventures of Sherlock Holmes,
> the detective is repeatedly asked to diagnose the origin of a speck of mud,
> which is nothing but moist dust.

"I must confess," he concludes, "that if, in the police laboratory of Lyon, we are interested in any unusual way in this problem of dust, it is because of having absorbed the ideas found in Gross and in Conan Doyle."[63]

Two features of dust were central to its forensic significance. First was its ubiquity: "There is not a single object that is not covered with it, since, from the moment that one removes a layer of deposited dust, new dust immediately begins to fall on the places just wiped clean." Second was its capacity to retain in qualitative form essential characteristics of its originary source. Locard defines dust as "an accumulation of debris" from any organic or inorganic body "in a state of pulverization."[64] Yet pulverization did not obliterate all qualitative vestige of the object from which it originated. To illustrate dust's surprising resilience, he invites his reader to consider a most unlikely evidentiary source, the body—and in particular the wings—of a dead butterfly:

> Its body rapidly decomposes, falling into dust. The greater portion of its elements (those which are putrifiable) undergo a chemical evolution, through which one is later unable to determine their origin. On the other hand, certain other imperishable elements become mechanically crushed without chemical alteration, and their minute debris are still recognizable, with the right technique and adequate equipment. For example, the dust originating from the wings of butterflies can be determined, whereas the digestive organs undergo alterations which radically transform them. As a result of this knowledge we may state that dust preserves sufficient distinctive characters, so that one is able, almost invariably, to identify its origin.[65]

Both in source and in its ubiquitous distribution, dust was a virtually limitless species of potential trace evidence: to enumerate the former, Locard observes, would entail listing "all the substances, organic or inorganic, existing on the earth."[66] Yet, for the purposes of criminal investigation, it was dust's compositional or contextual dimensions that governed its utility. The identification of plant matter on a victim's clothing not found growing at the scene of the crime, for example, opened up a line of inquiry as to the spatial and personal interactions that had caused matter out of place to settle where it did.[67] To categorize this infinite world of dust and to provide guidelines for determining the evidential significance of the equally infinite locations on which it might rest, Locard follows Gross in highlighting occupational dust as a key analytical filter, enumerating for example characteristic compositions of dust found under the nails of just under fifty types of worker and on the eyebrows of fourteen.[68]

To realize dust's analytical promise as a striking example of crime scene "exchange," however, a systematic approach to searching and sorting was essential. Locard echoes and extends Gross's instructions on the former, adding instructions on searching body zones (skin, hair, eyebrows, nails, ears, and nostrils) to Gross's list of characteristic dust-collecting sites. On dust recovery, Locard proposes a significant modification of Grossian crime scene technique. Gross had recommended placing a dust-laden object in a bag and beating it, but this in Locard's view negated the potential value of mapping its pattern of distribution over the object in question: "The distribution of the dust," he insists, "may possess an interest at least equal to that of its final identification."[69] To capture this dimension, he outlines a strict regime of collection and recording, in which dust from each of the "interesting zones" is first photographed and, once harvested, isolated in packets numbered to correspond with a card-index record.[70] This painstaking work is facilitated by instrumental innovations, most notably a purpose-built vacuum cleaner to extract dust not visible to the naked eye.

Locard's approach aligned the crime scene with practices associated with a range of contemporaneous field sciences, including geology, paleontology, and especially archeology. Most obviously, his concern with dust distribution drew on the importance of interpreting layers of matter and therefore necessitated an "orderly method" of excavation and preservation. When investigating shoes, for example, "successive layers may be found under the sole of the shoe, each of which has its own significance." He cites one case in which a layer of flour dust between two layers of earth provided evidence of entry into a mill. "In such circumstances," he observes, "the removal of the dirt en masse would destroy all possibility of a stratigraphic study, which could be made only by taking one layer at a time." In such instances he suggests drilling "a perpendicular incision into the shoe to obtain a good view of the respective strata."[71]

The overlap between Locardian crime scene excavation and contemporary archeological practice is worth some further consideration. In the latter decades of the nineteenth century, a new generation, led on the continent by Conze in Austria, Curtius in Germany, and Fiorelli in Italy, and in England by Pitt-Rivers and Flinders Petrie, were forging a program of scientific excavation based on a number of characteristics whose affinity with crime scene investigation is evident.[72] Most obvious was the emphasis on the need to produce an exhaustive audit of a site irrespective of any prior hierarchy of value assigned to the objects that lay within any field. This new sensibility demanded, and enacted, a set of disciplines based on suspension of preconceived judgment as to what was worthy of note and, consequently, a willingness to embrace the tedium of "total recording."

Pitt-Rivers's celebrated fieldwork on his Dorset estate, chronicled in his multivolume *Excavations in Cranborne Chase*, exemplifies this approach. In introducing his enterprise, he alerts readers that his methods and his account of them are of a piece, and that both necessitate an expositional style at odds with conventional narratives:

> It will, perhaps, be thought by some that I have recorded the excavations of this village and the finds that have been made in it with unnecessary fulness, and I am aware that I have done it in greater detail than has been customary, but my experience as an excavator has led me to think that investigations of this nature are not generally sufficiently searching and that much valuable evidence is lost by omitting to record them carefully.[73]

As a rule, he explains, excavators limited their accounts to "only those things which appear to them important at the time," but as a dynamic practice in which fresh discoveries—physical and perspectival—were continuously generated, such limited accounts stifled productive reengagement: "On turning back to old accounts in search of evidence, the points which would have been most valuable have been passed over from being thought uninteresting at the time. Every detail should, therefore, be recorded in the manner most conducive to the facility of reference."[74]

The new archeology, then, defined itself by its concern with "trivial details" and their meticulous recording: it was by careful attention to "odds and ends that have, no doubt, been thrown away by their owners as rubbish," that practitioners produced knowledge of real value.[75] The emphasis on the value of everyday objects and their relations in space and time, and their systematic excavation and recording was in these texts set in stark opposition to the unscientific and destructive practices of the "treasure hunter." Petrie's 1904 *Methods and Aims in Archaeology* stands as a model moralizing articulation of this contrast, in which traditional practitioners are criticized as being "still attracted by pretty things, rather than by real knowledge."[76] In their quest for buried treasure, these old-style diggers fetishized objects of superficial value and in so doing overlooked—and indeed destroyed—the more complex analytical possibilities of an excavation site. Achieving knowledge at this level, Petrie insists, entailed

> the power of conserving material and information; of observing all that can be gleaned; of noticing trifling details which may imply a great deal else; of acquiring and building up a mental picture; of fitting everything into place, and not losing or missing any possible clues; all this is the soul of the work, and without it excavating is mere dumb plodding.[77]

As with the systematic investigation of the crime scene, all this labor would be for naught without submission to a further field requirement: "Recording," Petrie intones, "is the absolute dividing line between plundering and scientific work."[78]

This attention to unremarkable objects as evidentiary traces of some more fundamental set of events that had previously transpired thus links archeology and crime scene investigation at the conceptual and practical levels. In turn, this emphasis on the value of the "incidental" is part of a more fundamental shift in the interpretive methodologies entailed in a range of nineteenth-century historically based field sciences. In the geology of Charles Lyell, the paleontology of Georges Cuvier, and the evolutionary biology of Charles Darwin, historical narrative was properly anchored in unintentional material sources rather than in those constructed (physically or verbally) for explanatory purposes.[79] Each of these depended on a node of related attributes—restraint of thought and deed, interpretive openness, representational fidelity—that enabled commonplace matter to testify more eloquently than could more obvious evidential "treasure." For Locard, the connection was clear: "the detective, one might say, reconstructs the culprit's identity from the traces he leaves behind, just as the paleontologist reconstitutes a fossil from its fragments."[80]

In the third and final installment of his series, Locard exemplifies the principles of a forensics of dust by reviewing twenty-two criminal cases,

taken from the Lyon lab files and elsewhere, in which dust was a telling feature of the investigation.[81] Three of these—all cases of homicide—are
worth brief consideration by way of conclusion, as they exemplify key features of the Grossian and Locardian regime of traces that we have outlined
in this chapter.

The first case, reported by the Frankfurt chemist Georg Popp in 1908,
opens with the discovery of the body of a decapitated woman in a forest but
quickly turns to a rich vein of dust matter that marginalized the state of the
corpse as a matter of interest to investigators. Aided by a geologist, the in
vestigator identified fifteen species of trace evidence, which signified both
in its distribution (remnants of hawthorn and myrtle leaves where neither
tree grew) and more compellingly in its layering. Detailed stratigraphic
analysis of the boots of a suspect told the full story of his movements before and after the murder—his departure along the greyish mineral and
excrement-laden village street, across a porphyry-based path to a field of
grass, moss, oat straw, and pink quartz, and so on, to the scene and back. But
the boots captured not merely the murderer's passage from home to scene;
they also preserved a sedimented record of the murderous act itself. In the
layer corresponding to the soil of the woods where the attack had taken
place, investigators identified "fibres of reddish brown wool, which were
from the dress of the victim."[82]

The two other cases were reported by the Nancy-based professor of
legal medicine Pierre Parisot, and they are significant for our purposes in
reflecting, even in the context of a homicide investigation, the priority of
trace over body evidence. The first involves a male corpse found beside a
canal next to a gas works, near to which was also a stone yard containing
huts that provided workmen with shelter. The thighs and chest were covered with a grayish-white dust; a darker substance coated the hands and
feet; the ear canal, scalp, and fingernails contained further distinctive debris. Laboratory analysis determined a peculiar combination of organic
and inorganic sources of this dust, which was subsequently found repli-
cated in the stone yard. Of particular significance was the discovery of a
bag of coal in one of the huts, the particles of which matched the dust distributed across the corpse's thighs and chest. This match corroborated the account given by the case's preliminary suspect, who claimed to have used an
old coal bag to cover the corpse that he had chanced to come across. In this
way, attention to the surface coating of the corpse and its contextual mapping, rather than its external and internal examination for cause of death,

confirmed its value as a quasi–crime scene laden with analyzable trace evidence.[83]

In Parisot's other case, the corpse of an elderly female was found lying in a shed, covered with straw and wood. External medical inspection revealed numerous wounds inflicted pre-mortem to the face and scalp, with marks on the neck suggesting strangulation as the cause of death. The case was thus off to a classic medico-legal start, but this shifted when, on internal inspection, examiners discovered "small, black, foreign bodies" in and about the eye and penetrating the lacrimal sacs. On analysis these turned out to be straw debris, analogous to that found in the straw covering the victim's body. The post-mortem also revealed a quantity of blood pooled in the stomach, which on analysis was found to contain additional straw dust. The presence of dust in the body's interior strongly indicated that the victim had been buried under the straw while still alive, a supposition ultimately corroborated by the assailant's confession. Medico-legal examination had thus been turned into an exercise in trace hunting, blood and bodily orifices serving as the media in which the presence and distribution of dust could be identified and analyzed. The lesson of this case, in Locard's concluding summation, was that trace evidence of the greatest importance could be recovered during the course of an autopsy.[84]

The aim of this chapter has been to establish the conceptual and practical features of the core subject of this book: CSI. To this end it has devoted extensive and intensive attention to the work of two leading theorists of the modern crime scene, Hans Gross and, to a lesser degree, Edmond Locard. This level of engagement was necessary in large part because, in it was the detailed articulation of practices, gestures, protocols, and cognitive awareness that turned a place in which a crime had taken place into a "crime scene."

The themes and concepts articulated in this chapter will recur throughout the rest of the book, both as an analytical framework as we seek out the place of a forensics of traces in the development of twentieth-century English homicide investigation and as an actors' category and reference point for those engaged in, commenting on, and seeking to transform, this investigative work. The following chapter begins this mapping exercise, by considering the kind of advice available to nineteenth- and early twentieth-century English forensic investigators and how this differed from what has been outlined here.

CHAPTER TWO

Crime Scenes before CSI

In the English context, there were no manuals on criminal investigation produced in the nineteenth and early twentieth centuries that even approximated either the depth or breadth achieved by Gross.[1] The nearest equivalent handbook was Howard Vincent's *Police Code and Manual of the Criminal Law*, first published in 1881 and reaching its sixteenth edition by 1924. In 1878, after a French sojourn where he studied and produced a report on Parisian policing, Vincent was appointed head of the Metropolitan Police's newly constituted Criminal Investigation Department.[2] Vincent followed a reformist agenda, with mixed results: his attempt to open up detective recruitment to candidates who had not come up through the police rank and file, for instance, met with concerted resistance and was ultimately abandoned. Efforts to codify police conduct as a way of bolstering procedural and behavioral discipline were longer lasting, with his *Code* as its most enduring textual legacy.

Vincent's *Code* was designed as a portable pocket reference for use by police officers in action, and it provided guidance on practical topics arranged alphabetically for ease of reference. Over its multiple editions the *Code* expanded from its original length of roughly two hundred octavo pages to more than three hundred in the 1924 version. Though clearly a different order of text from Gross's *Handbook* in aims, scope, and ambition, Vincent's guide, as a quasi-official advice manual extending from the late Victorian to the interwar periods, provides a useful contrast to the approach to crime scene rigor outlined in the previous chapter. There are a series of obvious omissions that mark the contrast starkly: Vincent has no entry for "Crime Scene" in any of its derivative forms nor any for forms of trace evidence or the instrumental means by which such traces might be investigated.[3] The *Code* does have an entry for "Experts," substantively unchanged throughout the first sixteen editions, consisting of a comparatively ano-dyne single sentence: "when there is a question on any subject on which a course of special study or experience is necessary to the formation of an opinion, including handwriting, the opinions thereon of persons specially skilled in any such matters are relevant, and the persons are called experts."[4] The entry for "Detectives," the English counterpart to Gross's much-scrutinized investigating officer, was longer, roughly four hundred words by the 1924 edition but, perhaps reflecting Vincent's original aim of instilling stricter standards of professional conduct, was exclusively devoted to ques-tions of personal character and comportment: modesty, discretion, and fair dealing with the public and the criminal classes alike—including advice on the relative merits of providing informants with remuneration or alcoholic refreshments in public houses.

There are only two entries in the numerous editions of the *Code* that directly connect with Gross's interest in crime scene procedure: "Dead Bodies" and "Murder." The former consists of one page of advice primarily concerned with the police officer's duties with respect to the handling of found bodies (notification of the coroner, transport to the mortuary, search of clothing for indications of identity in the case of unknown corpses) and a list of obvious signs of death (rigidity, surface temperature, cessation of breathing and heart action). It does, however, begin with a short statement—which remained unembellished in subsequent editions—covering the rudi-ments of crime scene management:

> When a dead body is found, and there is no doubt that life is extinct, it should never be touched until the arrival of a constable, who should forthwith care-fully note its appearance and everything surrounding it. If he suspects that death was caused by violence, he should not move the body, or allow any part of the clothing, or any article about it to be touched, or moved, by any person, until the arrival of a Sergeant or Inspector, who should be sent for by the quickest possible means.[5]

For more on this topic the reader is referred to the entry for "Murder," which contains the closest equivalent to Gross's concern for systematic CSI. It consisted of a single page of advice on not moving found bodies or anything surrounding them until the arrival of an inspector; on not creating extrane-ous footmarks at the scene; on taking careful notes on the position of the body, condition of the clothing, and the appearance of wounds. More than four decades and sixteen editions later, little had changed: by 1924, the admonishment that the constable "should on no account move it or anything surrounding it; or allow any other person to do so; or in any way confuse footmarks in its vicinity" had been italicized for greater emphasis, and advice on the need for photographing the body exactly as it had been discovered had been inserted into the duties of the superior officer once he arrived on the scene.[6]

INVESTIGATING MURDER SCENES IN THE ENGLISH MEDICO-LEGAL TRADITION

In neither substance nor form, then, was there an English equivalent to Gross's *Handbook*. This is not to say that elements of Gross's approach to crime scene investigation were entirely absent in the English advice literature. To find them, however, it is necessary to turn not to police guides but instead to medico-legal textbooks that had, since the early to mid-nineteenth century, served as the primary resource for expert guidance on the investigation of crimes against the person.

These texts were generally written by recognized "authorities," those with an institutional position in either or both a university or hospital that conferred and confirmed a distinct expertise. Yet their target audience was not a cadre of fellow experts but rather general medical practitioners with no claim to officially sanctioned medico-legal authority. This circumstance derives in large measure from the decentralized structure of England's long-standing institution of first resort for the investigation of cases of suspicious death—the coroner's inquest. Compared to their Continental counterparts—statutorily recognized and remunerated *Gerichtsarzts* or *médecin-légistes*, who served courts of inquiry according to well delineated codes of practice—medical witnesses at inquests were of marginal standing. They did not hold public office, and until the passage of the 1836 Medical Witnesses Act they were not statutorily entitled to payment for their services. The terms of this act, moreover, did little to confer official standing upon witnesses. Provided they met the requirement of being legally qualified medical practitioners, witnesses were chosen not on the basis of special skill or experience but on proximity to the death in question—either by virtue of having been the deceased's attending practitioner or, failing that, being "at the time in actual practice in or near the place where the death has happened."[7] This localist and episodic structure informed the expositional relationship between author and presumed reader: the author, from his (ostensibly) secure and sanctioned position in the medico-legal firmament provided practical advice and encouragment to nonexperts who, in the course of their everyday medical activities, might be thrust into a case of suspected homicide.

Given this orientation, it comes as no surprise that English medico-legal treatises focused on medical practitioners' responsibilities in cases of suspicous death, and in particular on their examination of dead bodies. The advice varied in degree of emphasis and specific content from text to text, but a number of core themes were common. The main categories of death were introduced: poisoning, hanging, suffocation, drowning, wounding. Readers were also instructed on how to interpret the body across these different modes of death. This included advice on the form and conduct of post-mortems and how to use the external and internal signs on the body to shed light on the cause and circumstances of death. The interpretation of marks on and in the body featured prominently—how to recognize a bruise and how to differentiate bruising from post-mortem lividity and other artifacts of death, for example. Attention was drawn to the evidentiary value of physiological markers, such as degree of rigor mortis, putrefaction, and surface temperature, generated in and on the body, as indicators of an approximate time since death.

This highly abstracted synopsis indicates the (unsurprising) body centeredness of the nineteenth-century English medico-legal advice literature. Though by no means static in content, depth, or form, it provided a recognizable repertoire of actions and resources with which the would-be medical investigator could approach a case of suspected homicide and, relatedly, a set of expectations as to what he might be able to offer in pursuit of a resolution. It is here that the rudiments of a Grossian regime of crime scene investigation is discernible, though again one in which the body, rather than the trace, was dominant.

Take, for example, the advice given to practitioners who were called to view a body where it was found. This advice characteristically distinguished between the medical man's core post-mortem responsibilities and his broader, more contextual, responsibilities, the latter cast as occasional and supplemental. The King's College professor of forensic medicine William Guy, in his "brief directions" for observing and collecting facts related to persons found dead, explicitly affirms this distinction between core and peripheral medico-legal responsibilities by differentiating "common" from "skilled" witnesses. When approaching a dead body, a medical observer combined both of these functions, Guy explains, but it was only with respect to his investigation of the corpse that he acted in a skilled capacity. If called to the place where a body lay, he continues, the medical man "must of necessity observe many things connected with the body itself—the position in which it is placed, and the objects by which it is surrounded—which might just as well be observed and stated in evidence by any other person." This contextual observation, a matter of "common" witnessing, stood in stark contrast to his duties with respect to the post-mortem inspection of the corpse, which "can be made by himself alone."[8]

At the crime scene, then, and in explicit contrast to his role at the post-mortem table, the medical man acted like an ordinary observer. Any difference, Guy continues, derived not from access to a specialized set of skills but from his putative qualities of mental refinement: "The medical man is not only one of the first witnesses of these facts; he is also in most cases by far the best educated and most intelligent witness." It is on this basis that Guy exhorts the medical man to be "alive to all that is passing around him, that no object, however trifling, which may possibly throw light on the cause of death, may be overlooked."[9] Thus for Guy the exhortation to keen observation of the environment surrounding the body is based on the observer's general intellectual assets rather than on mastery of a distinct method. As such, he casts expert medical engagement with the crime scene as a matter of individual virtuosity that could not be reduced to, or even guided by, a set of explicit protocols: "each man's own judgment and foresight must prompt the particular points to be observed in individual instances."[10]

Guy's emphasis on the medical witness's competence at the scene of a homicide as derived from a general capacity for observation maps onto a commonplace contemporary ideal of medical identity: the virtuoso clinician. At the top of the nineteenth-century medical hierarchy, as the medical historian Chris Lawrence has shown, stood the elite clinical consultant, armed with "incommunicable" observational skill—in part experiential, in part innate—from which he was able to draw singular diagnostic conclusions on the basis of obscure symptoms.[11] In this sense, the medical witness was a natural authority at the scene of a crime, and the advice contained in contemporary medico-legal texts both traded on this idealized medical identity and urged the ordinary practitioner to live up to the observational acumen attributed to his professional standing.

This combination of assumption and exhortation is evident in the most widely read and cited English textbook of the century, Alfred Swaine

Taylor's *Principles and Practice of Medical Jurisprudence*. Taylor, Fellow of the Royal College of Physicians, lecturer in medical jurisprudence at Guy's Hospital, and the most visible expert witness in the Victorian criminal courtroom, published the first edition of *Principles* in 1865. Taylor's opening chapter stipulates that the "first duty" of a medical jurist was "to cultivate a faculty of minute observation of medical and moral circumstances." This faculty, Taylor continues, was for some elite practitioners possessed as "a natural gift," and he illustrates this by recalling the story of the eminent surgeon Sir Astley Cooper, who, called in to tend to a shooting victim, concluded from the nature of the wound, the position of the victim, and the presumed direction from which the pistol had been fired that the assailant had been left-handed.[12] Cooper's skilled judgment stood as an inspirational model for Taylor's target audience. In approaching such cases, Taylor exhorts his readers to heed the advice of a "learned judge" who remarked from the bench that "a medical man, when he sees a dead body, should notice everything."[13]

Taylor's concept of medical expertise is thus introduced with reference to an epistemological ideal that existed prior to any forensic training—a consequence of professional competence rather than the outcome of specially acquired skills. In this respect, his text is emblematic of the tacit assumptions of a traditionally sanctioned medical omnicompetence at crime scenes that, as we have seen, Gross seeks to textually and conceptually displace.

To be sure, Taylor's text is not devoid of advice on how his readers might encounter and engage with crime scene traces, but in both form and content this confirmed the body as their focal point. The most systematic treatment of this topic, tellingly, is contained within a chapter on "circumstantial evidence," a chapter marked by the language of supplemental, rather than essential, significance. It opens by noting that evidence was "*sometimes* derived" from the circumstances under which a body was discovered, after which Taylor advises a restrained approach to this form of evidence: "a practitioner would certainly be wrong to base his professional opinion exclusively on circumstantial proofs; but it is scarcely possible for him to avoid drawing an inference from these, as they fall under his observation." However, if such inferential indications were approached with "a proper degree of caution," a practitioner was "bound to observe and record them; for being commonly the first person called to the deceased, many facts, capable of throwing an important light on the case, would remain unnoticed or unknown, but for his attention to them."[14]

Over the next twenty pages Taylor provides illustrative guidance on eight scenarios in which a medical witness might be called to take trace evidence into consideration: (1) the position of the body, (2) the position of the weapon, (3) blood on weapons, (4) hair and other substances on weapons, (5) foreign substances in wounds, (6) marks of blood on clothing or furniture, (7) marks of blood or other substances on the deceased, and (8) marks of blood on the assailant. Several themes emerge. First, Taylor continues to cast this form of evidence in supplemental terms, introducing several sections by observing that evidence of the sort discussed "may occasionally" or "sometimes" be of use. Second, his focus is almost exclusively on biomatter, and thus his account of trace evidence is anchored in subject matter designed to resonate directly with the professional interests of his readership. Third, Taylor's advice provides scant procedural detail, the investigation of traces being cast largely as an activity that flowed from general medical skill and required no particular adherence to task-specific protocol.

Blood dominates Taylor's discussion of trace evidence, and it is in his treatment of this topic that he is both most similar to, and most different from, Gross. His similarity derives from a recognition of the need for medical witnesses to consider crime scene blood in spatial and dynamic terms.

> It is proper to notice all marks of blood on the clothes of the deceased or in the apartment, and to observe where the greatest quantity of blood has been effused; this is generally found on the spot where the deceased has died. The deceased may have bled in more places than one; if so, it is proper to notice whether there is any communication in blood between these different places. Blood on distant clothes or furniture will show whether the deceased has moved about, and whether he has struggled much after receiving the wound.[15]

He also shares Gross's interest in correcting commonplace preconceptions about the appearance and significance of such stains. The "popular view" that "if much blood is found about a dead body, the weapon ought always to be more or less bloody," he observes, was not necessarily the case: heavy blunt instruments forcibly striking the victim's head, for example, could produce contusions and fractures without blood-letting; knives used in stabbing were also frequently free of blood.

However, in both these discussions Taylor's terms of engagement differ from Gross's in the priority they give to the body, as opposed to the space in which the body lay. In correcting popular expectations of blood-soaked crime scenes, for example, Taylor invokes general physiology:

> In a rapid blow or plunge the vessels are compressed, so that a bleeding takes place only after the sudden withdrawal, when the pressure is removed. Even if blood should be effused, the weapon, in being withdrawn, is sometimes cleanly wiped against the edges of the wound, owing to the elasticity of the skin.[16]

Taylor's treatment of crime scene blood, though embracing elements of Gross's emphasis on space, again prioritizes physiological questions. The prime example is his advice on how the medical witness should interpret the shape and distribution of blood found at a scene of violence. Blood found spattered against surfaces at a distance from the body, he explains, derived from breached arterial vessels that "sprinkled" blood with each heartbeat. As the heart ceased to beat, these damaged arteries lost the power to send blood out in jets from wounds, and this in turn altered their shape in discernible ways.[17] Moreover, only certain kinds of wounds created the right conditions for such an event: blood spatter tended to be caused by a small puncture wound, which provided the optimum conditions for maximizing blood pressure to cause effusion of blood "at a distance." Thus, on the basis of their physiologically grounded understanding of how blood exited wounds, medical practitioners were ideally placed for the task of assessing the "*form and direction*" of crime scene blood: where and how it landed, its consistency, and its size and shape.[18]

Taylor's treatment of blood found at the scene of a crime differs from Gross's in two important respects. First, Gross's priority is spatial, aimed at reconstructing the physical dynamics of an act of bloodletting independent of any physiological explanation. His approach to blood spatter—what was significant about it and how to acquire knowledge about it—is instructive on this point. It was, he writes, frequently important to know "whether the person from whom the blood has dropped was, at the time when the drop fell standing still or moving, and in the latter case in which direction and how fast." To gain insight into this physical question, Gross advises his IO to "make a study of the pavements and road ways in the immediate vicinity of large hospitals, to which many people go daily, soon or immediately after receiving an injury." This medical site was chosen not for its ability to convey the sort of specialist knowledge provided by Taylor but rather on simple empirical grounds: since injuries were either badly bound up or not bound up at all, patients lost varying quantities of blood that would register as differentiated shapes on the ground over which they traveled. To supplement this empirically derived knowledge, Gross advises a set of physical experiments designed to reproduce the conditions from which different blood shapes derived. Dropping blood from varying heights resulted in distinct patterns—some circular, some elongated. Adding horizontal movement yielded further information of potential value in reconstructing the circumstances that would have produced any given scene confronting the investigator:

> We shall find, as a rule, that the extension of the drop lies in the direction of our movement; and further, the splashes are now found only in the same direction; that is, the splashes point in the direction whither the person from whom the blood dropped was at the moment proceeding. If we now in making the experiment alter our pace, we find that the faster the movement the longer the spot or blot. This is explained by the spherical shape of the falling drop which, when it strikes the paper, continues its forward movement. In the same way, the faster the motion the more are the splashes prolonged in the same direction.[19]

The second, and for our purposes more significant, difference between these two treatments of the crime scene is the absence in Taylor's account of any protocols governing practice. As shown in the previous chapter, Gross outlines in meticulous detail the best means of detaching, packaging, labeling, and transporting blood and other trace material so as to retain their physical and evidentiary integrity. This framework is cognitive as well as procedural: in insisting upon the mechanics of harvesting, he embeds blood as an irreducibly physical artefact whose location in space is its essential feature—and challenge. Taylor's blood, though clearly existing in space, serves to underscore the interpretive potential of a medically informed observer rather than to illustrate the exacting requirements of trace-centered investigation itself. Though Taylor's blood is at scenes of crimes, and is interpretable therein, its handling as a physical substance in specific spaces and under specific conditions is absent. As against the thirty-odd pages of detailed advice in Gross's handbook on how to search, register and describe, detach and preserve crime scene blood, Taylor limits himself to a single, rudimentary statement of the need for investigative care in such cases: "A practitioner, in noticing and recording the circumstances involved in them, ought to exercise due caution."[20] It is in the generality of this advice, and its lack of supporting material and mental apparatus, that the difference between Taylor and Gross can be best appreciated.

GROSS ABROAD: EARLY DEBATES ON ENGLISH CSI

When Gross's *Handbook* was translated in 1906, commentators immediately recognized it—for good or evil—as a groundbreaking contribution to English criminal investigation. Writing in the *Illustrated London News*, the science columnist Andrew Wilson described it as a "remarkable volume" that had no domestic equivalent: "It is a novel idea, in Britain at least, to find such a work published as a police text book," Wilson observed, noting that this textual novelty reflected the broader absence of an institutional framework for scientific policing like those already established on the Continent:

> As yet in this country we have no schools of criminology other than our great police establishments present, but abroad, where, as in France particularly, the pursuit of the evidence, and its identification likewise, are conducted on scientific principles, the police training is systematised in a high degree. What would be thought of a British University which included in its listing of chairs one of "Criminology"? Yet such a chair exists in the University of Prague, and Dr. Hans Gross is its occupant.

Parts of Gross's text, Wilson continued, served the needs of what he recognized as the contemporary lynchpin of English forensic expertise—the medical witness—but Gross's contribution reached well beyond that of standard medico-legal texts:

> No doubt certain phases of this work concern the medical jurist equally with the magistrate and police officer, and every British medical man requires to study medical jurisprudence as an essential part of his curriculum. But Dr. Gross goes far outside the purely medical aspects of criminology. He has chapters on the detective officer himself, on the examination of witnesses, and on inspection of localities.

Yet, as innovative and praiseworthy as Gross's contribution might be, Wilson expressed doubt about its reception amongst English readers who, in his view, were overly protective of detection as an "art": "Even if the detective, like the poet, is held to be born and not made, it is obviously equally worthy of consideration that aptitude in the detection of crime is a matter in which education, practice and training must count much in evolving the astute sleuth-hound."[21]

Resistance to Gross's systematizing and scientizing message was also anticipated in a *Times Literary Supplement* review written by the prison governor and future head of the CID, Sir Basil Home Thomson. Like Wilson, Thomson viewed Gross's work as essentially foreign:

> In England criminology has never been treated as a science. There is a fairly
> wide literature on the punishment of crime, but beyond two or three works
> on medical jurisprudence there are no handbooks in the detection of the
> criminal. For these works we must go to France, Italy, Germany, and Austria.

Thomson also found much to admire in Gross's investigation techniques, and in particular their capacity to render meaningful the most unpromising of crime-scene traces: "In the practical methods of obtaining a clue to the perpetrator of a crime there is nothing more fascinating than the treatment of dust under the microscope. The dust in a pocket, or in the crevices of a pocket knife, may tell more of the movements of the owner than he himself can remember."[22]

Yet English police were generally resistant to the procedural rigor and analytical magic of dust-driven CSI, and for Thomson, unlike Wilson, this was an entirely appropriate attitude. The Continental approach stemmed in large part from the central role of legally trained officials (like Gross's IO) whose investigations were driven by explicit procedural rules and whose work was both amenable to and aided by systematic codification.[23] Moreover, the traditional English approach, which eschewed "scientific method" in favor of working from "information received," yielded positive results. Continental "erudition" notwithstanding, Thomson insisted, the English police were regarded as "the most effective in Europe." Indeed, the translation of works like Gross's might pose a risk to the felicitous status quo by shifting public attitudes to, and raising unrealistic expectations of, criminal investigation: "while it may not be very useful to the official detective it will stimulate the zeal of the amateur and so contribute to the growing practice of trial by newspaper."[24]

The threat of scientific policing to native practice had to an extent already come to pass, with some contemporary commentators identifying a lack of rigor as a prime contributor to a spate of recent high-profile unsolved cases. Writing in the wake of the unsolved Ripper murders in Whitechapel, the retired police officer Charles Tempest Clarkson and crime journalist

J. Hall Richardson criticized English reliance on uniformed police officers as scene investigators, whose lack of "detective instinct" had resulted in "terrible bungling in the observation of little points of the utmost value." It was not until several murders had been perpetrated, for example, "that the police thought it advisable to photograph the corpse, before removal, and thus preserve a permanent record of it position."[25] Major Arthur Griffiths, inspector of prisons from 1878 to 1896 and author of a two-volume account of English policing, shared this concern. Though wary of a Continental flair for trace-based "speculative evidence," Griffiths nevertheless conceded that "modern police methods" were properly characterized by a "quick wit to seize almost imperceptible clues, the faculty of analysis, the power of inductive reasoning." Citing several contemporary failures, including the Whitechapel atrocities, Griffiths admitted that "our otherwise excellent and admirably effective police have been far less successful than those of other countries in the unravelling of such mysteries."[26]

This avowed tension between regard for native sensibilities and the benefits of reform was voiced episodically in the years following the publication of Gross's translated *Handbook*, and in a manner that fully realized Thomson's fears about the text's potential to stoke unrealistic public and journalistic criticism of English policing practice. Take, for example, the attention devoted by reporters, editors, and correspondents in the *Daily Mail* to a now-forgotten 1908 murder investigation. On August 24, 1908, the body of Caroline Mary Luard was found by her husband, Major General Charles Edward Luard, and two companions on the veranda of their isolated summerhouse in a heavily wooded area near Sevenoaks, Kent. She had been shot, and Luard, a retired Army officer, immediately summoned the local police. The initial reports of the discovery and police response, though heavily draped in melodrama, depicted an orderly approach to the scene of the crime:

> The local constable was sent for. He insisted on the body remaining as it was found until he could summon his superiors. The three men, the general incoherent with grief, watched the body in the silent wood for nearly two hours. The vicar of the parish, who also had been summoned, uttered a solemn prayer over the body of the murdered lady. The police superintendent and the doctor made their observations, and then as night was falling the body of Mrs. Luard was carried reverently through the undergrowth and the fragrant pines to the general's house on the hill. . . . The bungalow in the wood pre-

sented a strange scene this afternoon. All the approaches were carefully guarded by policemen, and inquisitive visitors were kept not only out of touch, but also out of view of the summer house. . . . The bungalow was closed, a place of the dead.[27]

However, chinks in procedure soon began to emerge. In its August 31 edition, the newspaper reported on the failure of the local police both to find any "tangible clue" and, despite their best intentions, to secure the crime scene: "No one was allowed, however, to enter the wood which was the scene of the crime by the gates, but some persons secretly made their way in from the neighbouring fields. Many of the more morbid took away heather, bracken, and twigs as souvenirs."[28]

Lack of progress soon became interpreted as a structural deficiency: an editorial on September 3 raised the concern that, as the police seemed to have "abandoned all immediate hope of bringing to justice the murderer of Mrs. Luard," the case was destined to become yet another entry in the "long record of mysterious crimes." The editorial blamed "the methods—not the men": it was unreasonable to expect local constables to possess the requisite skills for "detecting and tracing intricate and often almost imperceptible clues." It then turned to the Continent for an alternative regime that, though not without its faults, was nonetheless "free from some of our vices":

> In the first place, every precaution is taken to preserve intact the circumstantial evidence afforded by the scene and material of the crime. No one is permitted to disturb these evidences or to incur the slightest risk of obliterating a clue that may be manifest only to the eye of trained intelligence. In France, for example, not a foot would have trodden the wood in which the body of Mrs. Luard was found until the agents of the central police force had made the most minute inspection of every inch of the ground.[29]

Over the course of the next several days, as the investigation continued and the mystery deepened, letters poured in, some defending and others condemning the investigation in particular and the English model more generally. One critical letter, commenting on a published interview with a former CID chief, linked the events at Sevenoaks back to those at Whitechapel decades earlier, when "distinct clues were absolutely wiped out" by investigators, and drew particular attention to the hasty removal of Mrs. Luard's body from the scene of first discovery to the mortuary: "the proper course would have been to guard everything till the expert investigator was on the scene."[30] This prompted a vigorous "defence of the old system" the following day by the veteran journalist George R. Sims. Those calling for Continental-style reform, Sims argued, were pursuing an unrealistic council of perfection and underestimating the virtues of prompt, locally informed inquiry.[31] Another correspondent expressed concern about the breach in traditional English liberties—in particular the sanctity of the home—that would result from an embrace of foreign practice, invoking as a nightmare scenario the importation of Continental standard procedure in which the investigator "at once proceeds to the house and sets seal on all doors and drawers, examines inmates, sets watch upon every person likely to throw light upon the investigation, and every scrap of writing is at once seized, photographed, and, if advisable, circulated."[32]

By the second decade of the twentieth century, concerns over the English deficiencies were being voiced by individuals who identified themselves with the ideals of modern scientific policing. One of the earliest to adopt this stance was the London analytical chemist C. Ainsworth Mitchell, who opens his 1911 book *Science and the Criminal* with a plea for the creation of "a department specially trained for the work of criminal investigations." Scientific training of those first called to crime scenes, Mitchell argues, might have avoided the numerous "unsolved mysteries" of recent years. In a telling observation that we will follow up shortly, Mitchell likens the present system to "that under which doctors acquired their knowledge of medicine in the early part of last century. Their mistakes taught them what not to do, but in the meantime the patient sometimes died."[33] This criticism of the outdated empiricism of English practice was underscored a few years later when the New York City police investigator Raymond Fosdick published a survey of European practice on behalf of the newly established Rockefeller Foundation: while Continental policing had advanced in recent years from "old-time rule-of-thumb procedure" to a new "scientific spirit"—a shift for which Fosdick gave Gross significant credit—when he looked across the Channel he found a very different model: "In England the influence of Dr. Gross and his disciples is not yet perceptible. Indeed there are but few English officials who know anything of the work that is being done on the Continent."[34]

_◊ ◊_

As was recognized by contemporary commentators, the revelatory potential of trace-driven CSI, though present in outline, was not a prominent

CRIME SCENES BEFORE CSI   53

feature of the English textbook literature in the Victorian and Edwardian periods. Medico-legal treatises throughout maintained a primary focus on questions of the body: on the way the crime scene might yield clues about cause of death and identity of the corpse. Analysis of the crime scene for the purpose of reconstructing the events leading up to the crime were not isolated as a special consideration requiring a specific set of skills. However, if we turn to another contemporary genre—the detective story—we enter a substantively different world, one in which the disciplined search for and analysis of minute and ostensibly insignificant matter was projected as the cutting edge of forensic investigation.

GUARDING THE PALACE OF THE SLEEPING BEAUTY: DETECTIVE FICTION, DETECTING CULTURES

The interpenetration of detective fiction with real-world methods was a self-conscious feature of turn-of-the-century criminalist texts on both sides of the Channel. As noted in chapter 1, Locard is unabashed in acknowledging fictional counterparts as an imaginative springboard for his program of scientific policing, nowhere more explicitly than in his 1924 *Policiers de roman et policies de laboratoire*, the first half of which is devoted to the exploits of Edgar Allan Poe's C. Auguste Dupin, Emile Gaboriau's Monsieur Lecoq, and Arthur Conan Doyle's Sherlock Holmes. Locard's purpose is clear: to use these most publicly recognizable crime fighters to stimulate a practical program of reform by "drawing attention to what the police can do and what they might do if they were to break out of their habitual routines."[35] Their power, in Locard's view, derives from the contemporary public's "passion for the art of the detective," which he compares to the influence of earlier literary genres: just as Goethe and Chateaubriand spawned a generation of neurasthenics, and Hugo and de Musset caused the romantic spirit to bloom, so did Locard's trio ingrain for their public the essential lesson of scientific policing: that, no matter how cunning, the criminal "always leaves behind involuntary signs of his movements, and that this testimony is the only kind that never lies."[36]

Though Locard celebrates the logical acumen of Dupin's and Lecoq's enthusiastic approaches to crime scene investigation, he reserves his fullest praise for Sherlock Holmes as the unsurpassed master of trace-centered police science, a judgment that Locard admiringly illustrates through classic examples of Holmesian CSI.[37] "The Boscombe Valley Mystery" crime scene, for example, showcases both virtuoso technique and its potential to drive practical reform—Holmes's lament about the "herd of buffalos" that had defaced the crime scene, Locard observes, should "serve as an epigraph to every manual addressed to police agents."[38] And of course Locard is quick to highlight Holmes's credentials as a pioneer of modern dust analysis, admiring his identification of the Trichinopoly cigar ash at the murder scene in *A Study in Scarlet* and of the Wigmore Street post office's distinctive red clay in *The Sign of Four*.

By pairing his appreciative survey of *policiers de roman* with one featuring those of the *laboratoire*, Locard underscores—and turns to his own purposes—the blurred boundary between detective fiction and the methods that he and Gross promote. Elsewhere, we have reviewed in some detail recent discussions by literary scholars of a wider self-conscious imbrication of detective fact and fiction: Ronald Thomas, for instance, has noted the "indistinct boundary between truth and fantasy, imaginative literature and journalistic reportage," which, in Melissa Littlefield's view, rendered them in part "literary advertisements for the sciences they employed."[39] Moreover, as Thomas and (more fully) Lawrence Frank have argued, detective fiction served as an important model for working out and illustrating the logic and practices of the historically grounded sciences—geology, paleontology, evolutionary biology, archeology—that grew to prominence in the nineteenth century and that were predicated on reconstructing a narrative of past events out of incomplete and unintentional physical traces.[40]

From the vantage point of its Continental champions, the detective story thus featured as a natural and entirely appropriate ally in proselytizing for a modern framework of crime investigation. In England, given the relative absence of a corresponding professional literature, this function was more significant still and is thus crucial for our account. Space permitting, we would here undertake a comparative assessment of how a range of characters (including the canonical trio of Dupin, Lecoq, and Holmes) interacted with and helped to articulate a new trace-laden forensic landscape. However, given present limitations, and our previous discussion of dust as an exemplary object of a forensics of traces, we adopt a different approach, one focusing on a selection of early twentieth-century cases featuring Richard Austin Freeman's dust-hunting hero—Dr. John Evelyn Thorndyke.[41]

In a career spanning three decades following his 1907 debut, Freeman's creation earned a reputation as "the scientific detective par excellence, . . . [whose] power comes not from a superhuman intellect, but from specialized knowledge, technology and method."[42] In eschewing Holmes's often eccentric conclusions in favor of ones grounded in carefully delineated and demonstrated scientific methods, Freeman is following an explicit pedagogic agenda with two principal aims: first, to instruct police officials on their proper duties in criminal investigations and, second, to educate the public about the powers of modern crime scene investigation. Freeman employs a range of devices in this effort. The best remembered of these is his formal innovation—the "inverted detective story"—which, by providing at the outset a detailed account of the crime and its perpetrator, shifts narrative emphasis from the traditional "whodunit" question to the "how" and in so doing foregrounds the analytical techniques performed by the character.[43] Freeman also showcases the workings of crime scene investigation and its analysis of a world of minute trace evidence by inserting into the text photomicrographs that at once illustrate the story, enhance its scientific verisimilitude, and enable the reader to experience the regime of trace visuality that Freeman seeks to promote (see figs. 2.1 and 2.2).[44]

From the outset of Thorndyke's career, Freeman is explicit about the ultimate objective of such strategies. In the preface to his first anthology of stories, published in 1909 and dedicated to his friend Frank Stanfield "in memory of many a pleasant evening spent with a microscope and camera," Freeman explains his working principles:

> I have been scrupulous in confining myself to authentic facts and practicable methods. The stories have, for the most part, a medico-legal motive, and the methods of solution described in them are similar to those employed in actual practice by medical jurists. The stories illustrate, in fact, the application to the detection of crime of the ordinary methods of scientific research. I may add

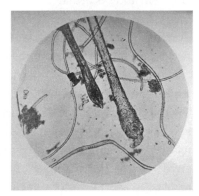

Figure 2.1. Fluff from key-barrel, magnified 77 diameters. R. Austin Freeman, "The Stranger's Latchkey," in *John Thorndyke's Cases*, 1909.

Figure 2.2. Sand from the murdered woman's pillow, magnified 25 diameters. R. Austin Freeman, "A Message from the Deep Sea," in *John Thorndyke's Cases*, 1909.

that the experiments described have in all cases been performed by me, and that the micro-photographs are, of course, from the actual specimens.[45]

As a self-anointed apostle of forensic modernity, Freeman reflects and amplifies many of the core themes discussed thus far. He fully embraces the Grossian and Locardian dictates of crime scene investigation and management, and he illustrates these with serial virtuoso demonstrations of the evidentiary potential of dust. In "The Stranger's Latchkey," Thorndyke rescues an otherwise unpromising crime scene by extracting, "with much coaxing, a large ball of grey fluff" out of a keyhole, which he then folds up in paper "with infinite care" and submits to microscopic examination. For Thorndyke, the fluff yields a "curious and instructive" assortment of fibers and hairs, a harvest lost on his ever-baffled sidekick, Jervis.[46] In his first of many "sermons in dust," Thorndyke declares, "You will have, Jervis, to study the minute properties of dust and dirt. Their evidential value is immense."[47] The next story in the anthology features Thorndyke in a race against time to secure crime scene dust against the depredations of undisciplined police investigation, which would inevitably "rob us of our treasure," and introduces a novel instrument to facilitate the process: a "patent dust-extractor, . . . made from a bicycle foot-pump . . . fitted with a glass nozzle and a small detachable glass receiver for collecting the dust." When passed over suspect clothing, the white coating of dust "vanished as if by magic, . . . and simultaneously the glass receiver became clouded over with a white deposit," which Thorndyke then detaches and labels so as to preserve a record of the part of the clothing from which the dust had been extracted.[18]

Of Thorndyke's early adventures, however, the most comprehensive example of dust analysis as a model of trace-driven and crime scene–based forensic investigation is "A Message from the Deep Sea," which opens with a chance encounter between Thorndyke and Dr. Hart, a distressed former student on his way to the scene of a murder in his capacity as newly appointed assistant to an East End police surgeon. Accompanying the inexperienced medical investigator, Thorndyke enters a lodging-house room in which a young girl is lying dead in bed, her neck displaying a "savagely" inflicted wound. Examining the bedclothes Thorndyke identifies particles of "silver sand" sprinkled over parts of the pillow. Asked by the astonished Jervis for an explanation of how it got there and what it might signify, Thorndyke is noncommittal:

> "We will consider the explanation later," was his reply. He had produced from his pocket a small metal box which he always carried, and which contained such requisites as cover-slips, capillary tubes, moulding wax, and other "diagnostic materials." He now took from it a seed-envelope, into which he neatly shovelled the little pinch of sand with his knife. He had closed the envelope, and was writing a pencilled description on the outside, when we were startled by a cry from Hart. "Good God, sir! Look at this! It was done by a woman!" He had drawn back the bedclothes, and was staring aghast at the dead girl's left hand. It held a thin tress of long, red hair.[49]

Pocketing the sand-laden envelope, Thorndyke turns his attention to the hair, carefully scrutinizing it as it lay in the rigid fingers of the girl's hand until interrupted by Hart's superior and a police detective who, on seeing the hair, removes it from the hand and places it a paper packet, which he then puts in his breast pocket. The detective's subsequent discovery that a red-headed love rival of the deceased was a fellow lodger concludes his interest in the investigation.

Thorndyke's investigation, of course, continues in two distinct venues and centers on two distinct objects: first, in his microscope-equipped chambers where he examines the "silver sand," and, second, at the local mortuary, where he examines the corpse. Thorndyke's microscopy leaves Jervis enchanted and amazed:

> Mingled with crystalline grains of quartz, glassy spicules, and water-worn fragments of coral, were a number of lovely little shells, some of the texture of fine porcelain, others like blown Venetian glass. "These are Foraminifera!" I exclaimed. "Yes." "Then it is not silver sand, after all?" "Certainly not." "But what is it, then?" Thorndyke smiled. "It is a message to us from the deep sea, Jervis; from the floor of the Eastern Mediterranean." "And can you read the message?" "I think I can," he replied, "but I shall know soon, I hope."[50]

At the mortuary later that same day Thorndyke encounters the police surgeon in a dismissive mood; he had just concluded his post-mortem examination, which he considers "a mere farce in a case like this; you have seen all that there was to see." Undeterred, Thorndyke gains access to the corpse "to verify one or two points," but his "post-mortem" is highly unorthodox in nature—though adopting a suitably solemn affect with respect to the corpse, it interests him not as singular case of mortal flesh to be probed for pathophysiological clues but as a subsidiary crime scene to be searched for trace evidence:

> Removing his hat, [he] advanced to the long slate table, and bent over its burden of pitiful tragedy. For some time he remained motionless, running his eye gravely over the corpse, in search, no doubt, of bruises and indications of a struggle. Then he stooped and narrowly examined the wound, especially at its commencement and end. Suddenly he drew nearer, peering intently as if something had attracted his attention, and having taken out his lens, fetched a small sponge, with which he dried an exposed process of the spine. Holding his lens before the dried spot, he again scrutinized it closely, and then, with a scalpel and forceps, detached some object, which he carefully washed, and then once more examined through his lens as it lay in the palm of his hand. Finally, as I expected, he brought forth his "collecting-box," took from it a seed-envelope, into which he dropped the object—evidently something quite small—closed up the envelope, wrote on the outside of it, and replaced it in the box.[51]

At the inquest, the fruits of Thorndyke's engagement with scene traces are revealed. The bunched hair clasped in the victim's hand has roots at both ends, suggesting that they had not ended up in there as the result of a death struggle but had been planted post-mortem; the state of their root sheaths confirms this—they were shed, not torn from the scalp, indicating that they had been taken from the accused's brush. His "post-mortem" find had been a small particle of steel, which corresponded exactly to a missing fragment from the real culprit's knife. But it was the revelation of the foraminifera that most enthralls the inquest, prompting the perplexed coroner to ask how this exotic species of deep-sea dust could have made its way to the pillow of an East End lodging room:

> "The explanation," replied Thorndyke, "is really quite simple. Sand of this kind is contained in considerable quantities in Turkey sponges. The warehouses in which the sponges are unpacked are often strewn with it ankle deep; the men who unpack the cases become dusted over with it, their clothes saturated and their pockets filled with it. If such a person, with his clothes and pockets full of sand, had committed this murder, it is pretty certain that in leaning over the head of the bed in a partly inverted position he would have let fall a certain quantity of the sand from his pockets and the interstices of his clothing."[52]

On ascertaining the nature of the sand, Thorndyke reviews the list of persons acquainted with the deceased and discovers that one is employed as a packer in a local warehouse which had taken delivery of Mediterranean sponges a few days before the murder.

With the sponge packer arrested, the detective and police surgeon suitably chastened, and the public gallery awed at the evidentiary potential of a world of infinitesimal traces properly handled, all that remains for Thorndyke to do is to reinforce the story's core lessons. His concluding message also serves as a perfect summation of this chapter, for it captures all the essential features of the fin de siècle project of constituting a regime of disciplined CSI:

> "An instructive case, Jervis," remarked Thorndyke, as we walked homewards—"a case that reiterates the lesson that the authorities still refuse to learn." "What is that?" I asked.
>
> "It is this. When it is discovered that a murder has been committed, the scene of that murder should instantly become as the Palace of the Sleeping

Beauty. Not a grain of dust should be moved, not a soul should be allowed to approach it, until the scientific observer has seen everything *in situ* and absolutely undisturbed. No tramplings of excited constables, no rummaging by detectives, no scrambling to and fro of bloodhounds. Consider what would have happened in this case if we had arrived a few hours later. The corpse would have been in the mortuary, the hair in the sergeant's pocket, the bed rummaged and the sand scattered abroad . . . There would not have been the vestige of a clue." "And," I added, "the deep sea would have uttered its message in vain."[53]

BERNARD SPILSBURY AND THE RISE
OF CELEBRITY PATHOLOGY

This chapter concludes by introducing Bernard Spilsbury, a pathologist who, from his first publicly noted appearance at the 1910 trial of Hawley Harvey Crippen to his death in 1946, dominated the landscape of English homicide investigation in a manner not seen before or since. Biographical accounts of Spilsbury are numerous though problematic in their depiction of the specific nature of his work.[54] Having qualified in medicine at St. Mary's Hospital in 1905, Spilsbury took up a hospital lectureship in pathology in 1907. At the start of the twentieth century, St. Mary's had emerged as England's preeminent center for forensic science and medicine, largely eclipsing Taylor's home institution of Guy's. It boasted the services of three prominent members of the London-based Medico-Legal Society whose expertise was regularly sought by the Home Office in cases of special difficulty: its lecturer in forensic medicine and toxicology Arthur P. Luff, the physician and toxicologist William Willcox, and the pathologist Augustus Pepper.

To a large extent the role and responsibilities of the medico-legal expert at the turn of the century were similar to those outlined in the nineteenth-century medico-legal literature: primarily charged with conducting postmortem examinations of a victim of suspected homicide, he was also given some responsibility for taking cognizance of the wider material circumstances surrounding the body. For much of the nineteenth century this figure was not cast in specialist terms. Instead, duties of investigation and testifying devolved to the first medical practitioner on the scene. Even if one considers widely publicized late-century murder investigations (the Ripper murders at Whitechapel, most obviously), victims' bodies were examined by more or less faceless investigators, often local practitioners with no claims to special forensic expertise.

However, a few developments arguably had the effect of elevating the standing of the forensic pathologists as a recognizable subgroup of homicide investigators. In the context of debates about the qualifications that should be required for those conducting inquest post-mortems, proponents of a more rigorous regime of expertise had begun to argue for official recognition of a list of qualified specialist pathologists as the cornerstone of a reformed system. In London, these calls were heeded by the County Council's newly constituted Public Control Committee, which, in 1893, compiled an informal list of hospital practitioners (including Luff and Pepper) and experienced police surgeons available for the use of coroners. At the same time the committee initiated a program of mortuary construction, seeking to abolish the haphazard and "undignified" practice of post-mortems conducted in public house outbuildings and other ad hoc sites that had previously prevailed.[55]

Such developments, though by no means revolutionary, introduced a new layer of distinction between ordinary practitioners traditionally identified in medico-legal texts like Taylor's as qualified investigators on the basis of their general medical acumen, and those with a specialist cognitive and institutional grounding in the conduct of post-mortem examinations in cases of possible criminal violence. Spilsbury's rise to professional and public prominence, in this sense, was part of a broader trend that, as Norman Ambage and Michael Clark have observed, extended the "Victorian tradition of all-round forensic expertise."[56] As the coming chapters will argue, the significance of Spilsbury's innovations as a forensic pathologist lay less in the nature of his post-mortem investigative practices than in the way he transformed the role of the medico-legal expert into a singularly personalized, powerful, and celebrated one, with him as the unsurpassed exemplar.

To understand this aspect of Spilsbury's achievement, it is crucial to recognize that he was riding not merely a gentle wave of specialist reform but also a second, and higher-cresting, one. This involved the rise to professional and public prominence of a model of homicide investigation that, while not ignoring the body, generated evidence grounded in the context of the suspected act, focused on material traces, often minute, found at the scene of the crime. This model, the one that we have traced from its articulation by Gross and Locard to its projection onto the English stage in newspaper accounts and, more prominently, in detective fiction, was anchored in the practices and competencies that we now associate with CSI: acute powers of observation, systematic attention to detail, appreciation of ostensibly trivial objects and relations, and physical engagement with the material realities of the scene.

Spilsbury's "celebrity" derived from a conflation of two forensic roles: that of general medical witness and that of crime scene investigator. This conflation has two dimensions—a historical one, fostered by contemporary observers of Spilsbury "in action," and a historiographical one, developed and nurtured by a legion of biographers who recycle heroic accounts of his famous cases. This hybrid construction—its source, its function, and its legacy—will be the main preoccupation of the next two chapters, which examine in detail Spilsbury's involvement in the 1924 case of *R v. Mahon*. It was the Mahon case that secured his ascendency by fusing the distinct, and indeed in many respects conflicting, epistemic structures and practical deployment of forensic pathology and forensic science. Both were on the rise in the Edwardian period, and it was this conflation that created the cult of celebrity that he enjoyed. Yet at the same time, in Mahon as in his career more broadly, fissures appeared between these two sets of practices. It is only by careful attention to what Spilsbury actually did, rather than what others have projected onto him, that we can appreciate the unique space that he occupied as a forensic practitioner at a unique point in the history of English homicide investigation.

CHAPTER THREE

Murder at "the Crumbles"

W e now turn to the first of this book's "flash moments"—the investigation of the 1924 murder of Emily Kaye by Patrick Mahon in a holiday bungalow on a stretch of beach near Eastbourne known as "the Crumbles." Both at the time and ever since, it has stood as a pivotal moment in the making of English CSI. Bernard Spilsbury took the starring role, and in biographical accounts of his career his contributions to the investigation are often taken as evidence of his commitment to a trace-centered forensics. In *The Father of Forensics: How Sir Bernard Spilsbury Invented Modern CSI*, the crime writer Colin Evans presents Spilsbury's actions as an indication of his trace-hunting credentials:

> Spilsbury didn't touch anything at the moment, rather moved from room to room, hands pushed firmly into pockets—his invariable attitude at any crime scene. . . . Spilsbury reined in his curiosity, determined to complete his "big picture" analysis. . . . In the lounge where Mahon said the fight had occurred, Spilsbury went over every inch of the door with a magnifying glass.[1]

Performances such as this, for Evans, stake Spilsbury's claim as the "invent[or] of Modern CSI." By extending Spilsbury's core medico-legal repertoire to embrace the sensibilities of a hands-on harvester of traces, the Crumbles case thus gave rise to a new kind of forensic creature, a hybrid practitioner of the mortuary and of the crime scene.

Spilsbury's performance at the Crumbles is crucial to understanding the historical development of English CSI, although for reasons that differ substantially from conventional accounts. Though his forensic contributions came to dominate the Mahon investigation, these did not stem from any systematic engagement with the crime scene. He was instead working within, and at the same time reaching beyond, the nineteenth-century tradition of the medical jurist discussed in the previous chapter. Spilsbury's standing as a pioneering exponent of CSI is largely based on a projection of the modern fascination with an ensemble of forensic practices onto the past. But at the same time this projection is not without historical basis, for it is itself an echo of an earlier discourse that was assembled and showcased by the contemporary press as it observed and reported on the investigation in real time. Indeed, a significant form of cultural "domestication" of CSI, albeit partial and provisional, was accomplished in this journalistic framing of Spilsbury's engagement with the Crumbles crime scene.

Our analysis explores how the scripts of trace hunting and crime scene discipline, implicitly and explicitly, permeated accounts of Spilsbury's work at the Crumbles bungalow, which in turn had a profound effect on contemporary understandings of the nature of his forensic persona. The Mahon case marked a transition in Spilsbury's identity from a well-known Home Office consultant pathologist to an iconic public personality, establishing a new figure on the forensic landscape—the "celebrity pathologist"—whose image both transcended the nature of his actual work in the case and shaped understandings of English homicide investigation for decades to come.[2] The Crumbles investigation in this sense acted as an incubator for the celebrity that surrounded (and still surrounds) Spilsbury. This legacy is significant for the overall story, as it served as a reference point for a subsequent cohort of reformers attempting to establish an alternative model of CSI in the English context, one that was closer in spirit and practice to the model laid out by its continental exponents.

Our account will be developed over two chapters. The first carefully reconstructs the murder investigation itself, describing its main elements, introducing its principal actors, and exploring their practices and interactions. The second focuses on contemporaneous representations and resonances of the investigation as assembled and relayed by the media. By attending to the messy tangle of reality and fiction, these two chapters, when taken together, provide a layered account which reflects the centrality and ambiguity of Spilsbury, celebrity pathology, and the Mahon case in the making of English CSI.

MURDER AT THE CRUMBLES

The investigation into the death of Emily Kaye began with the police surveillance of a locker room at Waterloo Station containing a Gladstone bag.[3]

In the bag were various articles of clothing and a knife stained with blood.[4] On May 2, 1924, when sales manager and handsome thirty-four-year-old adulterer Patrick Mahon opened the locker to retrieve the bag, police investigators immediately took him into custody for questioning, during which he admitted involvement in the death of his thirty-seven-year-old lover Kaye.

During his interrogation by detectives, Mahon gave two versions of events, one on the day of his arrest, and a second one on May 5. Both statements insisted that Kaye's death at the holiday cottage they had shared on the Crumbles, a stretch of shingled beach near Eastbourne, was a terrible accident. However, there were significant differences between the statements. In the first, Mahon recalled that on the night of the April 16 the pair had quarreled, and in a violent rage Kaye threw a coal axe at him. A fierce struggle ensued, during which she fatally struck her head as she fell on an iron coal cauldron. Fearing he would be charged with her murder, Mahon dismembered her body and attempted to destroy the remains.[5] In his second statement Mahon gave a more complex account of the events surrounding Kaye's death. After she threw the coal axe, Kaye dashed at him and clutched at his face, and in order to defend himself, he explained, he had no option but to "fight back and loosen her hold."[6] While he reemphasized that Kaye's head had come into "violent contact with the round cauldron," causing her head to "ooze" blood, Mahon now introduced the possibility that he might also have accidentally strangled her during the struggle. The story of his attempted disposal of Kaye's body remained the same.

The first police interrogation of Mahon lasted into the early hours of May 3, immediately after which Scotland Yard detectives rushed to the Crumbles, arriving at around 7 a.m. The Yard's Chief Inspector Savage and his accompanying officers were met by Superintendent Sinclair of the East Sussex Constabulary, who escorted them to the cottage, known locally as the "Officers' House," to establish the existence of human remains.[7] Investigators unlocked the front door and entered the living room. They then explored the bedrooms until they reached one—a small dark room—which one investigator later recalled "had a very offensive smell" emanating from a cargo trunk. They opened the trunk and peered inside.

On the top was a tray containing three pairs of shoes and a pair of slippers. We took the tray out, and underneath found four parcels, which appeared to be human remains. We then examined the contents and found wrapped in articles of wearing apparel one of the breasts. In another parcel done up in brown paper was the other breast. In another, also done up in brown paper, was the left of the pelvis. In a piece of sacking was the right of the pelvis. In a biscuit tin was the intestines, liver, lungs, heart, and other parts or organs. We then had the whole trunk taken out into the back [yard] and photographed. We made a further search and found in this same bedroom a hat box which was found to contain, done up in under-clothing, 38 pieces of human flesh, ranging from 2–8 inches, some with bones, muscle and fat, all of which had been boiled.[8]

The horrible discoveries continued to mount. Searches of the remaining rooms yielded a large saucepan and an enamel bath full of "reddish liquid" layered with "fatty matter," partly incinerated bone residue in several fireplace grates, and a three-legged coal cauldron with a bent leg, against which Kaye had allegedly fallen. As Savage wrote in one of his reports from the scene, May 3 was a grisly and labor-intensive day for scene investigators: "[the] search of the house and the unpacking of the boiled and unboiled portions of her body was a gruesome and sickening task, the stench was appalling and we did not complete the work until a late hour in the afternoon, when we returned to the town in the lorry."[9]

Spilsbury arrived at the bungalow the following morning. Savage met him and his secretary, Hilda Bainbridge, at Victoria Station and escorted them to the scene. Spilsbury's presence at the Crumbles in several respects marked a departure from his usual interventions in cases of suspected murder. Up until the Mahon case (and indeed subsequently) Spilsbury featured in a continuous series of publicized homicide investigations that followed a common pattern. His interventions typically commenced not at the crime scene but at the post-mortem table where, faced with an often mutilated and decomposing corpse, he single-handedly assembled its story from within the enclosed space of the mortuary and then emerged to defend it in polished courtroom testimony, where he spoke in accessible language about the ultimate decipherability of the bodily chaos that had initially confronted him.

The Mahon case, however, represented an anomaly in Spilsbury's career, as his role in the investigation started at the crime scene.[10] His presence at the Crumbles bungalow was dictated by the state of his core object of scrutiny. The condition of Kaye's body rendered impossible a conventional mortuary-based inquiry removed from the crime scene: comprehensively

Figure 3.1. Police photograph of Emily Kaye's dismembered remains. East Sussex Record Office, SPA 2/37/34, piece 6. Courtesy of East Sussex Record Office and East Sussex Police.

mutilated and dispersed throughout the bungalow, the corpse could not be moved to the mortuary following the normal procedure for transport (fig. 3.1). Spilsbury thus had no choice but to engage firsthand with the physical space in which the remains had been discovered. Accordingly, a makeshift mortuary was erected at the scene: a kitchen table from the house was placed in the exterior courtyard of the bungalow and covered with a cloth, to serve as a post-mortem slab. In an attempt to conceal the spectacle from the gathering crowds, wicker screens were erected across the bungalow's perimeter walls. This work was designed to confirm and accommodate, in the necessary but unorthodox space of the crime scene, Spilsbury's core identity as a forensic pathologist.

Spilsbury's autopsy practices served as a powerful and productive resource in the early stages of the Crumbles investigation, enabling him to assess the mass of calcified bones, pieces of boiled flesh, and putrescent bodily organs that had been discovered by police investigators. In channeling and performing the well-established scripts of the medico-legal practitioner,

Spilsbury sought to reconstruct, identify, and interpret mutilated flesh. His most pressing task was to establish positive identification by examining the remains for indicators such as weight, height, hair color, and sex. But because of the butchered state of the bodily remains, conclusively determining individual identity proved difficult. As a consequence, he began by seeking merely to confirm whether these were the remains of a single individual matching Kaye's general profile or the dismembered and commingled remains of multiple bodies, human, animal, or both.

Spilsbury turned his attention to the remains that the police had discovered and inventoried on the first day of the investigation. He fit the pieces of chest and abdominal wall together to form a single human torso, and found that the organs formed an (almost) complete set with no duplicates. From the bone fragments he reassembled portions of the legs, arms, and hands. There was, however, a vital missing piece of what he later described as a challenging "human jig-saw"—Spilsbury could find neither a skull nor the upper neck bones. Nonetheless, his reconstruction enabled him to deliver a general profile that fit the physical description of Emily Kaye: the body of "an adult female of big build and fair hair."[11]

After establishing a degree of identity, Spilsbury then turned to the question of the cause of death, but here he faced another set of challenges. Post-mortem examinations usually commenced with an external inspection of the surface of the body before opening up the body for an internal examination and subsequent dissection. The Kaye autopsy, however, was no ordinary one: the dismembered and traumatized state of the body and organs compromised standard procedures and protocol in that there was no easy distinction between the exterior and interior of the body. Yet Spilsbury persisted in structuring his examination in accordance with convention, first attending to external signs and then to interior ones. He closely scrutinized the surfaces of the large collection of boiled skin and the portions of skin attached to the reconstructed torso for any visible indications of injury received in life, such as bruising or puncturing wounds to the skin, which might account for death. He detected no such external signs of violent trauma. The only injury he observed on the (partially) reassembled body was "a bruise at the back of the left shoulder about 2 inches long" that, he surmised, could have been caused by a struggle but was not of sufficient severity to cause death.[12]

Turning to interior signs, Spilsbury carefully examined the bodily organs for indications of potentially fatal disease. Once again, his findings were negative: despite their putrefied appearance, they belonged to a person in full health. Spilsbury's internal examination also allowed him to explore the possibility of whether Mahon stabbed his lover to death with a knife. Though it was no longer possible to determine the existence of wounds caused by a knife attack on skin that had been subjected to multiple cuts caused by the victim's post-mortem dismemberment, Spilsbury reasoned that it would still be possible to identify any stab wounds to the intact organs. However, from his examination, Spilsbury concluded that there was no "indication of injury inflicted during life in the organs."[13] Close inspection of the edges of the organs, the skin, and the bones enabled him to determine the type and degree of the sharpness of the instrument that had been used to dismember the body. The clean cuts visible on the pieces of boiled flesh and the organs suggested to him that "a very sharp knife" had been used to render them, while the bones had been cut through with a saw.[14]

Without the head or the upper neck bones, Spilsbury's investigation into the cause of Kaye's death seemed to have reached an impasse, yet their absence suggested to him an inferential way forward: "the absence of any cause of death in the parts which I have examined indicates, in my view, that the cause of death would have been found in the head or neck, which are missing."[15] In the wake of Spilsbury's stymied autopsy findings, police investigators, working on the possibility that Mahon had buried Kaye's head in the vicinity of the bungalow, launched a series of targeted searches at the Crumbles to unearth and deliver the crucial evidence to the pathologist. In his report from the scene, Savage explained how, enrolling a local pack of hounds for "six or seven mornings," police returned to the beach and searched it "from 4 am until 8 am in the hope of finding the victim's missing head."[16] Despite these efforts, the crucial parts were not found. These searches nevertheless draw attention to an important point: that the police worked within a framework of investigation in which the corpse was positioned as, and was expected to be, the primary evidentiary resource for unraveling what happened to Kaye, with the forensic pathologist as its core orchestrator and interpreter.

The failed hunt for Kaye's head and neck significantly curtailed Spilsbury's ability to assess the veracity of the two accounts that Mahon had given to police to explain Kaye's "accidental" death. On Mahon's story of a lethal collision with the cauldron, Spilsbury, without the head, was unable to gauge the severity of the injuries Kaye might have received from any such blow. On the second scenario, Spilsbury's hands were similarly tied. Without the neck, he could not inspect the surrounding tissue for strangulation marks, or the hyoid bone for evidence of a lethal fracture.[17] Nor was it possible to identify other physiological indicators in the available bodily organs—petechial hemorrhages, for instance—as their putrid state prevented "the [pathological] signs of death from strangulation being detected."[18]

One might expect that Spilsbury's failure to establish a cause of death from his post-mortem inquiries would have reduced the subsequent role he played in resolving the case. The reverse was true. The reach of his interpretative powers, as we will soon demonstrate, was by no means limited by the inconclusive outcomes of his autopsy.

FROM PATHOLOGIST TO CSI PRACTITIONER?

As the Crumbles investigation progressed, Spilsbury's engagement with the crime scene deepened in two important respects: first, he reflected on a blood stain that had been identified by Chief Inspector Savage and Superintendent Sinclair at the scene; second, he assessed the significance of the material state of one object at the scene: the cauldron that Mahon, in one of his accounts, claimed had caused Kaye's death. A superficial reading of these two engagements would suggest that here Spilsbury had significantly shifted the terms of his work from pathologist to trace hunter, thereby self-consciously adopting the mantle of an active and physically engaged crime scene investigator. However, in characterizing his work at the Crumbles over the course of a series of legal hearings up to and including Mahon's trial, Spilsbury positioned himself in a decidedly more passive and semidetached role. In testimony based on his post-mortem work, Spilsbury unsurprisingly cast himself as the singular source of agency: observations and conclusions were his and his alone. In his crime scene testimony, by contrast, he was content to cede narrative agency with respect to crime scene management and engagement to others by repeatedly employing language such as "I was shown" and referring to a general investigative gaze rather than one generated from and by him.[19]

These linguistic formulations reflect the reality of the sequence of events in the initial phase of the investigation. Spilsbury arrived on the second day and proceeded to operate and move in a space that had already been surveyed and managed by police investigators. Reading through their reports, it is clear that, unlike Spilsbury, Savage and Sinclair presented themselves as engaged scene practitioners, using the active voice ("we found" and "we searched") to describe their movements and findings.[20] In the first arduous day of the investigation, Savage and Sinclair determined exactly where human remains could be found and detected and gathered the most obvious objects of value, including potential murder weapons, blood stains, and blood-stained clothing. In the process, they quantified, recorded, photographed, and sought to determine the identity of the putrefying human remains.

These detailed accounts of scene labor are also useful as they allow a re-interpretation of the framework established at the Crumbles bungalow within which Spilsbury would conduct his own inquiries. Spilsbury's spatiotemporal distance from the work carried out by police investigators is strikingly clear in his engagement with crime scene blood.[21] Following Mahon's second statement featuring Kaye's bloody fall against the cauldron, police investigators returned to the bungalow to see whether they could corroborate his story. In their courtroom testimony, Savage and Sinclair recalled how, unaccompanied by Spilsbury, they had pulled up a stain-free carpet to reveal a blood stain on the underfelt, nine inches from the door.[22] On lifting the felt they detected a further stain on the floorboards, almost exactly the same shape and size as that on the felt, which suggested to them that the blood had leaked through the layers of carpet and felt and onto the floorboards.[23] They cut out the felt, carpet, floorboards, and the bottom panel from the door and sent them not to Spilsbury but to the Home Office analyst and St. Mary's Hospital chemist Dr. John Webster.[24] Webster tested these blood-stained articles to determine whether the blood was or was not human. In Webster's view, it was.

Though they were the authors of the Crumbles bloodstain work, neither Savage nor Sinclair was invited by either the defense or prosecution to comment on their findings or to use them to evaluate the plausibility of Mahon's story. This kind of interpretative exercise was judged to fall within Spilsbury's remit alone, and he readily accepted the challenge. With a confidence undiminished by the fact that he had played no part in its detection, Spilsbury drew upon the bloodstain evidence to supplement his post-mortem inquiries into the cause of Kaye's death. This becomes clear in his cross-examination by defense counsel James Dale Cassels. Cassels sought to elicit Spilsbury's agreement that the stain had been made by blood flowing out from an injury caused by a blunt object, and not by blood spurting from a knife wound. His intent was to eliminate the scenario that Mahon had slit Kaye's throat and thus to substantiate Mahon's cauldron story. Cassels presented Spilsbury with the bloody courtroom exhibits, and after examining them, Spilsbury agreed that there was "no evidence of blood spurting," which would be expected in a fatal stabbing case.[25]

Having eliminated a knife attack, Spilsbury then used the bloodstain as the basis for imaginatively reconstructing the final minutes of Kaye's life. From its shape and size, and its concentration in one area on the floor, he concluded that the bloodstain was consistent with a "lacerated" wound to the head by a blunt object, after which the victim fell to the floor, bleeding for "four or five minutes" until "the heart stopped beating."[26] In doing so Spilsbury harnessed and enacted a distinctive repertoire of forensic practices and levels of observation, one rooted in the medico-legal tradition of blood hunting discussed in the previous chapter. His account of crime scene blood, though interpretatively spatial, was predominantly centered on questions emanating from the body: his primary reasoning on the shape and distribution of the Crumbles blood was determined by his consideration of how bodily injuries and physiological processes (involving the heart and blood pressure and circulation) might have shaped the flow of blood exiting the body into space. This focus on the body thus enabled him to recreate the violent choreography of the victim's death through a projection of the possible reciprocities between traces of blood in space and the kinds of bodily injuries that had most likely created them.

In delivering this interpretation, Spilsbury acknowledged his lack of engagement with scene-harvesting practices, a fact that he freely admitted in court. As he had explained under cross-examination, "I only saw it after it [the bloodstain] had been produced as an exhibit in Court."[27] Spilsbury's mediated relationship with the scene as a supplement to his post-mortem investigation is also evident in his second ostensible act of CSI virtuosity—his interpretation of the three-legged, blood-specked cauldron. In his courtroom testimony he acknowledged the limits of his post-mortem findings: he had been confronted "by the body of a healthy person," and "[with] the head and neck missing there was no evidence of the cause of death being some unnatural cause." It was in this context that he turned his attention to the cauldron, appropriating this inorganic object as a means to extend his post-mortem inquiries. In effect, Spilsbury transformed it into a proxy for the missing head. If Kaye had died in the living room by striking her head against it in a high-impact collision as Mahon had claimed, Spilsbury reasoned, both head and cauldron would bear a significant imprint of the blow. If, by contrast, the collision had been minor, the damage to both would be slight.[28] Substituting the cauldron for Kaye's missing head, then, gave Spilsbury a paired object which he could use to conjure the severity of the injuries that the latter would have displayed had it been available to him at his post-mortem.

When he turned to the cauldron itself, however, rather than finding a sturdy object against which a fall might easily inflict lethal injuries, Spilsbury discovered the reverse. Held together by a recently fitted false bottom, with wholly defective and inadequately fused welding, it was, in his words, "very flimsy in construction"; thus, he concluded, it was highly unlikely that it could absorb the energy produced by a significant collision without breaking apart.[29] As he put it, "No fall upon the coal cauldron which has been produced [as a court exhibit] would have been sufficiently severe to cause fatal results without crumbling up the cauldron."[30] Its structural weakness, Spilsbury concluded, revealed a core weakness in Mahon's story about its part in Kaye's accidental death: the fact that it was still in one piece after its alleged contact with Kaye's head suggested that any such impact must have been of a nonlethal nature.

Spilsbury's assessment of the cauldron's material integrity is significant in several respects. First, it showed him adopting the synoptic consultant role of the medico-legal witness rather than the empirical and consultative position of a Grossian investigating officer. In testing his theory, Spilsbury did not invite the opinion of a metallurgist on the material qualities of the cauldron, nor did he commission or pursue physical tests to generate experimental data in support of his assessment. Instead, he projected medical expertise as the singular authoritative voice on the evidentiary value of this core crime scene exhibit.

Spilsbury's self-contained interpretive command over the cauldron's physicality extended to its status as a crime scene object.[31] As with the detection and subsequent harvesting of the bloodstain mentioned above, he was not involved in its retrieval from the scene. Nor, more strikingly, did he visit the living room to attempt a spatial reconstruction of the alleged struggle in order to explore the physical dynamics of Kaye's fall with reference to the actual material dimensions and layout of the living room. Instead, he focused on the cauldron in its relationship with the body: the wider physical realities within which the alleged struggle took place did not concern him.

In cross-examination, Mahon's defense counsel challenged Spilsbury on his apparent lack of interest in the specific physical configuration of the murder scene and the different scenarios that might have arisen within it. In a series of questions designed to prompt Spilsbury to broaden his analysis and to go beyond the issue of the material state of the cauldron, Cassels sought to establish a multifactorial framework for understanding the dynamics of the violent struggle between Kaye and Mahon.

> CASSELS: What I am suggesting is this, you have to take into consideration the fall, the chair, the cauldron, supplying more or less a leverage, with the pressure of the body and a hand on the neck: would not that have the effect of possibly fracturing one of the neck bones. . . . [So] there is no magic is there about the cauldron as a cauldron?
>
> SPILSBURY: Only this, that with regard to that particular cauldron any blow which was struck by a falling body must have been only of the nature of a glancing blow to produce that bending [in one of its legs].[32]

In his reply, Spilsbury reasserted his interpretive command of the cauldron, and from that, of the relevant circumstances leading to Kaye's death. Cassels did not let the medical virtuoso's transformation from the master of flesh to the master of the cauldron go entirely unchallenged, in the process reminding the courtroom of the nature and limits of the star pathologist's expertise in this case:

> CASSELS: You are in a difficulty in this case, one knows, because you have not got the organs from which you can make your deductions, have you?
>
> SPILSBURY: No.
>
> CASSELS: You can only go upon speculation?
>
> SPILSBURY: Yes.[33]

Through such hostile questioning, Cassels attempted to cast doubt on Spilsbury's deductions and theorizing, challenging them as overreaching his core base of expertise: his theories concerning Kaye's death could be not grounded in a conclusive post-mortem.

Spilsbury's reply suggests that he was unfazed by Cassels's interrogation, and the trial judge's closing statement to the jury mirrored—and supported—Spilsbury's position. Mr. Justice Avory singled out Spilsbury's forensic skills and deductions as fundamental to "ascertaining direct evidence of the injury inflicted on the person alleged to have been killed":[34]

In considering this account given by the prisoner, you will bear in mind the evidence of Dr. Spilsbury, than whom there is no greater expert on matters of this description, and who tells you that in his opinion, having seen that coal cauldron, having heard the description given by the prisoner of the fall upon the coal cauldron, he is satisfied that such a fall could not have caused her immediate death.[35]

If Spilsbury was wrong about the cauldron, Avory reasoned, why would Mahon have gone to such lengths to destroy the head entirely but not the rest of the bodily remains, "unless it were for the purpose of concealing the injuries on the bone of this head which might afford conclusive testimony to what had really happened on that night, instead of the mere fall on this rickety old coal cauldron?"[36]

—◦ ◦—

There is a further story still to tell about the cauldron, one that highlights some of the broader structural features of English homicide investigation in the mid-1920s: that is, Cassels's use of Spilsbury's "rickety" object to probe the protocols of the investigation of the Crumbles bungalow. In his cross-examination of Chief Inspector Savage, Cassels asked three interrelated questions about the procedural regime surrounding the cauldron: "Has that coal cauldron remained in the same condition in which it was discovered by the police in the dining room?" "It is exactly as it was received?" "Has it been used for any purpose at all since the visit of the police to the bungalow?"[37] In responding to these questions, Savage stipulated that the cauldron had remained in "exactly" the same condition in which it had been discovered.

Reminding the courtroom that Savage first went to the bungalow on May 3, Cassels then theatrically invited the inspector to approach the cauldron, asking him to peer inside and tell the court what he could see. Savage stated that it contained pieces of a newspaper covered with coal dust, after which Cassels invited him to look closer at the date of the newspaper. When Savage announced the newspaper was dated May 23, nearly three weeks after police investigators had first unlocked, and then sealed under protective custody, the front door to the Crumbles holiday cottage, Cassels challenged him to explain the presence of "a piece of [that] newspaper with coal dust on the top."[38] Savage's answers were imprecise. He recalled that it had been taken to Webster at St. Mary's Hospital on two or three occasions, brought from the Police Court hearing at Hailsham, then taken back to London, and finally produced at the Police Court. As the date of the newspaper corresponded to the Hailsham hearing, it was, Savage surmised, likely there that the newspaper found its way into the prosecution's primary crime scene exhibit.[39]

Savage's testimony makes it clear that, in its movement through its intermediary destinations, and ultimately to its physical presence in the courtroom, the cauldron had not been kept within a formal chain of protective custody. That Justice Avory expressed little interest in or concern with police investigators' failure to protect it from contamination may strike modern readers as surprising. Yet, as chapter 5 will show, it would not be until a decade later that English police investigators developed a bureaucratic regime to document the handling, transportation, and storage of scene evidence across crime scenes, crime labs, and courtrooms.[40] Apparently satisfied by Savage's explanation, the judge closed down Cassels's line of questioning with the vague observation that "it is quite clear anybody may have put that newspaper in it."[41] Thus, while Cassels's critique demonstrates that lapses in police protocol could be raised as an issue at trials in the 1920s, it equally shows that the force of the argument did not compel a reevaluation of the bona fides of crime scene objects. Avory accepted Savage's verbal account of the handling and transfer of physical evidence, revealing a less exacting set of legal expectations concerning the preservation of physical evidence than the one suggested by Cassels' questions. For Avory, the auditing of routine police protocols and the identification of inadequate safeguards against the contamination of physical evidence were not matters for the court: the cauldron was retained as the central court exhibit in the prosecution's case against Mahon, and Spilsbury's reading of it remained intact.

MAHON'S MATERIAL LEGACY: THE "MURDER BAG"

As a coda, we expand our analysis of the complex and ambiguous place of the Mahon case, Spilsbury, and celebrity pathology in the history of English CSI by turning to one of the investigation's lasting material legacies: England's first officially sanctioned "murder bag." The story of the post-Crumbles murder bag can be told in two ways and from two source bases: first, as a historical artifact and from police and Home Office administrative records, and, second, as a presentist-inspired artifact generated by crime writers and Spilsbury biographers.

We start with the administrative origins of the murder bag. In a report composed in the aftermath of the Crumbles investigation, Chief Inspector Savage emphasized the dangerous task faced by police on its first day, when they handled and sorted fragmented and decaying human flesh with their bare hands. The gruesome nature of their activities, he insisted, was such that it even shocked the eminent pathologist Bernard Spilsbury:

> On the following day I accompanied Sir Bernard Spilsbury to the Officer's House and was present during the seven or eight hours which he took to examine the remains, and he said he could not understand how we had managed to do what had been done on the previous day, as although he was properly equipped for the task and has had long experience of post-mortem examinations he found the work extremely difficult and unpleasant, hence the long time it took him to complete it. He pointed out that not only must it have been unpleasant but that it was also dangerous for the Officers to have handled the putrid matter without proper clothing and appliances.[42]

Police investigators had not been issued with protective equipment—rubber gloves, carbolic acid, and the like—which, in Spilsbury's view, were essential items for handling bodily remains at murder scenes. Scotland Yard officers used Spilsbury's authoritative criticisms to strengthen their concerns about the sanitary risks of homicide investigation. A letter commending police investigators for their dedicated scene work explained that the Mahon case had reinvigorated the drive for the provision of such dedicated equipment:

> The case brings up again the point as to whether we should not have available for the use of Officers sent out on enquiry a bag containing articles which might be useful to assist in the examination of the scene of a crime, and of surgical appliances which would enable officers to handle dangerous matter with comparative safety.[43]

Scotland Yard's anxieties concerning the horrific and unsafe labor undertaken at the Crumbles, strengthened by Spilsbury's warnings about the wholly unsuitable manner in which investigators had been forced to handle decaying human remains, persuaded police authorities to assemble a murder bag and the Home Office to finance it.

According to this administrative paper trail in the period up to its creation, then, the roots of England's first officially sanctioned murder bag lay in the pressing need to protect investigators when physically handling dangerous human remains. But the murder bag has a second origin story, one that has been assembled by modern popular accounts that present its creation as a mark of the arrival of English CSI and Spilsbury's privileged role within it. The crime writer and Spilsbury biographer Colin Evans again serves as a clear example. The Crumbles bungalow investigation, in his view, exposed Scotland Yard's inadequate material and conceptual preparation for crime scene discipline:

> If they [police investigators] wished to preserve human hair or clothing, or soil or dust on boots, they simply picked it up with their fingers and put it on a piece of paper. They had no tapes to measure distances, no compass to determine direction, no apparatus to take fingerprints . . . , no magnifying glass. In short, they had no appliances whatsoever for immediate use at the crime scene.[44]

In this reading, the murder bag is a response to what another modern author claims to be a further set of criticisms made by Spilsbury: this time of the police investigators' lack of "a proper understanding of crime scene practice" and their consequent lack of "proper equipment that minimised the possibility of the contamination and cross-transference of evidence."[45] In these accounts, Spilsbury successfully campaigned for a bag filled with Holmesian paraphernalia to provide murder investigators with vital equipment for revealing and processing hidden crime scene traces. The murder bag created in the aftermath of the Mahon case thus serves as a fitting legacy and reminder of Spilsbury's zeal for systematic trace hunting.[46]

To assess the relative merits of these divergent accounts, let us now peer inside the murder bag: What do we actually see? In its initial version, released in October 1924, the clear majority of items were designed to shield the investigator from the body, rather than to protect the scene from the investigator or to facilitate the systematic search of the scene for telling traces. Though the bag included some equipment for trace hunting (a large magnifying glass) and for recording the scene (a surveyor's tape measure), two-thirds of its contents were for processing potentially dangerous body parts, including two pairs of thick rubber gloves, two towels, two pairs of large forceps, antiseptic soap, a mackintosh apron of full length and a tin of the corrosive disinfectant Lysol.[47] Its contents, then, reflected the interests of a body-centered pathologist worried about the sanitary dangers stemming from a riot of putrefying human remains rather than those of the inventor of modern CSI.

However, if we return to the murder bag ten years after its initial appearance, we see a significant shift in the balance of items, one that is suggestive of an intervening shift in the forensic landscape. In its 1934 reissue, the murder bag still registered efforts to mitigate the disagreeable and dangerous engagement with the corpse, with smelling salts added to the list of contents. However, most of new items—including steel tape, a boxwood rule, and a steel micrometer caliper square—were designed to support trace hunting and the spatial capture of the crime scene.[48] The revised murder bag of the 1930s thus announced and embodied a forensic regime anchored in the crime lab and new crime scene protocols and discipline, the emergence of which will be explored in coming chapters.

CHAPTER FOUR

Celebrity Pathology and the Spectacle
of Murder Investigation

The focus on the Crumbles investigation thus far has been on analyzing Spilsbury's post-mortem and crime scene contributions. Based on these contributions the argument that he is the inventor of CSI does not hold up. In our reconstruction, the Mahon case turns out to be a story less about the dawning of English CSI and more about the ascendance of the figure of the forensic pathologist, whose practices of investigation represent an extension and amplification of the authority of the nineteenth-century medical jurist. This chapter will replot the activities at the Crumbles in order to bring out a different storyline, one that engages with press projections and imaginings. It was in media representations of his work that Spilsbury's standing as a unique forensic practitioner, a master of both the mortuary and the crime scene, emerged and gained remarkable momentum.

REPORTING MURDER AT THE CRUMBLES

The press was at the scene from the very start. Scotland Yard's rush to the scene attracted reporters and photographers—as well as curious members of the public—to observe and record events. As we saw in the last chapter, within the cottage a predominantly body-centered forensic regime held sway. But, as far as the press was concerned, the activities in and around the bungalow were being absorbed and reconfigured by another framework of investigation, driven by the dictates of Continental-inspired CSI. Journalists, in other words, produced a version of the murder investigation that was largely of their own imagining, in line with their expectations of and presumptions about how a modern murder inquiry should be carried out.[1] In these representations, the investigation was driven by the promise of slow revelation, resulting from a search of the scene for hidden traces. The anchor point for this drama was Bernard Spilsbury, universally acclaimed as the figurehead of this new model of scientific trace hunting. This media-inspired forensic imaginary opened a discrete cultural space for extending and projecting the authority, powers, and personality of the forensic pathologist in a way not seen before.

In bringing the Crumbles murder and Spilsbury to the attention of the English reading public, news stories drew upon a long-established media preoccupation with crime, gruesome violence, and melodrama. However, in setting the scene within this familiar formula, press reports from the Crumbles also reflected more recent journalistic developments, most notably the populist and engaging editorial tone adopted by leading newspapers.[2] Readers in this interwar media landscape were increasingly invited into a dynamic relationship with the newspaper, fostering a new kind of imaginative association with public figures through the human interest story that encouraged readers to identify with those "in the news." Photojournalism further personalized and aestheticized sensational news stories, enhancing the potential for audiences to achieve a close connection with people caught up in an event.

This new media culture transformed the Crumbles crime scene into an intensive site of imaginative engagement. From the moment the body was discovered, the press turned readers into amateur detectives: up-to-date reports on evidential discoveries, suspects, investigators, and witnesses punctuated coverage and piqued public interest. Photography lent the investigation a modern visual lexicon, as newspapers incorporated images of the activities at the bungalow into their pages, documenting the inquiry's temporal sequence. Such accounts communicated a journalistic readiness to extend the story in fresh and exciting ways, encouraging readers to keep returning to the "bungalow of death" with continuously renewed excitement.[3]

By dramatizing the forensic personnel and methods deployed at the crime scene, newspapers also provided ample material for storytelling and fantasy, often blurring the boundary between journalistic fact and crime fiction.[4] Consider, for example, the *Daily Mirror* advertisement in August 1923 for a competition to solve a series of fictionalized criminal mysteries. Promising a handsome prize of £250 and adorned with a suggestive Thorndykian image depicting the minute properties of a single strand of hair under a microscope, the competition had been organized by a new publication, the

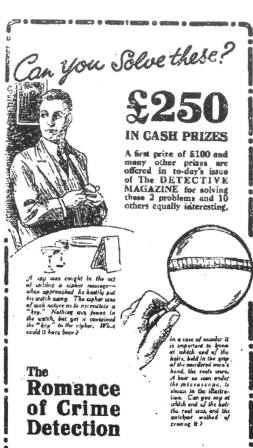

Figure 4.1. "Can you solve these?" *Daily Express,* July 20, 1923, 5. Courtesy of Time Inc.

Detective Magazine. Its pages were dedicated to showcasing the possibilities created by the application of scientific methods to understanding the world of trace analysis, as clearly illustrated by the highly suggestive caption for the competition:

> A pair of footmarks, a hair seen under a magnifying glass, a couple of tracks made by a vehicle, a man glancing at his watch. Do they convey anything to you? With the pictures and their letter-press that will accompany them you will have the opportunity of exercising your common-sense, your observation, and your deductive faculties to the full. Sherlock Holmes would, of course, solve them at a glance. Scotland Yard would work them out by the light of experience and organisation. . . . You will, if you apply the methods that will be explained, find that there is a scientific principle in each problem. Yet no abstruse knowledge beyond the reach of all will be called upon. All that will be necessary will be common-sense and a little ingenuity and imagination.[5]

Thus the *Detective Magazine* instructed its readers in the observational promise of the new complex world of trace forensics, a world in which Sherlock Holmes, with his lightning powers of deduction, was cast as the unequalled master. As we will soon see, the press reportage of the Crumbles murder investigation created a cultural dynamo through which Spilsbury's identity as a real-life Holmesian sleuth was amplified, transmitted, and energized, significantly altering and expanding public expectations about his powers of detection.

CSI: CRUMBLES

Let us reset the scene. At the center of the journalistic accounts of the investigation was the Officer's House—now transformed into the "cottage of doom" and suggestively set on the wide coastal wasteland of the Crumbles. Beyond providing a background to the investigation, the beach became a metaphorical and discursive plane onto which newspapers inscribed certain cultural values and projected representations of the homicide investigation and investigators. In the initial news reports of the murder, front-page photographs combined with textual descriptions contrasting the emptiness of the Crumbles to the tomb-like claustrophobia of the bungalow. Set apart from a row of twelve nearby cottages (fig. 4.2), its detached

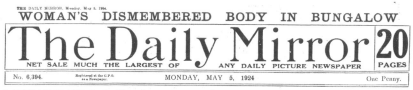

The Officers' House, a bungalow on the Crumbles, Eastbourne, in which the mutilated remains of a woman were found by police who forced an entry.

Figure 4.2. Crumbles in the headlines. *Daily Mirror,* May 5, 1924, 1. Courtesy of Mirrorpix.

position suggested a vulnerability onto which the imagination could imprint supernatural tropes: neighbors were overheard referring to it as "the haunted house."[6] The isolation of the "fearsome" beach provided ample scope for dramatic narrative: evocations of the isolation of the area, the cold temperature, darkness, thick scrubby terrain, and shingled beach established the landscape as an appropriately brutal setting for the horrific events that had transpired.[7] Newspapers generated a multifaceted narrative focusing on the conduct of scene investigators, identifying and directing the attention of readers to what the papers selected as the main features of the drama of modern homicide investigation. A close analysis of these press projections reveals how they collectively communicated a new version of forensic investigation that was coming into view.

The first recurring motif in the press coverage was its emphasis on Scotland Yard's dramatic race through the night to the crime scene. The *Western Daily Press*, for example, vividly described how "Chief Inspector Savage and Detective Inspector Thomas Hall travelled through the night by motor car to a lonely stretch of land a short distance from Eastbourne, where in a house they discovered the dismembered portions of a woman's body."[8] This

was the stuff of sensation, an exhilarating, fast-moving drama that adver-
tised a forensic regime in which time was of the essence: "the detectives arrived on the lonely coast just as dawn was breaking," according to another
report, "but they immediately set to work on their gruesome task."[9]

Having captured this "weird night drive,"[10] journalists turned to detailing elements of recognizably Grossian activity, starting with detectives'
efforts to secure the crime scene. They reported on how the bungalow had
been turned into an enclosed, rarefied space in which, at least formally, the
public was relegated to the role of passive observer. "The police," according
to one report, "are taking no risks. All entrance to the house is barred by
wicker fences fastened securely to the outer gate and a police patrol night
and day will be maintained."[11] Stories abounded of how investigators assid-
uously kept the bungalow under lock and key. For example, at the end of the
first day, it was widely reported that Detective Savage sealed the bungalow
from trespassers, so the investigators could resume their search on the following morning knowing the scene was in the exact condition they had left
it.[12] Other accounts hailed the discipline of officers stationed outside the
bungalow, who proved impervious to bribes offered by members of the public insisting upon having access to its interiors.[13]

Such reports suggest a straightforward correspondence between what
actually took place during the investigation and the principles advanced
by CSI enthusiasts. If we look more closely, however, there were also
some significant discontinuities. Take, for example, the following account
of the handling of trace-laden artifacts retrieved from the interior of the
bungalow:

Later this afternoon, Scotland Yard detectives removed by motor-car to
London the remains of Miss Kaye and a number of exhibits in the case. First of
all, Detective Inspector Hall brought out of the bungalow a coal scuttle, the
two legs of which are said to be blood-stained. Next he carried under his arms
a couple of biscuit tins, in which were the remains of the dead woman. A small
trunk, bearing the initials E. B. K., [was] also removed. Assisted by a constable, the inspector carried out a large fish boiler, and they were followed by another constable with a large iron saucepan, the lid of which was tied on with
string. Spectators watched the proceedings in silence, which was broken by
the inspector's query, "Has anyone in the crowd got a piece of string?" A man
standing near supplied the wanted string.[14]

This moment is worth highlighting as it shows that the press projections of the Crumbles investigation did not always easily map onto the ideals espoused by advocates of CSI rigor. Gross would no doubt have been seized by one of his "involuntarily shivers" at the thought of the inspector calling out to the crowd for string so he could secure his crime scene exhibits. Absent, too, is any indication of adherence to the guidance on careful packing outlined in chapter 1. As items emerged from inside the bungalow, the reporter identifies each unwrapped discovery—even reporting bloodstains on the cauldron and the victim's initials on the trunk. Such press commentary thus revealed a permeable boundary between the exterior and interior of the crime scene and between the investigator and the public.

Nevertheless, the overall effect of press reports from the crime scene was to create and cement the symbolic links between CSI and the Crumbles procedure, blurring the line between journalistic fact and crime fiction, and clue and trace. The investigation, in the eyes of admiring reporters, was remarkable less for the body-centered practices outlined in the previous chapter than for its focus on mundane traces. A *Daily Mirror* correspondent speculated extensively on this feature of the investigation of the bungalow, which in his account was literally being taken to pieces in order to reveal hidden clues: "Carpets were searched for any traces of blood or other evidence. Even small chips were taken from the floorboards and examined under glass with as much care as an analyst would examine portions of a body for a trace of poison."[15] The image of the toxicologist waging war on a dreaded secret poisoner had of course long been a staple of the popular fascination with forensic investigations.[16] Now, however, this fascination was being displaced by the promise of a new mode of forensic expertise, rooted not in close examination of the viscera but in physical interrogation of the environment in which they had been found.

Finally, and in language infused with Grossian imagery, accounts of the scene investigation emphasized the significance of ordinary objects and traces. As the same *Daily Mail* correspondent reported: "the police are convinced that unless every possible item of rubbish and clothing, and all articles are personally examined, there is still a possibility of losing a valuable clue."[17] Through such commentary, journalists confirmed that modern criminal mysteries were resolved by the revelatory potential of the most unpromising of crime scene artifacts and locations. Such vivid images of the Crumbles trace hunting served to enhance the newsworthiness of the murder—and thus to prolong its media lifespan—and at the same time created and symbolized new expectations about how crime scenes were to be investigated.

BERNARD SPILSBURY: INVESTIGATING OFFICER AND SCREEN IDOL

The final, and most pervasive, feature of the press imaginings of the Crumbles crime scene was their identification of Spilsbury as the embodiment of investigative oversight. The press featured Spilsbury as the focal point of an unfolding drama, his activities, achievements, and performances within and around the bungalow towering above all others. Indeed, from the moment Spilsbury arrived at the scene to the guilty verdict delivered at the conclusion of Mahon's trial, the press—in headlines such as "Sir Bernard Spilsbury Tells of His Finds at Bungalow" and "What Dr Spilsbury Found"—shone a spotlight on his singular forensic skills.[18]

In light of the achievements attributed to him in his work on the Mahon case, Spilsbury's past cases acquired an interlinked, rearticulated, and retrospective coherence that at once conveyed and encapsulated the remarkable and highly individualized acuity that had come into view at the Crumbles. Crucial here is how the English reading public's knowledge of and encounters with Spilsbury's capacities had, to date, derived almost exclusively from his courtroom appearances as an expert witness, appearances that were made visible by press characterizations of his testimony. His public identity was thus tied to the specific manifestations of his expertise at inquests, committal hearings, and murder trials, which lent an episodic and fluid character to perceptions of his work: a histologist in the 1910 Crippen case, a blood hunter and analyst in the 1917 Voisin case, a toxicologist in the 1922 Armstrong case. Each of these demanded a unique courtroom performance from Spilsbury, reflective of the contingencies of the case in question. These contingencies in turn determined the role that was, and could be, ascribed to him in press reports.

Mahon in this respect liberated Spilsbury from the shackles of circumstance: depicted as an all-purpose detective, moving from case to case, Spilsbury emerged as a unique crime-fighting force who, when enrolled into a police investigation, single-handedly unmasked Britain's most "daring, ingenious, cold-blooded murderers."[19] He was "more than a mere witness to medical facts, he [was] something of a super-detective," whose forensic powers were rooted not only in the mortuary and the witness box but now, and crucially, at the crime scene:[20]

> He does a great deal of the most difficult and technical work before any great trial which involves a charge of murder. It is his job to ascertain the cause of death. Sometimes—as with the remains of Crippen's wife—he has but a small part of the body to work on. His investigations are made in the laboratory *after several visits to the scene of the crime as a rule.* And there he makes the scientific tests which undo the poisoner, the suffocater, the killer by violence.[21]

Toxicologist, trace-hunting detective, laboratory scientist, pathologist, and now crime scene investigator, Spilsbury's developing public identity merged with the long-established fictionalized figure of the private detective.[22] Mobilizing this prior set of literary associations, the press invited readers to see Spilsbury as the real-life equivalent of the Holmesian sleuth, someone always ahead of the police, anticipating events and appreciating crucial details as well as the overall picture. Spilsbury's cultural profile was, in this sense, predicated upon incorporating and reenergizing long-standing literary tropes. These cultural representations of Spilsbury absorbed the "fantastical" nature of Holmes's eccentric genius, which endowed him with a specific individuality. Through a persuasive combination of the marvelous and the mundane, media representations used Spilsbury to facilitate fantasies of control over the chaos and horrors within the "bungalow of death." Separated out from and lifted above the ordinary, the presence and powers of Spilsbury enchanted modern murder investigation.[23]

The theatrical press photographs and news copy of Spilsbury arriving at the bungalow are particularly striking. The *Daily Mail* reported that once the dramatic discoveries of human remains had been made by Savage and Sinclair, "the keys were turned and [the] door heavily sealed . . . [that is] until the following morning," when "Sir Bernard Spilsbury with his young woman assistant drove through a crowd of sightseers to investigate."[24] That Spilsbury's arrival occurred on the second day of the investigation neither detracted from his significance as the lead investigator nor dampened expectation of his impending exploits. By separating him from the initial wave of scene activity in this way, the press projected Spilsbury as an independent observer, a gifted outside consultant.

Public fascination with Spilsbury's presence at the Crumbles bungalow did not end with his disappearance through its front door. For reporters, the inscrutability of his activities inside in fact amplified excitement and anticipation, heightening the spectacle of the murder investigation and his role within it. The *Daily Mail*, by observing that "Spilsbury['s] forensic work had taken place behind firmly shut blinds, involving a solemn and gruesome task which he had to perform in examining the remains," invited readers to imagine the macabre details of his hidden working practices.[25] The press and its readers clamored for what they could not see, the shrouded presence of Spilsbury helping to ensure a compelling and mesmerizing spectacle. The *Eastbourne Gazette* reported that he had entered the bungalow at precisely 11:21 a.m., and from that moment his presence was felt all the more for his absence from view:

> The blinds were drawn and for a long time there was no sign from within. Meanwhile, there was a constant stream of sightseers who stared in idle curiosity at the motor [Spilsbury's transport] at the gate, the policeman on guard and the low white house with the closely drawn curtains. There was nothing else to be seen but the great shingly expanse of the Crumbles ... Larks were singing overhead in the sunshine. Inside the bungalow, Sir Bernard Spilsbury was conducting [a] minute examination of the dismembered corpse.[26]

The reference to the sublime in this passage—the sound of larks bathed in sunshine—suggests the absolute stillness of the watching crowd, their attention apparently absorbed by the thought of Spilsbury at work within the bungalow's inner sanctum.

There were openings in the cloak of secrecy through which the press was able to project Spilsbury as a crime scene virtuoso. The *Daily Mail* described impatient spectators climbing onto the garden walls to observe the masterful practitioner at work, catching "occasional glimpses of those engaged in the awful task within."[27] For a moment, every reader following the investigation was put in the position of these sightseers seduced by Spilsbury's forensic aura. It is worth considering at length the *Daily Mail*'s representational tableaux of text and image capturing his enigmatic performance, through which we get a sense of how his public image was achieving a greater level of individualization in the public narrative and spectacle of a homicide investigation:

> For a time Sir Bernard was framed in one of the tiny windows that looks towards the sea a few hundreds of yards distant. Cigarette in mouth, he was scrutinising sheets, clothing and other articles that were being handed to him. Later, in a part of the garden that is surrounded by a still higher wall and is away from prying eyes, the remains were assembled on a table in the open

Figure 4.3. Spilsbury and Miss Bainbridge exit the stage. *Daily Mail,* May 5, 1924, 9. Courtesy of the *Daily Mail* / Solo Syndication.

air. Meanwhile the police were making the most thorough examination of the floors and walls and drawing Sir Bernard's attention to every fresh discovery. Other officers searched cupboards and even put their arms into the drains.[28]

The report and accompanying photograph worked together to create a number of interrelated readings. The passage itself conveys press imaginings of the division of labor at the Crumbles bungalow. Spilsbury is unambiguously portrayed as an analyst engaged in assessing the evidentiary status of objects presented to him by others—police field workers—placing him at a distance from the routine of physical searching. The image recycled Holmesian tropes to cast Spilsbury in the role of the omniscient consultant, against whom police officers were little more than worker drones. Report-ers' observations of the interaction between Spilsbury and the police, as they shifted their attention to the outside of the bungalow, continued to tes-tify to the centrality of the consultant investigator. Accounts emphasized that the search for the missing body parts on the beach and digging of the bungalow yard was conducted by investigators almost entirely "under his supervision" and that it was he who determined the value of any clues uncovered.[29]

Turning to the image, we can gauge the press's cultivation of Spilsbury's celebrity aura, which could be read through his gestures, appearance, and demeanor. In particular, his averted gaze as he exits the bungalow—tipping his hat to cover his face—registers a cool indifference to the spectators. Spilsbury's refusal to engage with his starstruck audience, resisting the photographic gaze and its potential for garnering publicity, only made his spectators adore him more.

In this respect, the image of Spilsbury in this scene evokes the conven-tions that were being contemporaneously established to describe and proj-ect the glamor of the screen idol.[30] The arrival of the screen celebrity by the 1920s provided significant cultural resources for reimagining and extend-ing Spilsbury's identity—in some respects leading to the "celebrification" of his public image. The "stars" and the industry surrounding them extended their public image in a paradoxical fashion, on the one hand creating off-set personae as absorbing as anything witnessed on the screen itself but on the other hand endowing them with an aloof quality.[31] Among the rising gener-ation of Hollywood icons it was Greta Garbo who particularly epitomized this construct, her appeal deriving in no small part from the fact that she remained "a resolute mystery to her public, allowing no interviews, no pub-licity shots, offering no details about her life."[32]

Considered in this light, the onstage and offstage actions attributed to Spilsbury at the Crumbles bungalow represented not merely an investigator working and exiting a crime scence. It constituted a "performance," implic-itly evoking and registering Garbo-esque qualities and enabling the press to project, in his averted gaze and his evanescent appearance in the screen-like frame of the small window, a celebrity persona characterized by a mag-netic presence enhanced by absence of detail. If the Crumbles case was a movie, then Spilsbury was billed as its enigmatic and unerring star—one, moreover, who took his place in the pantheon of celebrated detective char-acters. In the weeks following the discovery of Emily Kaye's body, the

Hull Daily Mail dubbed him a "real-life Sherlock Holmes," claiming that his ingenious grasp of scientific methods and policing were uncannily reminiscent of the fictional superdetective, as was their striking physical resemblance:

> With his tall thin, athletic figure and strong clean-up features, he could play the role of Sherlock Holmes without any make-up and he is probably nearer the type of that popular fiction character than any other living man.[33]

By "casting" Spilsbury as Holmes, this passage makes an explicit reference to how the newly reconstituted celebrity landscape was recalibrating his identity. Moreover, newspapers increasingly endowed Spilsbury with a seductive surface befitting his screen celebrity, his gestures, mannerisms, and appearance lifting him above the ordinary:

> Tall and very distinguished in appearance, Sir Bernard Spilsbury has been described as the handsomest member of St Bartholomew's teaching staff. He is clean shaven, with a remarkably youthful face and figure. He dresses very well, affects a high single collar which emphasis[es] his firm, square chin and has a clear, penetrating voice.[34]

The visual and presentational elements of Spilsbury's persona—his appearance and voice—transcended his actual achievements and knowledge-making practices, helping to extend his fame and reputation beyond his specific forensic contributions to a homicide case.

Spilsbury's celebrification was also apparent in the press coverage of the Mahon trial. Like the murder investigation itself, the courtroom drama, according to the press, possessed film-like qualities that were passively consumed by audiences. In the courtroom setting Spilsbury's physical appearance impressed and transfixed his audience as much as his actual testimony. His photogenic charisma captured the attention of onlookers, eclipsing his forensic peers involved in the case. As one newspaper correspondent observed, "The tall, well-groomed worker of modern miracles, Sir Bernard Spilsbury, was eagerly sought." The same correspondent contrasted Spilsbury's star presence with the utterly forgettable appearance of forensic bit actors: "The senior analyst to the Home Office, Mr John Webster—a physical contrast to the great pathologist—was pointed out to the curious."[35] It was Spilsbury's "attractive" surface, rather than Webster's "everyman" appearance, that the packed courtroom audience had come to see, and to consume.[36]

CRIME SCENE MANAGEMENT AT THE
"SHILLING CHAMBER OF HORROR"

In the pages of his *Handbook*, Gross alerts investigators to the importance of murder scene management. Every homicide investigation, Gross observes, unfolded in a hazardous landscape of anxiety, fantasy, and sensation. In this understanding, the viability of a crime scene depended on its protection from emotional as much as physical assaults on its integrity. The act of demarcating a crime scene involved the exclusion of the public in part as a means of relegating such indiscipline to its perimeters. Yet this did not mean that the investigating officer should be unconcerned with the affective space outside of the crime scene. For Gross, the physical integrity of the scene and the calm investigative order within were under constant threat from the destabilizing emotional states that had been banished from its interior.

The most immediate external threat was homicide journalism, the conventions of which stoked disruptive public interest. So serious was the threat, Gross warns, that if the investigating officer failed to manage media interest appropriately, the crime scene and the investigation could be overwhelmed. To prevent this Gross advises against telling journalists nothing, because wrapping the investigation in "an impenetrable mantle of secrecy" created more problems than it solved.[37] In the absence of information from police investigators, journalists would become a law unto themselves: in the pursuit of a story, they would weave and disseminate sensational and dangerously misleading narratives based upon "witnesses and their relations, upon the jailors of the prison, upon the cabman who has driven the Investigating Officer to the scene, upon the people of the house, and upon other persons who have or may have some knowledge of the matter."[38]

For Gross, unmanaged press stories surrounding a homicide case constituted a contagion that threatened even official investigators:

> Not only the man in the street but Investigating Officers themselves have a certain confidence in everything in print and allow themselves in spite of many disillusions to be influenced by newspaper articles; "there must be some truth in it" one thinks, and if one reads several times over the account of the case otherwise than as one has seen it oneself, one ends by doubting oneself, and, in spite of the best will to speak the truth, one gives an account of the case different to what one would have given if not under exterior influence.[39]

It was therefore imperative for the investigating officer to insulate himself and his investigation from these external and corrupting influences. Press enthusiasm, for example, could be restrained by providing periodic updates on developments deemed suitable for public consumption. Here, as with the approach to and management of the crime scene more generally, restraint and considered judgement were essential. Choosing what information to release to the press made it necessary for the investigating officer to anticipate the possible consequences of this decision for his whole investigation: "The tact of the Investigating Officer," as Gross explains, "will guide him in *what* should be printed in a given case, and *how* and *when* it should be published."[40]

In the course of the Crumbles murder inquiry, no such effort was made to manage the press by keeping reporters abreast of its progress. Journalists working the case were positioned at the borders of the crime scene, where they combined investigative reporting with on-the-spot impressions to make sense of ongoing developments. This included observing and following investigators at work and interviewing neighbors and other potential witnesses. When the investigation widened beyond the perimeters of the bungalow, the press, while boasting of stealthily pursuing detectives during their investigations in and around Eastbourne, also conducted inquiries of their own, which often diverged from the lines pursued in the official investigation.

The spectacle generated by such reporting practices triggered widespread criticism, which eventually reached the floor of the House of Commons. On May 12, 1924, several members of Parliament, alarmed by published images of the crime scene investigation, implored the home secretary to issue instructions ensuring that press photographers would be excluded from any future murder scene until "the police have control of premises for the purpose of investigating alleged crimes."[41] In response, the Home Secretary Arthur Henderson explained that, as yet, the police had no authority to ban photographers from crime scenes but that practical regulation measures would be considered. Within the context of this political debate, others pressed the point that the police investigators lacked sufficient power to protect the crime scene from troublesome crowds, whose presence was evident in the published Crumbles photographs. "Are we to understand that there is no redress against the large crowds and disgraceful scenes that have occurred recently?" the MP Lieutenant Commander Kentworthy demanded. "Can nothing be done at all on that matter?"[42] By raising concerns about how murder investigation was becoming a potentially dangerous spectacle, Kentworthy issued a warning that sensation-seeking crowds threatened to overwhelm the crime scene and its investigators.

Newspaper editors and reporters professed to share in this concern with crime scene protection, yet from their perspective the problem lay not with their own news-making practices but with the irresponsible and unrestrained behavior of the crowd. In their reports of the throng of spectators that gathered around the Crumbles bungalow, journalists set out appropriate and inappropriate ways of behaving around a crime scene, highlighting the inherent dangers of the public fixation with murder scenes and their artifacts by introducing a new cast of characters into public discourse: "souvenir hunters"[43] and "amateur detectives"[44]—characters associated with what we might call "murder tourism."[45] By alerting its readers' attention to the dangers of public fascination with murder scenes in this manner, the press assembled an image of the crime scene as a physically and cognitively fragile entity, one that could easily be compromised by members of the public gripped by unrestrained excitement. In this way, reports on Crumbles tourism symbolically reaffirmed Gross's warning that the expulsion of emotion from the interior of a crime scene simultaneously served as the precondition for the scene's operational viability and as a threat to its integrity.

One of the first elaborations of murder tourism appeared on the front page of the *Daily Mirror* on May 8. A photograph shows the exterior of the bungalow jammed with enthusiastic spectators, while inside the coroner's inquest into Emily Kaye's death was underway.[46] Although the viewer is able to isolate certain individuals, the majority of figures blur together in a composite amalgamation of hats and clothes, suggesting homogeneity in their thought and action. Indeed, the most striking characteristic of press reports of the Crumbles inquest was not so much the substance of the proceedings within the house as the repeated trope of an increasingly sensation-seeking public whose "morbid curiosity" threatened to overwhelm the entire event. The walls that ran on three sides of the bungalow, it was reported, had become "black with sightseers."[47] The same correspondent continued, "From the tops of taxi-cabs people looked down into the tiny garden through which the accused had to pass, and some hundreds lined the rough drive down to the main road. . . . For the space of half an hour the Crumbles was like a fair ground."[48] In the words of another journalist, for the swarming crowd, the bungalow was nothing less than a "first-class film attraction."[49]

To criticize the defacement of the scene by murder tourists, press reports invoked the specter of sightseers "intent on collecting 'souvenirs'" overwhelming the bungalow, either prizing thousands of pebbles out of its surrounding cement wall or pulling up flowers from the garden.[50] These stories sat alongside those of self-appointed amateur detectives delving into its "dustbin in feverish hope of finding something overlooked by the police" or picking over the beach in the hope of discovering missing body parts.[51] One of these trophy hunters—a young boy—discovered a five-inch-long human bone under a boulder, which, according to reports, he promptly handed over to investigators. Others were far less willing to relinquish their treasures, keeping the bones they found as a keepsake, much to the envy of those who "could find nothing more closely associated with the tragedy than pebbles from the shingly beach."[52] In this example of Crumbles murder tourism, the singularity of the episode of the boy's discovery and his subsequent cooperation with the police investigation served as a stark contrast to the crowd's indifference towards official investigators' efforts to locate the missing bodily remains.

As the Mahon trial came to end, another wave of murder tourism rolled onto the Crumbles, but this time there were no longer police defenses in place to hold back the sensation-seeking throng. According to reports, the Crumbles bungalow had become a charged scene, with hundreds of people threatening to break into the garden and smash up the bungalow. Trophy hunters were now able to cross the threshold of the bungalow and access its inner sanctum to vicariously (and indeed literally) consume its contents. Speaking to the press, the owner explained she had been given no choice but to open the building to the public.[53] Subsequently, an entrance fee was introduced, and a neighbor stepped in to run tours of the notorious cottage (fig. 4.4)—creating a new public attraction, what the *News of the World* dubbed the "shilling chamber of horror."[54] Tours of the interior of the notorious bungalow, it seemed, were now a recognized Eastbourne tourist activity; as one newspaper correspondent observed, "Hundreds and hundreds of people made the pilgrimage to the bungalow and gathered round its old-fashioned garden to wait for their turn inside."[55]

This latest spectacle at the Crumbles bungalow, in the eyes of the press, represented a stark inversion of the sensibilities and protocols that detectives had worked to instill over the previous months. As sightseers toured its various rooms, the calm and restraint required for CSI gave way to an orgy of cheap thrills, horror, and voyeurism. Commentators decried this development as a sinister and morally dubious kind of exploitation that had to

Figure 4.4. Shilling chamber of horrors. *News of the World*, July 7, 1924, 7. Courtesy of News Syndication.

be stopped, but to little immediate effect: a heightened emotional response and a fascination with death were the order of the day, and the sensational and dramatic murder plot was a selling point. The guide walked the "murder tourists" through the bungalow's rooms, pointing to noteworthy "exhibits." The visitors, it was derisively reported, could satisfy their appetite for souvenirs by purchasing sticks of candy with the words "Crumbles Bungalow Rock" printed on them. This particular exercise in commodification, according to an editorial in the *Sunday News*, constituted "one of the most disgraceful episodes of this fairground of death." Not only was the whole affair in bad taste, but this morbid tourism, the editorial continued, stimulated a fetishistic desire for crime scene relics:

> We entered the sitting-room, where Emily Kaye was said to have written her last letters and where, according to the prosecution's theory, she received the fatal blow. Then we were conducted through all the rooms of the bungalow and were allowed to examine their contents. We were shown brandy flasks. We were shown the bed "in which Mahon and Miss Kaye . . . slept"; we were shown the armchair [and] door which Mahon damaged in trying to fix a Yale lock to it, the blackened fireplaces (undisturbed since the crime) [and] the table on which he cut [up] the body.[56]

By portraying the behavior of the murder tourists and their engagements with the scene's "treasures" in this way, the press endowed upon the sightseeing crowds all the characteristics that a modern sleuth was meant to eschew. Such coverage confirmed that a murder scene was no place for public curiosity: its presence was a problem that required careful management. Crumbles murder tourism had become the symbolic other to a modern crime scene apparatus.

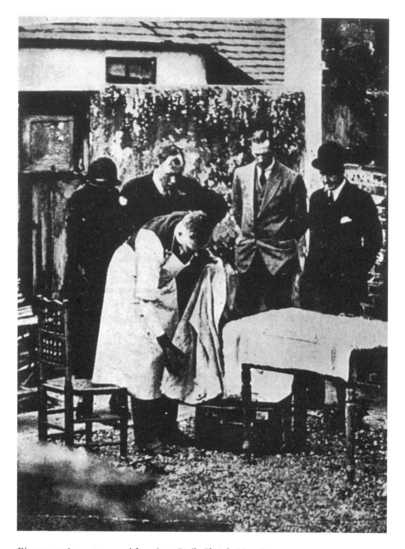

Figure 4.5. A mortuary with a view. *Daily Sketch*, May 6, 1924, 1.

The previous chapter ended with the murder bag as a way to destabilize historical and commonplace understandings of Spilsbury as the inventor of CSI. This one ends with a visual analogue—an iconic press image of Spilsbury—which captures the ambiguities that were produced by journalistic projections and imaginings discussed in this chapter. The photograph, depicting Spilsbury at work in his makeshift mortuary in the Crumbles courtyard (fig. 4.5), is significant because it permits contrasting readings of

Spilsbury's forensic practices and identity: in one reading, presenting him as a virtuoso of mortuary-based forensic pathology, while, in another, associating him with the demanding pursuit of trace material in the specially demarcated space of the crime scene, uncovering clues of equal significance to those derived from the corpse.

Filtered through the analysis of the actual investigative activities of the Crumbles case laid out in the previous chapter, the image brings Spilsbury the pathologist into sharp focus. It gives a rare but compelling glimpse into a set of forensic practices that was usually hidden by mortuary walls. In his outward demeanor and attire alone, Spilsbury strikes a formidable pose. He is dressed in his mortuary garb (autopsy apron and rubber gloves), standing next to the kitchen table-cum-mortuary slab, inspecting bodily remains and items of bloodstained clothing. Considered from this vantage point, the photograph can be read as exemplifying Spilsbury's highly individuated body-centered mode of forensic investigation, his presence at the Crumbles an artifact of the circumstances of the case rather than his commitment to firsthand engagement with the scene and its objects and traces.

But let us look at the image again and read it against this chapter's analysis of press representations. A product of mid-1920s photojournalism, it was produced by and circulated in a contemporaneous media discourse that assembled a sensational narrative of the Crumbles murder investigation and in the process blurred the line between fantasy and reality. From this perspective, Spilsbury the mortuary practitioner fades, and a new figure comes into focus: the pioneering hero of CSI, center stage at the crime scene, surrounded by police investigators and scene artifacts. Instead of the pathologist reassembling human remains for inspection, Spilsbury becomes the trace hunter examining the victim's clothing for telling clues. These readings of the photograph can exist as separate from each other, thus confirming either version of Spilsbury's expertise, or, by eliding the mortuary and the crime scene, the image can support a composite reading, in which he is the unique occupant of a borderland between two sets of forensic domains that at the Crumbles bungalow merged in a new and highly specific embrace of intertwined body, trace, and space.

CHAPTER FIVE

CSI in English Translation

B ernard Spilsbury entered the Crumbles bungalow as a rising star in the forensic firmament. His terms of publicly noted engagement (as histologist, toxicologist, or blood hunter, for example), however, were contingent on the nature of the case at hand. He exited as an unparalleled celebrity, a personality playing to a script that elevated him above mere circumstance and positioned him as the singular and heroic touchstone of interwar English homicide investigation. In this script Spilsbury was cast in two distinct roles. The first confirmed the conversion of the forensic pathologist from a largely anonymous nineteenth-century cast member to an individuated and personalized virtuoso. Spilsbury's exploits as interpreter of mutilated flesh were fundamental to this shift, yet in this new part, though he intensified the expectations for medico-legal expertise in matters relating to murder, he did not qualitatively transform them. The second role, by contrast, *was* transformative, in that it positioned him as master not of the mortuary and the body but of the crime scene and its traces. As shown in the analysis of the Mahon case, this version of Spilsbury was the result of a projection generated by contemporary interest in an emerging model of homicide investigation that, while not ignoring the body, sought out evidence generated in the context of the suspected act, focused on material traces at the scene of a crime.

Though different in their form, content, and long-term historical trajectories, forensic pathology and forensic science were *both* in the ascendancy in the Edwardian period, and their confluence forged the cult of celebrity that Spilsbury enjoyed. In creating and cementing this dual and mutually reinforcing image as master of body and trace, the Mahon case produced a peculiarly English exemplar of forensic modernity, which fused Continental advances in the scientific investigation of crime with medico-legal expertise.

An article in the *Daily Mail*, published as the Crumbles investigation drew to a close, neatly captures this conflation. "Dust as a Clue," written by the paper's medical correspondent Dr. Singleton, extolled the evidentiary possibilities of the eponymous species of trace evidence beloved of Continental crime scene theorists:

> Tobacco ash, the dust in a man's coat, and mud on boots have all at various times provided clues which have led to the unravelling of actual crimes. In fiction clues are made to order, but in real detective work they have to be unearthed.

This work, Singleton continued, had been given a noteworthy technical boost by Locard's announcement of a newly developed vacuum cleaner specially adapted for crime detection. For readers who might not be aware of developments in Continental "scientific policing," Singleton made what for him was the obvious connection: Locard, he observed, "is establishing a record as a criminologist in France equal to that of Sir Bernard Spilsbury in England."[1]

Singleton was not alone in forging such a celebratory association. Early in the following year a *Sunday News* headline declared Spilsbury the "Wizard of Criminology" and proceeded to specify the nature of his wizardry in the hybrid language of bodies, traces, and crime scene spaces:

> Nowadays the scene of any difficult murder case is not complete without the figure of Sir Bernard Spilsbury. . . . Sir Bernard is a man who can deduce much where others would deduce nothing. The smallest traces left by a murderer provide him with data that enable him to read the riddle of a crime. . . . A stain or a human hair, conveying nothing to others, tells him much. From little things he is often able to forge the vital link in the chain of evidence which has completed the case for the Crown.[2]

In public articulations of his forensic prowess, then, Spilsbury reached well beyond the confines of the mortuary: as the nation's leading exponent of modern criminology, no "difficult" murder scene could be properly investigated without his singular presence.

And yet in practice such scenes routinely *did* do without Spilsbury, and this was equally true of the post-Crumbles era as of before. As is clear in the case records of murder investigations in which he was involved throughout his career, his engagement typically began in the mortuary and ended in the courtroom. As noted in chapter 3, in only 10 percent of cases whose records we have been able to survey at the National Archives did Spilsbury visit the crime scene.[3] His involvement in the next in the sequence of his canonical "celebrated" cases immediately following the Crumbles—the 1925 trial of the Crowborough chicken farmer, Norman Thorne—provides a further striking illustration of this disjuncture between the work routinely attributed to Spilsbury and his actual practice.

The core question facing Spilsbury as a forensic pathologist in the Thorne case was how to derive evidence from a corpse that had been dismembered, buried for six weeks, exhumed, and examined in one state of putrefaction, and then reburied, reexhumed, and reexamined in a further state of decay.[4] However, there was another site of investigation in the case—the hut of the accused murderer, where Thorne was accused of delivering a fatal blow to his fiancée, Elsie Cameron, but where Thorne claimed Cameron had hung herself from one of the hut's ceiling beams after a lovers' quarrel. Following Thorne's statement, Scotland Yard's chief inspector John Gillian, accompanied by a local constable, entered the hut and took careful note of the state of its beams, paying particular attention to whether they bore traces of having had a heavy weight suspended from them by a rope. They found none. They later returned to the hut to conduct what Gillian described in court as a series of "experiments" involving the suspension of weights roughly equivalent to the weight of Cameron's body from one of the beams and then examining it for marks. At the trial, the beam was produced in court for Gillian to demonstrate to the jury the existence of clear groove marks in the wood produced by the rope during the course of the police experiments, in which traces of rope fiber could be discerned. Neither groove marks nor fiber traces, Gillian insisted, were present when the beams were originally examined.[5]

Concerted scene work thus featured as evidentiary elements in the Thorne case, but none of this involved Spilsbury. He never physically entered Thorne's hut and neither participated in nor commented on the crime scene work undertaken by the police. Tellingly, at one point in the trial he did address himself to the hut as a physical space, to deliver an opinion on what might have transpired within it. But he did so only indirectly and with reference to the same abstract and synoptic judgment that he had deployed at the Mahon trial. Asked for his views on the physical plausibility of Thorne's story given the dimensions of the hut and the arrangement of its furnishings, Spilsbury requested to "borrow the photograph of the hut." With this in hand he proceeded to detail a scenario of events and interactions that could best account for Cameron's post-mortem appearances. Under close cross-examination, Spilsbury stuck by the validity of his account, conceding only that others were possible "but that is how it occurs to me."[6] Thus, while he willingly engaged with the crime scene as an evidentiary locus, he did so on the basis of a mediated, imaginative projection into that space, rather than on firsthand experience. Even in the immediate aftermath of the Crumbles, then, at a time when his crime scene investigator persona was enjoying its greatest momentum—and in a case that involved clear and consequential interpretive engagement with the crime scene—Spilsbury stayed away, directly engaging only the elements of the case specific to his body-centered practices.

_ɔ ɔ_

We leave Spilsbury, for now, where we have placed him, not because from here he fades from the English forensic scene (in fact he continued as its dominant figure throughout the interwar period), but because his celebrity-driven version of body-centered homicide investigation served as a (critical) counterpoint to English reformers intent on inaugurating a more conventional and recognizably Continental model of scientific policing.[7] This project of translating CSI into English institutions and practices is the focus of the remainder of the chapter.

TEACHING THE DETECTIVES

This cohort of reformers cohered institutionally around the Departmental Committee on Detective Work and Procedure, established in May 1933 under the chairmanship of the Home Office assistant secretary Arthur Dixon and comprised largely of senior police officers and a number of provincial scientists with experience of criminal case work.[8] Dixon's interest in police science was part of a broader rationalizing and centralizing agenda, and in this he was willing to look elsewhere for inspiration. Addressing a 1934 conference of chief superintendents, he urged his audience to recognize the inadequacies of current crime scene practice:

> In this country we are far behind the Continent in taking adequate steps to prevent people who have no need to be there from visiting scenes of crime. It is all very well to mock at the Continental seals on doors and pieces of string and tape, but the idea behind these things, which is to preserve the scene of a

crime for the investigating officer in charge of the particular case, is a good idea.

Dixon illustrated the dangers of an unregulated crime scene with a recent case in which an officer moved a blood-stained mackintosh from under a bed and took it to his police station. When he was subsequently cross-examined in court he was unable to provide details on the circumstances in which it had been found. "People, including police officers and police surgeons, seem to be quite unable to keep their hands off things of interest," Dixon complained, concluding with a recognizably Grossian maxim on the danger of "moving things about at scenes of crime: nobody can ever be certain of what the exact position was before they were moved and that exact position may be quite vital."[9]

Between 1933 and 1938, when it published its five-volume final report, the Dixon committee, and especially its "D" section on scientific aids to police work, sought to enhance understanding and appreciation of the principles, methods, and powers of trace-centered investigation and to forge a network of forensic science laboratories able to generate useable results from trace matter derived from crime scenes. Among Dixon's supporters two stand out: the Hull University chemist F. G. Tryhorn, who became one of Dixon's leading exponents of CSI pedagogy, and C. T. Symons, who as Home Office forensic science adviser served as the architect of a new network of crime laboratories designed to cater to a burgeoning demand for trace analysis.

By the mid-1930s Tryhorn had developed a profile in the regional and, to a lesser extent, national press as a scientific trace hunter. His skills were showcased in a 1934 Leeds murder case in which he detailed his examination of the clothing of victim and accused, including the latter's trouser cuffs. This quintessentially Grossian locus of investigation yielded a suitably bountiful evidentiary harvest, including fragments of birch leaf that, Tryhorn confirmed, could be found in abundance at the scene of the murder.[10] He was also a local champion for Dixon's vision of scientific policing, which, as he told an audience at the Hull Chemical and Engineering Society, promised to empower a new cadre of forensic experts. "Until quite recently," he was reported as stating, "the medical witness dealt with all scientific matters in court, but with the splitting up of the sciences the individual sciences had now to play their full part in this side of police work."[11] Tryhorn's advocacy brought him to Dixon's attention—he was, Dixon noted in an October 1933 letter to a Home Office contact, "very keen to help," though also "very diffident about 'butting' in."[12] Dixon's letter was accompanied by a memorandum on the scientific instruction of police forces and the establishment of police laboratories that Dixon had asked Tryhorn to write, in which Tryhorn had noted the "keenness" of police officers of all ranks for such instruction. By March of the following year he had joined Dixon's Subcommittee D, and from this position he continued to vigorously promote the adaptation of key elements of Continental criminalistics to English conditions.

For two decades Symons served as assistant and then chief government analyst in Ceylon, where he developed a reputation for innovative crime scene and trace analysis work. In 1934, in poor health, he returned to England armed with a letter from the Ceylon inspector general of police recommending him to the Home Office as a leading exponent of the application of science to criminal investigation. Dixon met with Symons and was impressed with his enthusiasm, his considerable experience, and—on the strength of Symons's personal visits to Paris, Lyon, Lausanne, and Berlin—his familiarity with developments in Continental practice.[13] Dixon offered Symons a place on the scientific aids section of his committee. A few months later, Symons was appointed as the Home Office's first salaried "forensic science adviser."[14]

In the autumn of 1935, at Dixon's request, Tryhorn convened a training course for twenty-two detectives selected and sent by their constabularies at a cost in tuition, board, and lodging of £5/5- per head.[15] The course was delivered as a series of lectures and practical demonstrations over six days in September. The requirements of CSI practice are very much in evidence in the printed course syllabus. The first day began with a lecture introducing the principles of scientific aids to criminal investigation, followed by a practical session on methods of packing evidence. The afternoon lecture focused on the principles of searching and preservation of crime scene traces, after which the attendees engaged in hands-on work. The second day's pair of lectures introduced the material and technical referents for a forensics of infinitesimal traces, the first featuring the microscope as its key visualizing technology, the next populating this world of minute trace evidence with exemplary objects: fiber, hair, soil, and dust. The day's two practical sessions covered the processes of trace collection—featuring dust extraction techniques—and the principles of chemical and microscopic examination. Subsequent days followed this program of combined theory and practice as applied to a range of other traces and techniques.

Tryhorn considered the course a success. All the students, he reported, made good progress, with a handful showing "outstanding" aptitude. These would be "eminently suitable for propaganda work in their forces, and for receiving and packing exhibits at their headquarters," and if a few such individuals could be trained for each local force the future viability of the enterprise would be significantly enhanced. This favorable gloss was echoed in evaluation reports sent to the Home Office from individual attendees and their superiors in the weeks following the course. Birmingham's chief constable, in a letter to Dixon, reported that his two officers were very pleased and that he intended to send more students in future.[16]

Detective-Sergeant Frederick Carter of the Bristol Constabulary provided the most detailed reflections in reports to his superintendent in September and October 1935. Carter's first report praised Tryhorn's emphasis on training students to "recognise what 'traces' are likely to afford useful results from scientific analysis" and how to collect and preserve them in a suitable condition. This emphasis on trace matter, Carter pointedly observed, provided officers with detailed knowledge of how scientists, "as distinct from the pathologist," could aid in criminal investigation.[17] Carter proceeded to detail examples taken from the course lectures that illustrated the trace-evidentiary matrix at work in actual cases, starting with a German murder investigation that no doubt came from the 1906 Popp case described by Locard. Vegetation on the victim's clothing gave a clue as to the original location of the body. This led police to a suspect, and on examination of his boots they found that, though the boots had been superficially cleaned, thick layers of mud remained in the heel and instep. These layers were carefully removed to preserve their integrity and were found to include mud from the village street, goose droppings linked to the suspect's yard, traces of grass and moss of the type growing in his field, quartz residue from the grit stone that composed part of the hillside where the body was found, and reddish fibers of wool that were shown to correspond with the wool fibers of the victim's clothing. For Carter, the case "affords an extraordinarily complete record of the success of dust analysis. Much of the searching that was done would have been done in any event, but the examination of the mud deposit suggested a logical line of inquiry."[18]

In his second report, Carter elaborated on his suggestion that the pursuit of trace evidence itself was not entirely novel but that what Tryhorn was conveying was nonetheless substantively different from prior practice.

On the basis of his twelve years of service as a detective, Carter defended standard methods against overzealous champions of a "new" police science: "the methods of crime investigation employed by the general run of detective officers are not the haphazard, illogical and unscientific efforts that one is sometimes asked to believe."[19] Detectives were adept at learning from experience of what worked in criminal investigation and had evolved certain broad principles in the treatment of evidence and the need for expert assistance in analyzing blood and hair traces in murder and manslaughter cases, and blood, semen, and bruising in cases of rape and indecent assault. What was new, Carter continued, was the attention to procedural rigor, and the new cache of trace matter that this attitude in the field yielded:

> The type of scientific evidence that, in my experience, has not been looked for because of the ignorance on the part of police officers as to the extent to which the chemist can assist, is that which concerns minute traces, often of microscopic proportions and invisible to the naked eye, that may exist on garments and other articles found at, or near, the scenes of crimes, and upon the persons of victims and suspects.[20]

Carter's favorable evaluation of Tryhorn's detective school indicates that, for at least some in the police rank and file, the project of translating Continental crime scene methods into English practice was regarded as worthy of support. Further evidence of this attitude can be found in the pages of a new journal that served as an important outlet for scientists, administrators, and serving officers to articulate the virtues of trace-centered forensic investigation. Founded in 1928, the *Police Journal* entered a field previously dominated by the venerable *Transactions of the Medico-Legal Society*. *Transactions* had been published since the 1890s, and though it included contributions from toxicologists and other lab-based practitioners, it had been traditionally dominated by the concerns of a body-centered forensics and its mortuary-based perspective. The *Police Journal* set out a different agenda: to foster links in understanding and practice between the practitioners engaged at the two crucial ends of an emergent forensics of traces—police officers at the scene of a crime and scientists in (as yet unbuilt) crime laboratories. The *Journal*'s inaugural editorial highlighted its innovative objective, to link for the first time the "views of the professional police officer and the scientific authority on criminal matters."[21] Articles in the journal would all be directed to forging this link: "The scope of police work is steadily widening; and it is becoming in an increasing degree scientific," the editorial concluded, and thus all its articles would be designed to be "instructive from a police point of view."[22]

From the outset, the *Journal* made good on its promise to create a space for exchange between scientists and police. Its first volume featured articles by leading British practitioners of trace forensics: John Glaister Jr. on blood and hair analysis, William Willcox on toxicology, Sydney Smith on ballistics, C. Ainsworth Mitchell on the circumstantial nature of trace evidence, and Henry Rhodes on chemical evidence. This inaugural volume also published a version of Locard's series on dust analysis, accompanied by an advertisement featuring the Electrolux Suction Cleaner designed to enhance the efforts of forensic dust hunters (fig. 5.1).

Rank and file police officers were also regular contributors to the *Journal*, and their articles—much like those of the scientists—were cast in a composite language of CSI adapted from Continental writers. Police contributors, for example, demonstrated adherence to, and at times unselfconsciously reproduced, the classic dictates for crime scene management. In his 1934 outline of the qualifications of an investigating officer, the Liverpool detective sergeant James Healey proposed "a golden rule to be remembered. 'Never alter the position, pick up, or even touch anything, until minute notes have been made of them.' Experience teaches that one has not the slightest idea what turn a case will take, or what is of importance, or what will be denied."[23]

Three years later, the former Edinburgh detective-lieutenant John Duncan contributed a detailed account of a training lecture for senior police officers that featured a hypothetical murder scenario involving two elderly gentlemen found dead in their dining room by their maid—one apparently shot, the cause of the other's death unclear. Taking on the task of relaying the lessons of the scenario to his readership, Duncan first echoed Gross's emphasis on the need for the investigator to "maintain a quiet dignity" at the scene and to "appear confident and purposeful in all he does and says."[24] This attitude of quiet and purposeful confidence should then be imposed on the scene itself: "In entering the room where the bodies are, please do not let us all hurry in together. Such an entry is bound to be heedless, and someone is sure to disturb something that should not be disturbed." Protecting the integrity of the scene was particularly important in cases of murder, Duncan continued, which as a matter of course require "the scrutiny of experts" for whom pristine conditions were essential.[25]

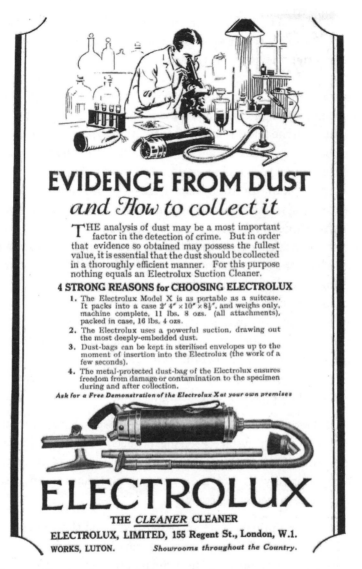

Figure 5.1. Cleaning the scene. *Police Journal*, vol. 1, 1928. Courtesy of Electrolux.

But as Duncan was quick to observe, the detective's work was not simply to secure the scene for other experts—he was also to comprehensively observe and exhaustively record:

We should be able to say what was the precise position of such articles as the door mat, the fire irons or the window blinds. We should be able to say what lay on the floor, and where, what on the table, what on the mantelpiece. We should be able to say who amongst us handled these things, who first discovered them, where they were finally placed.

Investigators often failed in this task, he continued, and though the omissions may appear slight, the implications could be significant: "a half-burned match on the floor, a clod of earth on the carpet, a picture askew on the wall, these may all have a tale to tell as important, and to a competent observer as eloquent, as a bloodstain or a bullet hole."[26] This comment evokes Gross's critique of trophy hunting, a point he reinforces by turning to the need for a systematic recording of the context in which the bodies lay. In doing this Duncan repeated his warning not to disturb the bodies in advance of the medical expert but at the same time insisted upon an independent role for the investigating officer: "The doctor when he comes will give particular heed to all these things, and will give evidence thereon; but we must observe and note them too."[27]

From the bodies as sources for trace evidence, Duncan turned his attention to the procedures for identifying, preserving, and transporting traces. He exhorted his imagined fellow officers to "get down on our knees" to hunt for traces "seemingly trivial, but of great importance," to take "careful measurements" of their precise position, urging completeness in this exercise:

A useful axiom is that while we may make a grave mistake by taking too little, we shall never make a mistake by taking too much. Most of the articles we collect will call for chemical and microscopic examination, and will find their way to the laboratory yct, but in the meantime it is our duty to get possession of them and see to their safe custody.[28]

Only with this preliminary work accomplished—and the bodies safely removed to the mortuary—can the investigator's attention turn to what might once have been considered his primary duty: gathering (human) witness testimony.

Police correspondents also engaged with the analysis of trace evidence as "mute witnesses" that, if properly approached, could circumvent the deficiencies inherent in human testimony. In a 1936 contribution with the generic title "Obtaining Information," the Scotland Yard detective-sergeant Arthur Cain provided a particularly subtle version of this analysis—one that echoed Gross's self-reflexive account of the investigating officer as a witness in need of perceptual discipline in order to enable mute evidence to "speak" objectively. Cain provided a complex analysis of the behavioral and psychological acts of cognition made at crime scenes. He initially outlined the sources of mediation separating object and perceiver: variable workings of sense organs, environmental conditions in which objects are framed, and mental disposition on the part of the observer. But, for Cain, these perceptual obstacles were the starting point for making the detective. By overcoming them through habit and training, the detective separated himself from the ordinary observer and became a reliable instrument of criminal investigation: "As a rule we tend to see and hear what we expect to see and hear. . . . But if this expectant attention is properly directed, the efficiency of your powers of observation will be greatly increased."[29]

Once acquired, this observational attitude required protection against sources of erosion and distortion. A prime example of this was the investigating officer's use of his notebook to record in detail without delay, and here Cain's observations resonate with Gross's view that recording not merely secured against the erosion of memory but also served as a bulwark against that which naturally enters to fill the void left by forgetting:

> Misrepresentation is brought about by the working of the imagination in an effort to overcome the loss of detail that has slipped from your memory. . . . [Y]our imagination will put in things which your memory has lost. Whatever you put in will be "plausible"; that is, the detail *might* have been there, or the occurrence *may* have happened.

Ordinarily, Cain observed, such plausible additions are innocuous—but not so in a criminal investigation, where "minor matters often prove to be important at a later stage of the inquiry." With this in mind, Cain offered a modified Grossian dictum: "The golden rule is: WRITE IT DOWN AS SOON AS POSSIBLE."[30]

The *Police Journal* crowned its early efforts to promote a reformed regime of trace-driven forensic investigation when in 1934 it published *The Detection of Crime: An Introduction to Some Methods of Scientific Aid in Criminal Investigation*, written by the Derbyshire superintendent Walter Martyn Garrow and his assistant chief constable James Main Else. Though at a comparatively slim 180 pages it was by no means a rival to Gross's *Handbook* in terms of detailed engagement, the text by Else and Garrow represents one of the first attempts to systematically outline the principles of CSI for an

English audience.[31] In both form and substance, the influence of Continental authorities is evident throughout. It opens with a recognizably heroic account of the range of intellectual, technical and behavioral attributes demanded of a modern investigator:

> The investigator of crime must be an astute reasoner and logician; he must be a profound student of human nature and a master in the analyses of the motives that guide human action; he must be a physiognomist, physiologist and psychologist, and for reliance on scientific aid in his work he must understand the requirements of the chemist, pathologist, toxicologist, biologist, physicist and metallurgist and must have a thorough and complete knowledge of police science. He must possess indomitable courage and be imbued with patience measured by infinity.[32]

Subsequent chapters introduce the investigator to a range of canonical topics: the search for blood and seminal stains, dust, and soils; the importance of fibers as evidence; the use of the microscope in criminal investigation; and the examination of vegetable matter and of feathers. Throughout, Else and Garrow offer practical instruction on methods of trace collection, packing, and transit, and technical subjects are broached to alert investigators to the evidential possibilities of trace analysis as developed and described by Continental theorists.

Their discussion of dust examination, which they associate with the work of Locard's police laboratory, is of particular interest. Citing differences in national criminal procedure and in particular the law of evidence, Else and Garrow initially adopt a restrained position on the value of dust: "There is no doubt that in some cases the determination of the origin of dust will (in connection with other circumstances) materially assist in the compilation of evidence, but whether it can be used in this country to the extent and certainty predicted by Dr. Locard for its use in France, is another matter."[33] Nevertheless, they acknowledge, and provide examples of, "considerable number of instances" in which the identification of dust has "played an important part in detection." One such instance is worth reflecting on, for it recalls the very form of dust evidence that chapter 1 highlighted as an exemplary instance of the unfettered Locardian imagination: "Almost everyone will at some time have held the wing of a butterfly between the fingers and, as a result, may have remarked the displacement from the wing of what appeared to be a kind of dust." By providing their readers with a visual representation of this most delicate of traces, moreover, Else and Garrow go

Fig. 24   The dust or scales from the
wing of a Butterfly
(Highly magnified)

Figure 5.2. Butterfly dust. W. M. Garrow and J. M. Else, *The Detection of Crime: An Introduction to Some Methods of Scientific Aid in Criminal Investigation*, 1934, 107.

a step further than Locard in positing the magic of dust analysis as a matter of attainable modern practice[34] (fig. 5.2).

⌒⌒

When Tryhorn sought to extend the principles of his training program beyond the confines of the classroom, he unsurprisingly selected the *Police Journal* as his means. In 1935, he published an article entitled "The Assessment of Circumstantial Scientific Evidence," in which he outlined a conceptual framework for understanding crime scene trace evidence with clear echoes from the Continent. Despite the general adage that every trace may prove of evidentiary value, he insisted, investigators had to exercise judgment in determining which traces to recover, and for this they required insight into the epistemology of crime scene traces as practiced in the forensic laboratory. "The examination of such traces involves usually the identification of the matter composing the 'trace,'" he explained, "followed by its comparison with other matter from which it may be derived, or with which it may be identical in character." These comparative results became significant against the backdrop of a specified, but flexible, distributional economy. For example, commonplace matter might under certain circumstances be recognized as possessing a telling individuality. By way of illustration,

Tryhorn invoked a scenario reminiscent of Thorndyke's analysis of the provenance of East End foraminifera, involving the identification of sand on a suspect's clothing and the finding of sand at the crime scene. Given the ubiquity of sand this in itself was not significant, Tryhorn observed:

> But if it can be shown that these two samples both contain iron and titanium and that both are in the form of rounded granules, indicating that the sand has been subjected to the action of wind or water for a long time, then a type of individuality is observed which raises greatly the evidential value of the comparison. The value will be raised still further if chemical analysis of the sand shows the presence of other impurities common to both samples.[35]

Alternatively, traces may take on significance due to their scarcity, but for this he acknowledged the need for prior systematic knowledge of local ecologies through which matter could be identified as out of place. This happened most often in the case of debris from rare or sparsely distributed plant or animal species, but it also pertained to chemical trace analysis. For this he drew upon an example from close to home:

> Ultramarine (washing blue), although a common substance, is rare in dusts; in Hull, however, where much of it is made, it is a common constituent of dust, particularly in the eastern part of the town. In Barrow, the only other place in England besides Hull where it is made, it is also likely to occur in local dusts; but in the same district in Hull where ultramarine is made large amounts of graphite are used, and this also finds its way into the dust of the district. The application of this second criterion indicates that that finding of both ultramarine and graphite in the clothes of a person living or working in East Hull would have small significance, but such a discovery in the case of a person resident, say, in Oxford, suspected of an offence in Hull, would be extremely significant.[36]

Past masters of CSI, from fact and from fiction, would wholeheartedly have concurred.

Tryhorn followed up on this foundational discussion by contributing a seven-part series of articles under the general title "Scientific Aids in Criminal Investigation," which tracked in sequence and substance the lectures outlined in his 1935 Hull training syllabus and made still more evident his sources of inspiration. The first installment established the importance of the small and ostensibly insignificant, and their dependence on disciplined handling at the scene:

The "clues" on which scientific evidence is based are often exceedingly minute: single hairs, a few fragments of leaves, some particles of dust, a splinter
of wood or metal, a small twist of fibres, and similar trifles have frequently
figured as the basis of crucial evidence in criminal cases. Such traces need
special care in handling and transport, and call for special methods of
packing.[37]

This world of fragile traces, Tryhorn argued, represented a departure, in the
English context, from prior understandings of scientific criminal investigation focused on medico-legal expertise: "to most people 'science' meant
something or everything within the scope of the medical practitioner: and
generally it was he alone of the men of science who played any part in bringing to justice the criminal." In cases involving crimes against the person, he
continued, the medical witness examined scenes of crime and brought
traces to light, but this expert's narrow field of interest meant that much
trace material escaped notice. Compared to Austria, Germany, and France,
he observed, the new English model of scientific policing—"though passing
through a period of rapid growth"—was still in its infancy.[38]

Tryhorn's allegiance to the Continental roots of his scheme was amplified in subsequent articles. The second saw him invoke two of its core principles. In advising the police on the nature of scene evidence, he turned to the
classic formulation: "Locard has stated, in effect, 'that every contact leaves
its traces.' This must not be interpreted too rigidly, but contains enough
truth to make it of value: and the rapid developments in police science add
continually to its importance." On the need to attend to the spatial dimension of trace harvesting, Tryhorn showcased his Grossian leanings: "The
exact position of the trace may be just as important as its nature. . . . It will
thus be realized that traces found at a scene of crime may possibly not carry
their full weight as evidence unless careful precautions have been taken to
note precisely the positions in which they occurred."[39]

This lesson was practically illustrated in the next article, devoted to the
searching and packing of potentially trace-bearing objects. Focusing on the
example of garments and footwear, Tryhorn emphasized the need to adopt
"some systematic procedure," for two reasons: to ensure a complete search
of the item and to "record unambiguously the positions on the garment in
which any traces occur."[40] When approaching items of clothing worn by a
suspect, Tryhorn highlighted the meticulous practical precautions required
to ensure their individual integrity and their ability to yield trace evidence:

Care must be taken to keep the individual garments free from contact with one another before the detailed search: thus, in taking garments from a suspect, each garment should be folded as little as possible, and separated from other garments by a sheet of paper. Footwear should be removed first and placed on a clean sheet of paper to avoid losing traces of soil, etc. If there is any reason to suspect the presence on the suspect's clothes of easily dislodged material, the removal of his garments should take place while he is standing on a clean floor or large sheet of paper. The floor or paper should be examined after the removal of each separate garment and any material found on it noted as having come from the garment last removed.[41]

To assist in the identification and recording of precise locations on which traces were discovered, Tryhorn recommended the use of a "searching board," comprising a grid of uniform and subdividable horizontal and vertical intervals (fig. 5.3). Garments pinned to the board could thus be searched and items discovered labeled by geometric coordinates, thereby lending both precision and reproducibility to search results.

Notes taken of a search needed to follow a similarly systematic format in order to both capture the search results and to demonstrate adherence to protocol. After pinning out a garment on the board, for example, "an entry should be made indicating how that pinning out was done, and, if conventions have been adopted for this particular type of garment, exactly what they were."[42] Any traces removed were to be given an exhibit number comprised of elements that denoted both their source and finder: "Thus, in an investigation, the third garment seized and searched by Detective Sergeant P.Q. would be given the exhibit-number P.Q.3; the first 'trace' removed and mounted by him during the search of this garment would receive the exhibit number P.Q.3/I."[43]

Tryhorn then turned to quintessentially Grossian themes, detailing instructions for collecting dust in trouser pockets and cuffs, and a method for maintaining the stratigraphic integrity of layered matter when examining footwear. On trouser dust, he noted the need for special care to "dislodge all the debris which usually clings tenaciously in the extreme corners of the pockets," as well as the requirement that "debris from each pocket shall be collected and packed separately."[44] Search for "evidence of layering" on footwear involved gentle scraping with a blade over glazed paper:

As soon as the scraped surface shows any sign of a change in colour scraping should be stopped and the scrapings collected on the glazed paper mounted.

Figure 5.3. Searching board. F. G. Tryhorn, "Scientific Aids to Criminal Investigation, Part 3," *Police Journal*, 1936, face 306. Courtesy of Sage Publications.

Scraping should be continued then over a fresh piece of paper and any second layer which appears should be separately collected: each successive layer in such a case must be separately collected.[45]

The discussion then turned to the "preservation of the integrity of exhibits," which focused attention on the ensemble of gestures, rules, and materials on which a successful regime of CSI was predicated. On material infrastructure, Tryhorn referred to an earlier contribution to the *Police Journal* in which he had introduced his version of a crime scene kit bag, which should be kept at each divisional headquarters. This contained more than forty items, *all* of which were devoted to the identification, recording, packing, and transport of trace evidence, and many of which received detailed descriptions and justifications for their inclusion. The crime scene counterpart to Spilsbury's "murder bag" had arrived.[46]

These physical aids participated in a broader framework of managerial care designed to secure the history of objects as they passed through the custodial chain from crime scene to courtroom. The value of an object, Tryhorn warned, depended on the investigator's ability to certify what had happened to it at every stage in the process. This in turn required a means of producing "a record of the persons who have handled it in any capacity since its first seizure." For this purpose he endorsed a recent Home Office recommendation for the use of exhibit labels with sufficient room for entering the signature or initials of all persons who had handled it: "This device will enable a check to be made at any time of the 'integrity' of an exhibit in the sense of continuity in its handling: the 'integrity' of an exhibit in the sense of its safeguarding from loss, damage, and contamination must equally be secured."[47] Set against the saga of the Crumbles cauldron recounted in chapter 3, this emphasis on a bureaucratically verifiable procedure for ensuring continuity and integrity of evidence serves as a striking indicator of how the landscape of CSI had shifted in little more than a decade.[48]

TAKING CSI INTO THE LABORATORY

Tryhorn's work to establish protocols for crime scene investigation was complemented by C. T. Symons's efforts to extend this discipline to, and embed it within, a new network of complementary spaces—forensic laboratories. Symons served as the key architect of this domain, working tirelessly until his death in April 1937 to lay the institutional groundwork able to support a modern version of trace-oriented forensics. He did this in two principal ways: by issuing a series of advisory memoranda and reports that served as a blueprint for Home Office sanctioned forensic laboratories, and by personally inspecting and advising a set of fledgling laboratories that had begun to appear in the early 1930s as the result of local initiatives inspired by the project of forging the new model of police science. By the end of the decade a network of regional labs catering to the burgeoning demand for trace analysis had been put in place.[49]

These institutions are less notable for the analytical procedures that took place within them or in the rules for determining how to translate the results of such procedures into viable units of evidence than in the development of rules governing the material and procedural interface between the crime scene and the crime lab—that is, the protocols of transfer from one site to the other designed to guarantee the continued authenticity of trace matter. In this we maintain our primary focus on the crime scene, and the laboratory is an auxiliary site that needed to adopt both the physical and cognitive restraint forged at the scene in order to preserve and extend the practices of CSI.[50] Through this discussion we seek to show how these new institutions served as further spaces in which the cardinal principles of a forensics of traces could be entrenched.

Symons's first substantive guidelines for model laboratory practice were laid out in "Some Notes on the Starting of Regional and Police Laboratories for Forensic Science," submitted to Dixon in January 1936. These notes contain recommendations on a range of topics, the most detailed of which were devoted to the requisite conditions for ensuring the harmonious relationship between the laboratory and the crime scene. Central to this exercise in harmonization were Symons's instructions relating to how objects brought to laboratories needed to be processed, stored, monitored, and handled while they remained in the lab in order to preserve their integrity within a chain of custody, whose crime scene origins had been so exactingly articulated by Tryhorn. In Symons's view, the creation of a series of bureaucratic protocols would permit laboratories to confirm (and extend) the physical and epistemic purity of the trace evidence harvested by trained field investigators:

> It is of the greatest importance that the identity of productions be established without any possibility of doubt from the time they reach the laboratory until they are despatched from it, and linked up at each end with the original source and eventual destination. No productions should be received into the laboratory without a covering letter identifying them or without some other sort of certain identification. When a parcel of productions comes from an outside source, it should be in the form of a sealed packet bearing a distinguishing mark, and accompanied by a cover letter, which should contain a copy of the seal. If so received, the intactness of the parcel and the seals should be verified at once, before any receipt is given.[51]

Symons here turned the material and gestural routines from the crime scene inward, positioning the laboratory as an additional location requiring temporal and spatial monitoring underscored by codified and verifiable procedural norms. The boundary between inside and outside was patrolled by intact seals and written certificates of provenance, which themselves required careful assessment and verification at this threshold stage: when a parcel is opened, Symons instructed, "each production and its label should be examined and compared with the details in the covering letter. If the packing has not been properly done, this should be noted and stated in the report."[52]

Having passed across this threshold the crime scene object became a ward of the laboratory. "Special steel lock-up cabinets" were to be provided to ensure their physical and conceptual integrity during their tenure.[53] Yet the very nature of laboratory investigation entailed new threats that could be mitigated only by strict adherence to protocol. The aim of the crime scene investigator was to excavate, record, and transport objects in as close to their found state as possible. In the laboratory, analytical examination might require alteration or even destruction of its prior material form. Thus, as the object made its way through the laboratory, each stage of handling and examination—and their consequences—required explicit documentation.

To enable this, Symons drew attention to the importance of a label "of standard form" that should be firmly affixed to any object identified and judged to be of potential evidential value at the crime scene. This label, Symons suggestively explained, functioned as "a sort of history sheet of that particular article from the time that it was found until it is finally disposed of in court or otherwise." The first stage of this history was written at the scene, but the recording of its subsequent stages were the responsibility of laboratory personnel. Space should be allocated "for recording how and by whom the item was handled in the lab, and the analytical results generated." Labels should provide room for recording the signature of absolutely everyone who handled or examined the object to which it was affixed. This would cover not only laboratory personnel but also any other authorized person who had been given permission to physically interact with it. In this latter case, a note was required explaining the reason for permitting this interaction.[54] The integral physical correspondence between label and object, Symons insisted, should be protected at all cost, up to and even at the moment of analysis: "If it is necessary to remove [the label] to make a complete examination (and this should very rarely be necessary), it should be carefully preserved and replaced."[55]

Once all laboratory operations had been completed, recorded, and reported, a final check was required to ensure compliance with this regime of care and thus the objects' readiness for subsequent use:

> When the productions in a case have been examined completely and the report typed, they will then be checked again to see that they correspond with

the descriptions given in the report, before they are made into a parcel and sealed up to be sent to their destination; the labels should also be examined to see that they have been initialled correctly.[56]

These procedures, if properly observed, simultaneously objectified the normative standards required of modern CSI and guaranteed that at every stage they had been faithfully observed.

—◦ ◦—

In his role as Home Office forensic science adviser, Symons visited the emerging police laboratories to assess their working practices and determine their readiness to be adopted into the Home Office regional network. He was thus able to issue informal and formal advice in response to the practices he observed and to develop written guidelines to encourage necessary changes in local practice. Symons's program of monitoring and intervention aimed to ensure that those who worked within these spaces were as disciplined as the objects that passed through them.

Symons's engagement with the Nottingham Police Laboratory, which in 1938 became the first to be incorporated into the Home Office network, serves as a prime illustration of these efforts to reshape the institutional landscape of CSI. The Nottingham lab had its roots in a local initiative driven by the city's innovating chief constable, Captain Athelstan Popkess, who had been an enthusiastic convert to scientific policing along Continental lines. After two years of self-professed "dabbling," Popkess made a tour of police laboratories in Paris, Lyon, Berlin, Dresden, Vienna, Budapest, and Prague, which provided both institutional and personal inspiration for his Nottingham project: "I regard Dr. Locard of Lyon as definitely the greatest criminologist in the world to-day," he informed a *Daily Express* reporter.[57]

In a 1935 article, fittingly published in the *Police Journal*, Popkess outlined his aspirations for the lab, including its ongoing work of compiling a "library of exhibits" that could serve as a data bank for turning Locard's exchange principle into practice: laboratory workers, he wrote, have been busy mounting on microscope slides

the seed of every grass that grows in Nottinghamshire and surrounding counties. We are at present mounting the hairs of animals, and to assist to this end we have recently received hairs of every animal in the London Zoo. We are also mounting soils and commercial dusts. Also fibres in commercial use.

Popkess's pursuit of a total reference archive of trace material at once vividly captures his personal zeal for scientific policing and evokes the imaginative scope and the daunting practical magnitude of the overall project. It was, he admitted, a task that stretched ahead for years, "and even then it will be by no means complete."[58]

In certain respects, Popkess was precisely the kind of forward-thinking innovator that Dixon and his allies were seeking to enroll in their reformist project. As they began to engage with the Nottingham setup, however, they identified deficiencies that required correction. Through site visits and reviews of laboratory case files, for example, they found unacceptably loose arrangements for handling and processing evidence. A 1935 report on an attempted murder investigation prompted a critical assessment by Symons. The description of the weapon—an axe whose head police found to be attached to its handle by a string—raised questions about the thoroughness of the work done both at the crime scene and in the lab: "Is the string stained with blood? Is it stained with coal? Where did the string come from? How was it cut? Is there any more like it at the spot?" Scene recording was equally poor: "There is no plan or photograph to show the court the various places where the articles etc. were found or the relations of the rooms or the means of exit from the house."[59] When Symons and Dixon visited the Nottingham laboratory later that year, they impressed upon Popkess the need for a far stricter institutional framework, "particularly as regards the handling, custody, marking, packing, etc. of 'productions.'"[60]

Alongside deficiencies in procedure, Symons and Dixon found Nottingham's epistemic culture in need of reform. The main source of the problem was easy to identify: "The scientific work and the police work," Dixon observed, "were too much mixed up together."[61] Part of the problem was physical—housed within the police headquarters, the work of laboratory staff was insufficiently differentiated from the interests of police investigators. The police orientation of the Nottingham lab, moreover, was exacerbated by Popkess's overzealous efforts to publicize its achievements. On his visit in August 1935, Symons held a private conversation with the lab's chief scientist Henry Holden about the detrimental consequences of Popkess's "advertising." Holden pointed to the recently published *Police Journal* article as a prime example of the problem, in which, alongside his promotion of the Nottingham library of samples, Popkess heralded the role played by trace analysis in the successful resolution of several criminal investigations. One such case involved the discovery of "squamous" biomatter scraped from under the nails of a suspect in a sexual assault case. When Popkess learned of the lab results, Holden reported, he "appeared to be elated and hurried out of the room to publish the fact that his officers had found definite support for the charge from the nail scrapings," despite having been told that their presence gave "no support for any connection" between suspect and victim.[62] For Holden, this was symptomatic of the lab's police-driven ethos that endangered scientific objectivity by encouraging conclusions "which were not justified by the material." Symons agreed: "The situation at Nottingham is a very difficult one," he wrote. "The officers undoubtedly can and do do their work efficiently, but they work under such conditions of interference and misrepresentation as are subversive to the correct and smooth working of the laboratories."[63]

A year later, matters had improved. Despite a discernible level of tension in their written exchanges, Popkess, in pursuit of Home Office support for his project, yielded to Symons's criticisms and invited him to "take the laboratory under his friendly supervision and guidance."[64] He agreed to Symons's draft protocols, undertook to divorce the lab "as far as practicable from a purely Police organization,"[65] and, in a significant symbolic capitulation to the Dixon vision of a network of disciplined forensic science laboratories, accepted Symons's suggestion to "suppress" the word "police" in the lab's title and replace it with the term "forensic science."[66] These rhetorical and physical strategies for separating lab from police activity echoed those used by Gross and his English disciples to transform the crime scene into a bounded, autonomous space for the detection of minute traces unencumbered by preconception.

Relations between Whitehall and the rebranded East Midlands Forensic Science Laboratory were also boosted by the development of a strong working relationship between Symons and Holden. They shared resources (Symons, for example, lending Holden his copy of Locard so that Holden could refresh himself on the analytics of dust[67]) and collaborated on developing notes on best practice that might serve as a guide not merely for Nottingham but for the other regional laboratories. Holden also freely complied with Home Office requests for a quarterly list of cases undertaken by the lab, and in both quantity and quality these were received without critical comment. The laboratory's statistical return of investigations carried out in the second half of 1936 showed a good spread of cases: of the fifty-four cases returned, twenty-nine involved biotraces, twenty-three physical or chemical methods, while only two featured pathological analysis.[68] In a further return providing brief particulars of the eighteen cases handled in the last quarter of the year, more than half featured trace analysis (hair, fiber, soil, and dust). At the bottom of the return Symons signaled his approval: "this shows good development in the area generally as a start."[69]

Four of the cases were sufficiently intriguing to prompt Symons to request further details, and these demonstrated the degree to which trace hunting was alive in the Nottingham lab. The first featured coarse and fine dried mud and grass fragments on the boots of the suspect. The coarse mud, on closer analysis, consisted of dung, animal hair, and brick and cinder fragments, which showed "striking similarity" to the mud in a field adjacent to his house. The finer mud and grass, under similar close inspection, "agre[ed] in detail" with the garden ecology, and the suspect's engagement with the garden was confirmed by the identification of a newly detached thorn on the suspect's clothing that could be linked to a rose bush found trampled at the scene. Muddied boots yielding differentiated evidence also featured in two other cases. One involved garden soil, wool fibers from a dining room carpet, and cotton, linen, and jute fibers from a bathroom mat. The other supplemented trace matching with stratigraphic analysis: the outer layer of mud contained traces of chaff, straw, and other withered plant fragments "essentially like" that found in a nearby stack yard, while the inner layer consisted of mud "like that from the drive." The suspect's coat bore a further significant environmental trace evidence—it was stained with a pronounced green patch that was found to derive from the *Pleurococcus vulgaris*, a microscopic plant commonly found on trees and palings. The significance of this stain became clear when the stash of stolen goods was found hidden up a *Pleurococcus*-laden tree. The final case was more impressive still:

A detailed examination of the coat for fibres etc. yielded the following results: (i) Rabbit hairs, abundant: from the colour range it was inferred that these were from tame rabbits: (ii) A number of chicken down feathers: (iii) Occasional cat and dog hairs: (iv) In the small outer breast pocket an isolated comb tooth, and a number of human hairs and powdered cindery material. The human hairs were of two kinds, namely darkish brown and grey and their appearance suggested that they were taken from a head which was showing signs of thinning hair or baldness as well as greyness. The cindery material was similar to that found commonly on allotment and garden paths. A number of fine wool fibres were present, chiefly on the inside of the collar of the coat suggesting that the wearer normally wore a scarf.[70]

In the reformed Nottingham lab, the pursuit of complex Grossian and Locardian trace linkages in criminal investigation had taken root.

___◦ ◦___

In June, 1936, Dixon's Subcommittee D issued a forty-page pamphlet entitled *Scientific Aids to Criminal Investigation*. Published as an official Home Office document, it was the result of several years' worth of work by committee members, and in particular Tryhorn and Symons, whose unpublished and published writings that we have reviewed in this chapter are excerpted and summarized throughout. From start to finish, it epitomized their joint embrace of Continental principles, its four sections—"Principles to be Applied in Judging the Value of Scientific Evidence," "Search for Material," "Examination of the Scene of a Crime," and "Handling, Labelling and Packing of Materials"—introducing readers to the core elements of CSI. Its first section's opening passage provides a clear orientation to what is to come:

> The methods used by scientists today are so very exact that many definite conclusions can be drawn from material which, owing to its diminutive size, might easily be overlooked. The criminal cannot approach the scene, commit the crime and make good his escape without leaving some evidence of his passing. It may be something he has dropped, something he has marked or scratched or worn in his passage; some minute personal fragment; a hair, a piece of skin, or some minute fragment from his clothing or the tools he has used. . . . It is not an exaggeration to say that every contact must leave its trace, sometimes readily visible, but at other times only discernible to a practised eye or discoverable by an expert. Even a few fine grains of dust may provide convincing evidence of guilt.[71]

This pamphlet reprised and reinforced the necessity of proper technique in collecting and preserving evidence, and as such needs no detailed analysis here. Instead of its content, we wish to draw attention to its circulation. On publication, *Scientific Aids to Criminal Investigation* was sent to every investigating police officer in England and Wales. This simple fact makes the pamphlet an appropriate end point for this chapter: as an officially generated and universally distributed set of guidelines for investigation, it serves as a measure of how far the project of "translating" the core principles of CSI had penetrated the forensic landscape of mid-1930s England.

CHAPTER SIX

Forensic Pathology in the Landscape of CSI

By the start of the Second World War, enthusiasm for Grossian and Locardian concepts was reshaping the principles and practices of English homicide investigation. Under the auspices of Dixon's Departmental Committee on Detective Work and Procedure, reformers had begun to put in place new institutions (detective training schools, laboratories) and had designed new technical aids and protocols (searching boards, chains of custody) with the aim of building an integrated regime of English CSI founded on the meticulous pursuit of trace linkages.

However, body forensics was by no means dead. In fact, while C. T. Symons and F. G. Tryhorn pursued their vision of a forensics of traces, a separate network of reformers was simultaneously attempting to extend the dominance of pathologists over the interwar forensic landscape. The symbolic centerpiece of these efforts was to be a London-based National Medico-Legal Institute. As the historians Norman Ambage and Michael Clark have argued, a medico-legal institute was to confirm, in bricks and mortar, the long-standing preeminence of forensic pathological investigation. The institute would establish England's first professorship in forensic medicine as an academic base for its director, enhance capacity for teaching and research, and provide state-of-the-art facilities for post-mortem and related pathological work.[1]

In contrast to the efforts of Dixon and his allies, this pathologist-driven initiative ended in failure, its prized Medico-Legal Institute, in the words of Ambage and Clark, remaining "unbuilt." As we have stated from the outset, however, our account of the making of English CSI does not follow a simple linear plot in which a forensics of bodies was eclipsed by a forensics of traces. Instead, the failure of the interwar project of institutionalizing Spilsbury's mortuary-based model of celebrity pathology led in the postwar period to a refashioned version of the pathologist as celebrated homicide investigator for whom, perhaps surprisingly, the newly regulated crime scene served as a key lever for raising his professional and cultural status. Attendance at the crime scene became written into the peculiar heroics of a reconstituted celebrity pathology, and the very difficulties associated with crime scene work emerged as a key source of its renewed and repositioned aura. Far from being marginalized by the emergent practices and protocols of CSI, the forensic pathologist took on a new and prominent role—as an integral, and most recognizably individuated, member of a disciplined ensemble of actors tasked with establishing physical and conceptual order at scenes of murderous violence.

THE DESIGNS OF INTERWAR FORENSIC PATHOLOGY

The campaign for a National Medico-Legal Institute was spearheaded by the London-based Medico-Legal Society, and, when in the early 1920s it established a committee to promote the cause, it made an unsurprising choice for its secretary and leading spokesman—Sir Bernard Spilsbury. The nation's most famous homicide investigator threw himself into the cause. The terms of his advocacy can be gauged by his contributions to a society meeting, held in June 1925, at which a ten-point list of recommendations in an interim report was debated. In his secretary's comments, Spilsbury drew attention to the three recommendations most relevant to his own forensic interests. First, harking back to the long tradition of pathological specimens as the foundation for teaching and research, he underscored the need for a medico-legal museum. Second, he urged the provision of resources for research into topics directly relevant to the questions traditionally (but often inadequately) tackled by forensic pathology—"the obscurity with regard to the nature of the post-mortem phenomena which occur in a body in conditions which modify the post-mortem changes," as a prime example. This clearly resonated with his recent involvement in the Thorne case, as did his final theme: improved facilities for the proper preservation of bodies. Other countries, he reminded his audience, had the means to preserve bodies "which render them available for further investigation whenever required." In London, he continued, "there is a complete lack of any such organisation."[2]

In the years that followed, society lecture topics provided members wide scope to comment on the state of English medico-legal arrangements, and, as a regular participant, Spilsbury took every opportunity to rehearse his case for an institute that would burnish the standing of his specialty. This partisanship is perhaps to be expected. Less expected, however, are his apparent indifferent responses to discussions about the theory and practice of CSI that were developing around (and so publicly associated with) him. Take, for example, his response to the homage to French police science offered to the society in 1931 by the Manchester police surgeon Thomas Blench. In his lecture, Blench had enthusiastically detailed the care and attention lavished on Parisian crime scenes: the routine exclusion of unnecessary persons, the use of metric photography to capture an objective record of the scene and all objects within it, and the *médecin-légiste*'s attention to the wider context in which the corpse lay:

> He searches for the presence in the hands of hairs, belonging perhaps to the murderer, and notes the position these occupy in the hands. He also notes the position of the victim, examines the wounds and takes the necessary measures for the transport of the body to the post-mortem room, where a minute examination of clothes and body takes place.[3]

On the face of it, Blench's outline of CSI across the Channel, and in particular the medical expert's integration within it, presented Spilsbury with an ideal prompt to reflect on his own experiences as England's most celebrated crime scene practitioner. Instead, he sought to turn the discussion to his favored topic:

> The subject is particularly interesting to this Society, because there are many of us who have for a long time been urging the needs of a medico-legal institute in this country. . . . It has been evident for a long time that we ought to have some means by which, in an important case at any rate, bodies could be preserved indefinitely for further investigation. . . . I should very much like to ask Dr. Blench in that respect, what facilities they have in the Medico-Legal Institute in Paris.[4]

England's putative crime scene wizard, it would seem, was more interested in the refrigeration of bodies than in the search for, and storage and interpretation of, crime scene traces.

The Medico-Legal Society's campaign for institutionally entrenching the preeminence of pathology in interwar English forensic investigation gained another champion in October 1931 with the appointment of former air chief marshall Hugh Trenchard as commissioner of the Metropolitan

Police. Trenchard's tenure was characterized by a vigorous reformist agenda aimed at improving the morale and efficiency of the force, including the enhancement of arrangements for the scientific investigation of crime.[5] In a letter to Sir Robert Scott, undersecretary of state to the Home Office, in February of 1934, Trenchard suggested that this could best be achieved by creating a crime laboratory within a proposed police college at Hendon, North London.

Having gained Home Office approval early in the following month, he canvased opinion on how best to advance the project. At the top of his list of questions was what qualifications should be required of a police laboratory director. Trenchard held meetings with high profile Metropolitan participants (including Spilsbury) and sent his assistant commissioner, Maurice Drummond, on a provincial consultation round that included stops in Hull for a meeting with the chemist Tryhorn and in Edinburgh and Glasgow, where Drummond discussed the plan with professors of forensic medicine John Glaister Jr. and Sydney Smith. Tryhorn, not surprisingly, strongly supported the idea of a scientist-director, preferably a chemist, but when this recommendation was taken north of the border it was summarily dismissed. Drummond reported that Glaister was especially adamant that such a laboratory would require a pathologist director. Glaister underscored this view by inviting Drummond to consider the fate of a chemist director attempting to give evidence in cases involving medical evidence—which, in his view, constituted the bulk of "important cases": "he would be opposed with the critical remark or question . . . 'Aren't you a chemist?'" This, Glaister warned, "would be bound to have a very deterrent effect on any jury."[6]

Trenchard required little persuasion: in an internal memorandum reflecting on the consultation process, he recorded his conclusion "that the head man should be a Doctor with considerable knowledge of medical jurisprudence and Forensic Medicine."[7] With the question of credentials settled, Trenchard launched a further round of consultations aimed at identifying a suitable candidate, which ultimately led to the appointment of the Edinburgh pathologist Dr. James Davidson in November 1934.[8]

Press coverage of the selection of Hendon's lab director emphasized the new facility's explicitly medico-legal orientation: the recruitment of James Davidson from Edinburgh's department of pathology, the *Daily Herald* observed, "is due directly to the intervention of Lord Trenchard, who has personally interviewed Dr. Davidson and other pathologists who were considered in connection with the post." As if not merely to confirm Trenchard's ideal for the appointment but to indicate the impossibility of thinking of a modern regime of scientific policing that did not include the nation's star forensic performer, the *Herald* reported its understanding "that Sir Bernard Spilsbury refused the appointment on account of the magnitude of his work for London coroners and for the Home Office."[9]

Trenchard's determination to install a pathologist director, as Ambage and Clark have argued, reflected his broader ambition to establish the national forensic medicine institute that Spilsbury and his colleagues at the Medico-Legal Society had long advocated. At a May 1934 meeting with the president of the Royal College of Physicians, Lord Dawson, Trenchard made it clear that the laboratory directorship "should be considered as a stepping stone to becoming the Professor at a Medico-Legal Institute." In a subsequent letter to Dawson informing him of the Home Office's approval of Davidson's nomination, Trenchard thanked Dawson for his support and looked forward to working with him to secure their ultimate ambitions:

> I am sure that this seed which, with your help, has been so carefully sown must be given all the daylight and sunshine that is possible, be carefully nourished and protected so that it may become the strong, fine plant which you and I desire and may produce many healthy seeds and plants, one of which I trust will outgrow it and become the Institute in London which will be looked up to as the authoritative place in England and Wales and be considered far in advance of those of all such institutions in other parts of the world.[10]

To ensure the transition from Hendon seedling to full-grown medico-legal institute, Trenchard formed a Home Office–sanctioned advisory committee, with him as chair and a membership heavily weighted toward medico-legal interests, including a former president of the Medico-Legal Society, the sitting president of the Royal College of Physicians, a council member of the Royal College of Surgeons, and the chief medical officers of the London County Council and the Ministry of Health. The prospects of a reformed regime of English forensic investigation, led by reinvigorated medico-legal expertise, appeared assured.

Appearances proved deceptive. By 1938, Trenchard had formally suspended his committee's pursuit of a medico-legal institute without having any meaningful progress to report. This failure stood in stark contrast to the fortunes of the Dixon committee discussed in the previous chapter, and the differing outcomes are by no means coincidental. It was clear that the Home Office considered Dixon's the more desirable of the two visions, in terms both of cost and of relevance to the development of a modern regime of criminal investigation. For example, in his letter to Trenchard approving arrangements for Davidson's appointment at Hendon, Robert Scott conveyed the secretary of state's support for Trenchard's declared interest in enhancing the application of scientific aids to police, the present state of which he agreed was "definitely backward." However, Scott continued, this need "is required not only in the field of forensic medicine *but equally, if not more urgently,* in other branches of science, such as chemistry and physics and various technical processes which may have important applications to police work." Scott concluded by delineating the nature and requirements of this new world of scientific policing, where "so much depends upon mere traces, such as a few fibres or few grains of dust, at the scene of a crime or on the clothing or person of a suspect, and on their preservation for laboratory examination where they exist."[11]

Within a year of the opening of Davidson's laboratory in April 1935, its performance came under critical scrutiny. Analysis of its work load showcased its shortcomings: in 1936 it processed a disappointing 160 cases, dropping to 101 the following year: "The 1936 return was bad enough," a Home Office docket note observed, "but that for 1937 is even worse, and indicates that the Metropolitan Police have not begun to realise the possibilities of scientific aids to criminal investigation."[12] Hendon's apparent failure was ascribed to several factors, starting with Davidson's personal shortcomings. Henry Holden, director of the East Midlands forensic laboratory, when invited to reflect on the comparative weakness of the Hendon regime, gave this view: "Davidson I consider weak, and like many weak men, obstinate."[13] Holden's assessment of the reasons for Davidson's shortcomings at Hendon identified a further set of explanations, centering less on his character than on his failure to instill a cooperative relationship between lab and scene workers: "Little or no attempt has been made to 'show the flag' in the area served by the Hendon Laboratory, and . . . the reception of visiting officers to Hendon has been so discouraging that case material has only been sent to them as a last resort."[14]

This, arguably, was not Davidson's responsibility alone, as Metropolitan Police correspondence suggests that senior officers actively sought to restrict the flow from crime scene to crime lab, to prevent Hendon from being "flooded with unnecessary requests for urgent examinations" by scene investigators who had developed "the habit of sending things to the Laboratory unnecessarily."[15] This tacit policy rankled some among the rank and file, whose protests echoed one of the cardinal principles of trace-oriented investigation:

> It is not very easy always to know exactly what should and should not go, and there may be some piece of cloth with a stain on it which looks perfectly innocent and yet may prove after careful examination to contain some evidence which may have an important bearing on some particular case.[16]

It is worth noting that, from his position as architect of the Home Office network of regional forensic laboratories, Symons also identified the restrictive scene-lab interaction as a key flaw in the Hendon regime: it was, he observed, "unfortunate from every point of view and there is, of course, an almost complete loss of contact between the outside man and the Laboratory."[17] In developing his own plans, he explicitly sought to establish a different dynamic. Though, as we showed in the previous chapter, Symons put detailed measures in place to create a controlled border between scene and lab, he was equally concerned to ensure that it was sufficiently permeable to prevent restrictions on interaction from sealing the two off from each other. Without such permeability, as the Hendon case demonstrated, a counterproductive gulf of communication and comprehension could emerge between denizens of the lab and scene investigators who were meant to supply them with material.

In his reports Symons continually stressed the need to enhance investigators' understanding and appreciation of trace analysis by providing them with opportunities to witness it in action. Symons underscored this ideal by expressing the hope that police officers would be encouraged to consult laboratory staff "fully and freely, and without any unnecessary formality."[18] A memorandum outlining the structure and functions of the proposed East Midlands laboratory affirmed his aspiration that there should be "no hesitation or reluctance" to submit crime scene material for an expert opinion, even if its value to the investigation was uncertain: "seeing that the minutest traces may yield invaluable information, it is best to be on the safe side and submit for expert examination any article which there is any reason to think may have an chance of yielding useful results."[19]

This encouragement to the police rank and file reflects a noteworthy parallel in approach to the treatment of crime scene material itself: Symons's labs renounced the stance of the trophy hunter who would welcome only recovered trace matter that was of immediate or obvious value. Instead, like Gross's investigating officer, his staff would suspend judgement on what may or may not prove to be significant and would accept the additional labor entailed by this more extensive approach. It is also worth noting that this liberal regime was seen as a way of preventing a common criticism voiced against Continental laboratories—that their pursuit of ever more refined techniques marginalized their relevance to and accessibility by case investigators, and resulted, in Dixon's view, "in the inadequate use of well-equipped laboratories."[20] Symons made the case in starker terms: "sitting in his laboratory surrounded by the finest and most expensive apparatus in the world, and equipped with the best academic training and experience, the expert may be ornamental and interesting, but he is useless unless he has the right material brought to him in the right condition."[21]

Criticism of Hendon also flowed from within—and from the very top of—the Metropolitan Police. When Trenchard resigned as commissioner in November 1935, Davidson lost a key supporter and gained a powerful critic in his successor, Sir Phillip Game. Game shared others' assessments of Davidson's personal limitations: he was, Game wrote, "a poor witness, does not impress the Courts, and the [director of public prosecution's] people have no faith in him. He is also said to be an uninspiring lecturer. It is certain, I'm afraid, that the Metropolitan Police Laboratory will never 'get anywhere' under his control."[22] But Game's evaluation of Hendon's prospects ultimately rested on two foundational questions: What was the proper professional qualification of its director, and was there a real need, in the specific context of London, for a dedicated police laboratory at all? Both questions led Game to engage with the relationship between the emerging system of forensic laboratories and the prior model of freelance consultancy exemplified by Spilsbury's dominance of high-profile murder investigations.

On the first issue, Game was soon convinced that the Met lab was being led by the wrong person. In a confidential letter to the Home Office in October 1938, Game aligned himself with the newly published views of the Dixon committee, which had issued a five-volume report earlier in the year in which it reiterated Dixon's insistence that a new lab-driven model of forensic investigation needed to disentangle itself from its traditional association with sensational cases and celebrated experts:

Experience shows that much the larger proportion of the work submitted to the regional laboratories is of a non-medical character. Moreover, other arrangements can be made for any post-mortem examinations that are necessary and, as a rule, for any pathological work that arises in cases of homicide and other serious offences against the purpose.[23]

Citing this view with approval, Game concluded, "It is probably wrong in principle to have a pathologist in charge."[24]

Game's criticism of Hendon's leadership led him to question whether London needed a lab of any kind. In a January 1939 letter to the Home Office's Sir Alexander Maxwell, Game urged the need "to go back to the beginning" and ask the question, "Do we want the Laboratory, and if so, for what?" Game's answer was no:

I personally, speaking without any detailed knowledge but more on first principles, very much doubt if we need a laboratory to assist us in dealing with cases in which scientific evidence, including pathological evidence, is really important. . . . In such cases, and their number is not large, the scientific knowledge needed will be of a highly specialised kind and the resources of the country in any case, and those of London in most, can nowadays produce a specialist of any and every variety. No reasonably and economically staffed Police laboratory can hope to do this.[25]

Game's model for forensic involvement in police investigations, then, was a restricted one, tied to rare and difficult cases that required the assistance of celebrated individual specialists. In London, he had these on call, without the need to finance and manage an in-house operation of dubious effectiveness.

Responding to Game's observations, the Home Office endorsed his doubts about pathology as the cornerstone of laboratory operations but questioned as "retrograde" his apparent willingness to embrace a system founded on celebrity freelancers.[26] In his formal reply, Maxwell reminded Game of the Dixon committee's conclusion that the value of forensic laboratory work lay in its capacity to align science with policing on an everyday level, to build skills, mutual understanding, and cooperation among an investigative cluster composed of scientists and police: "The police laboratory is not merely a place where a competent scientist does the kind of work which he could equally well do in his own laboratory. It is a place where a team of scientific workers develop their scientific knowledge along lines which are specifically valuable for police purposes."[27] From the Home Office's perspective, then, Game's position reflected an outmoded reliance upon insular virtuosity that placed the pathologist as the cornerstone of an episodic, spectacular, and homicide-centered conception of forensic expertise.

At a meeting between senior Metropolitan Police and Home Office officials in May 1939, several of these long-standing questions were, in principle, re-solved. The attendees agreed to work toward a reformed Metropolitan Lab-oratory that would be led by a scientist and that would have "no provision . . . for pathological work."[28] Some two years later, reflecting on the process through which these decisions were reached (though not yet implemented), a Home Office memorandum reiterated the root cause for Hendon's "some-what spectacular failure" in contrast to the provincial laboratories:

> The Metropolitan Police have of course always thought of scientific aid in terms of pathology, but actually pathological work is in some ways the least important side of the laboratory system. . . . Lord Trenchard's Committee also had a very strong medical bias and approached the problem from the point of view of the Medico-Legal Society; their grandiose scheme for the es-tablishment of a Medico-Legal Institute bound up with the Universities had very little bearing upon the work of the laboratories. It was in fact another of the misfortunes of the Metropolitan Laboratory that it started with such a strong medical bias.[29]

This bias stood in sharp contrast to the cooperative model of expertise pur-sued by Dixon and his collaborators, whose credibility derived from its in-stitutional rather than personal standing. The core attributes of a success-ful laboratory director followed from this alternative vision: not a man of "established reputation" but one of "acknowledged professional compe-tence who is a good and impartial witness, is able to get on with policemen and has the confidence of the Courts."[30]

RESITUATING FORENSIC PATHOLOGY
IN THE LANDSCAPE OF CSI

Davidson retained his position at the head of the nation's most prominent forensic laboratory for the duration of the war. He retired in 1946, as the first and last of its medical directors. His immediate successor was Symons's staunch ally Henry Holden of the East Midlands Laboratory, who served for five years until his own retirement from the service. The chemist Lewis Nickolls, who had started his forensic career as one of Hendon's staff scientists before assuming the directorship of the Wakefield lab when it was incorporated into the regional network, was named as the Metropolitan Laboratory's third director in 1951. With talk of a Medico-Legal Institute in abeyance, the outline of English homicide investigation had begun to conform to the vision advocated by Dixon and his allies.

To an extent this alignment represented a victory over the Spilsbury model of the all-knowing, solitary artist of the flesh and its displacement by a systematic, team-driven science of the crime scene. Spilsbury's life ended shortly after Davidson's exit. On December 17, 1947, he turned on the gas in his cramped, privately financed laboratory and was there found dead on the following day. The exemplary lone freelancer, who drew on an ensemble of personal resources and projected an image of omniscient virtuosity, perished in one of the offset spaces that helped to forge his celebrity. The demise of the Medico-Legal Institute, Davidson, and Spilsbury in one respect signaled the resolution of the long-simmering tension between the Trenchard and Dixon versions of scientific aids to criminal investigation. However, it was not so much a banishment of pathology from the landscape of forensic investigation as pathology's readjustment to a new dispensation, involving practitioners whose working lives were conducted in proximity to, and in direct relationship with, the idea of a disciplined trace-laden crime scene, and who were willing to seek a niche for themselves within a matrix of investigation demanded by such spaces.

This readjustment was led by a new generation of forensic pathologists, exemplified by the London-based duo of Francis Camps and Keith Simpson, who professed a set of shared, self-consciously post-Spilsbury values: regard for teamwork, integration of science and medicine, adherence to routine and rigor. Both in real time and in retrospective reflection, they identified their career trajectories as entailing a break with the earlier mold. Simpson's best-selling memoir, *Forty Years of Murder*, portrays the landscape of forensic pathology that he found as he entered the field in the 1930s.[31] A brilliant but flawed Spilsbury had at once dominated and deformed its practice, due in large part to his lack of engagement with it as a rigorous academic subject: he never wrote a practitioner's guide, neither contributed to the academic literature nor trained any students, and refused to consult with contemporaries abroad or at home: "He stood like a monolith, alone, aloof, respected but unloved."[32]

Critical comments of professional forebears are of course standard fare for retrospective autobiographical self-fashioning, but these also permeated the publications and activities of Simpson and his peers, and in this sense appear to have been adopted by them early in their careers as a way of identifying what was distinctive about their era of homicide investigation. In his "The Changing Face of Forensic Medicine, 1930–1960," for example, Simpson characterized the start date of his survey as "largely in the hands of a few 'figures' in the public field" who were rarely challenged; but, when they were, the confrontations were "often personal":

> The whole conception of forensic pathology badly needed re-shaping; experts had to be formed in the ranks of young pathologists and scientists who were prepared to tread the barer paths of laboratory and morbid anatomical training in the departments of pathology of university schools before practising their skill in forensic fields. They had to be "retained" by some kind of connection with their parent departments whilst developing their skill and maturity under the critical eye of chiefs who understood and were interested in the problems of obscure death, of trauma and disease, of reconstruction and crime analysis.[33]

As an index of this transformation, Simpson turned to shifts in crime scene practice, providing a comparative table of methods for "routine investigations" in 1930 and 1960. His outline of 1930 specified that bodies were seldom examined in the location they were found, that post-mortem examinations and the certification of the fact of death were both entrusted to nonspecialists (local practitioners and police surgeons), and that little laboratory work was undertaken. Thirty years later, he claimed, bodies were examined on the scene by practitioners trained to estimate the time of death and to search for any cause for suspicion; clothing and other material items were submitted for meticulous examination; an appointed pathologist conducted autopsies in the presence of a forensic science laboratory officer in cases of suspected criminal violence; and, after analysis, all laboratory specimens were preserved in deep freeze.[34]

Associating modern forensic pathology with the values of systematic crime scene practice did not mean abandoning its traditional and distinctive focus, a point made clear in the introduction to the 1947 edition of Simpson's

Forensic Medicine: "As it is around a body, often a dead body, that the chief interests of forensic medicine develop, it will not be unreasonable to set out the subject with this as the centre-piece."[35] However, there are clear differences between the expectations of an omniscient medical crime scene observer as found in traditional medico-legal textbooks and those specified by Simpson. For Taylor, recall, "a medical man, when he sees a dead body, should notice everything. . . . It should not be left to policemen to say whether there were any marks of blood on the dress or on the hands of the deceased, or on the furniture in the room."[36] In Simpson's view, this nineteenth-century assumption of medical observational supremacy both was outdated and tended to reinforce the unsubstantiated artistry that was Spilsbury's trademark. His advice on medic-body-scene interaction clearly assumes the existence of the kind of disciplined crime scene that had developed over the previous decade. Simpson's medical observer was enjoined to exercise restraint—to make sure not to disturb anything, to ask police permission to move or remove objects, for example. "Searching for weapons and finger-prints, and peering into furnishings for stains," Simpson declares, "is no part of the doctor's duty; he may safely leave such matters to the police."[37]

Reflecting on thirty years of change in crime scene protocol, Simpson's deputy, the Guy's pathologist Keith Mant, similarly points to a new world of action and affect. Mant notes that in the postwar period the crime scene had become a "sacred space," one in which the pathologist could participate but could equally defile.[38] Common mistakes were made "usually because the doctor becomes too absorbed in the general problems and forgets his specific duties and functions."[39] A properly focused medical attendant should avoid touching anything, aware that "any movement of the body may cause trace evidence to become dislodged or change its position"; he should wear disposable gloves and antistatic overshoes to "eliminate the exchange of trace evidence"; he should refrain from smoking so as not to contaminate the scene with saliva-laden butts.[40] "The longer the doctor stays at the scene," Mant warns in conclusion, "the more likely he is to disturb something which may interfere with the scientific examination."[41]

This new positioning of the pathologist at the scene—and his subsuming within a broader regime of systematic, sequential, and differentiated investigation—was itself framed as a practice that no longer was insular but was driven by the ethic and advantages of the "team." In the first postwar edition of the series *Recent Advances in Forensic Pathology*, its editor, Francis Camps, made this shift the substantive message of his opening statement:

"As the result of advances and of greater specialisation, medico-legal problems and their solutions now depend upon the closer co-operation and teamwork of experts, both in medicine and science."[42] For Simpson, even an article on that most insular of pathological practices—the autopsy—was a chance to extol these modern virtues: "An experienced pathologist will have learned to operate as a member of a team, not out on his own. . . . Good crime investigation is nearly always good teamwork."[43]

This cooperative ethos brought with it at least two clear benefits. By introducing a multisourced framework for the production of forensic evidence, it reduced the influence of conclusions based on individual virtuosity— thereby avoiding the danger of "relying upon experts and *not on what they know*," as Camps tartly observes.[44] Camps makes this imperative of knowledge grounded in the collective values of scientific research and experiment the cornerstone of his editorial recasting of the authoritative *Gradwohl's Legal Medicine*: "the book has been almost completely rewritten and redesigned to emphasize the fact that, in the future, statements from textbooks will be quoted in court on the basis of the latest scientific facts rather than on a tradition or reputation derived from the past."[45] A consequential benefit, in Simpson's view, was the comparative absence of courtroom controversy that he attributes to the days of the "private services" of Spilsbury and his ilk. The improved general standard of professional performance, he notes, had resulted "in the disappearance of those all too frequent undignified clashes of opinion at criminal trials." It was now rare, Simpson concludes with satisfaction, to "feel the jousting atmosphere" that characterized celebrated trials of the 1920s, "when personalities and skilled opinions clashed so violently."[46]

Simpson and Camps may have welcomed the retreat of "personality" as the defining feature of a bygone era, but in another sense they actively sought to fashion a reconstituted public identity for themselves and for their vocation. The cornerstone of this revised version of celebrity pathology was their embrace of the role of author, not merely of textbooks and specialist journal articles but of an autobiographical genre in which they represented and reified their place in the new landscape of investigation. Starting in the 1940s with published case accounts of their role in selected murder investigations and culminating some decades later in highly personalized "true crime" memoirs, both Simpson and Camps were actively engaged in crafting the terms of their public recognition in a way that the sphinxlike Spilsbury had left to the agency of journalists.[47]

Simpson was particularly prolific in this respect: between 1943 and 1953 he published articles on ten murder investigations, all adhering to a common script.[48] They opened with a didactic scene setting, in which the lessons to be taken from the case details were laid out in lively prose. The first in the series, his account of the 1943 Dobkin ("Baptist Cellar") case, for example, began with the claim that it provided "an ideal illustration of the striking results of the patient application of simple medico-legal principles of study, and it is because the case has this quality and is certain to remain a classic that it is recorded in this Journal."[49] His next installment—featuring his work on what was to become known as the "Wigwam murder"—was written up because it "provided such a remarkable example of the information to be gained by the patient reconstruction of body injuries from what was described as 'a rag and a bone and a hank of hair' that it will remain a classical case of scientific criminal detection."[50]

The reports then followed a generic structural formula, including accounts of initial discovery and scene of crime work (routinely placing Simp-

Figure 6.1. Body in space: murder victim in situ. Keith Simpson and Eric Gardner, "The Godalming Wigwam Girl Murder," *Police Journal*, 1944, face 216. Courtesy of Sage Publications.

son at the scene), the medico-legal autopsy, further criminal investigation, and the conclusion with closing reflections on its broader lessons. The cases included extensive detail on crime scene practice and the identification, retrieval, transportation and analysis of trace evidence (hair, fiber, soil, flora, and fauna), and the teamwork among police detectives, the pathologist, and lab scientists that enabled this trace matter to speak. Each report was fully illustrated with photographs of exhibits and invariably of the crime scene with body in situ. These photographs, as evident in the examples reproduced here from the 1944 "Wigwam" case, provided readers with a stark visual illustration of the emergent regime of interpenetrated bodies, scenes, and traces that Simpson was pursuing: in the first, body and space meld in a way that suggests an inextricable fusion (fig. 6.1); in the latter pair, trace-bearing natural object (sectioned birch log with adherent hair) and trace-bearing human body part (wounded forearm) are presented in a symmetrical graphic style that fosters an expectation of subsequent symmetry in the analytical regime that will interpret them (figs. 6.2, 6.3).

Though not reproduced in this series of articles, there is a further element of Simpson's visual and graphic engagement with crime scenes that provides a telling contrast to Spilsbury (and an echo of Gross): when he visited a crime scene, Simpson took extensive notes that he at times supplemented with a sketch of the body as it lay in space. The bulk of these crime scene documents have been destroyed, but a handful survive, preserved in the Gordon Museum at Guy's Hospital. The sketch reproduced in figure 6.4, from the 1964 *R v. Brittle* murder investigation, is the most detailed of those in the collection, and serves as a striking testament to Simpson's investment in the spatial analytics of CSI and his sense of the pathologist's key role in it. The drawing is supplemented by integrated observations on body, trace, and space: layers of turf from the opposite side of the road from where the body lay, beech leaf cuttings, and (possibly older) earth and beech debris are recorded alongside notes on the state of the body and its clothing, as is the body's subsequent removal from the scene to Guy's Hospital for further examination.[51]

In this series of articles Simpson asserted for pathologists a degree of narrative control over cases of homicide investigation. In one sense this represents a continuation of prior convention, in which press reports had projected onto Spilsbury the pivotal role in cases such as Mahon. But Simpson broke new ground, both by directly asserting that control himself (rather than through press reports) and by emphasizing the more populated and dynamic landscape in which these investigations were framed—one that

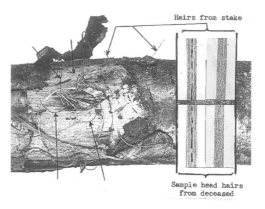

Figure 6.2. Body and trace: birch log with adherent hair. Keith Simpson and Eric Gardner, "The Godalming Wigwam Girl Murder," *Police Journal*, 1944, face 216. Courtesy of Sage Publications.

Figure 6.3. Body and trace: wounded forearm. Keith Simpson and Eric Gardner, "The Godalming Wigwam Girl Murder," *Police Journal*, 1944, face 216. Courtesy of Sage Publications.

entailed significant constraints on the pathologist's autonomy alongside opportunities to showcase his skills.

Two further innovations are worth noting. First, Simpson published his accounts not in the traditional outlet for forensic pathology, *Transactions of the Medico-Legal Society* (which by the late 1940s had been renamed the *Medico-Legal Journal*), but in the *Police Journal*—the mouthpiece for English CSI. As such, he positioned his authorial voice in conversation with the network of contributors and concepts explored in the previous chapter—a network that developed in large measure separately from that established around the Medico-Legal Society. Second, Simpson's interweaving of the established script of celebrated cases with the rigors of modern CSI was a way of asserting and projecting a new public version of forensic pathology. This version involved a distinct set of trademark gestures and positions that

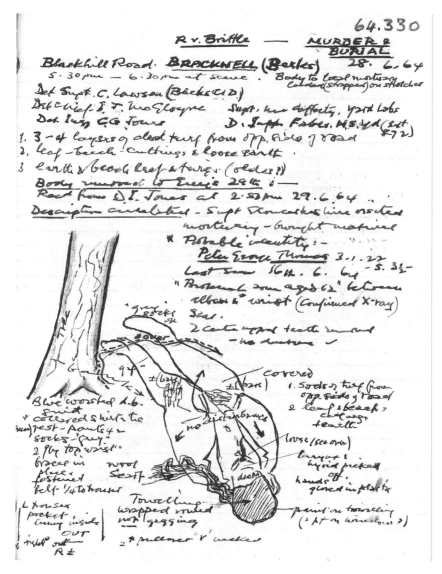

Figure 6.4. Sketching the scene. Simpson notebooks, Simpson archive, Gordon Museum of Pathology at Guy's Hospital. Courtesy of the Gordon Museum, King's College London.

added an arduous physical engagement with the crime scene to the pathologist's established mortuary heroics.

The press played its part in fashioning this revised model of celebrity pathology. Unlike newspaper accounts of Spilsbury, which did not characterize his (infrequent) visits to crime scenes in the language of urgency, those made

Figure 6.5. CSI by searchlight. "Arresting the Crime Wave." *Picture Post*, August 4, 1945, 17. Courtesy of the Kurt Hutton Archive / Getty Images.

by Simpson and his contemporaries were commonly described as taking place in the dead of night, following a midnight or early morning "rush" to the scene, to examine the body and its surroundings under high-powered arc lights. This reframed the dramaturgy of the murder investigation and the pathologist's role within it. The systematic application of forensic expertise began not in the mortuary but in a new space of horror, where the arduous conditions of the murder scene itself took on the quality of an obligatory trope that grounded and to a degree endorsed the pathologist's crucial role.

There is no better example of this new public iconography of the crime scene than the press coverage of the celebrated "Acid Bath" murder investigation of March 1949, in which Simpson played the undisputed star role (fig. 6.6). The case centered on a series of murders committed by John George Haigh, the most gripping of which involved the shooting of the wealthy widow Mrs. Durand Deacon in a London garage. It was Haigh's attempts to dispose of the body—by dissolving it in a vat of acid—and the immunity from prosecution that Haigh assumed this means of disposal had conferred on him, that captured the attention of the press. Questioned by Inspector Webb at the Chelsea Police Station on February 27, Haigh admitted to the crime, informed Webb of the location of the dissolved remains, and confidently asserted his position beyond the reach of the law: "Mrs. Durand-Deacon no longer exists. She has disappeared completely and no trace can ever be found. . . . I have destroyed her with acid. You will find the sludge that remains at Leopold Road. Every trace has gone. How can you prove a murder if there is no body?"[52]

Haigh's statement, unsurprisingly, prompted massive press interest in the investigation of the crime scene, and in particular the patch of earth on which sat some fifty pounds of "oily substance" and a forty-gallon drum soiled with an acrid greasy substance and containing partly dissolved debris. At the center of this drama was Simpson, with his secretary, captured in word and more strikingly still in image, across the front page of the March 2 editions of national newspapers. The *Daily Mail*'s account is typical: it informed its readers that on Haigh's confession Simpson had been called to the garage, where he spent an hour in the work shed where Haigh claimed to have shot Mrs. Durand Deacon, after which he turned his attention to the sludge-impregnated corner of the yard: "He went down on his hands and knees and carefully sifted soil and a pile of burned rubbish. He found a score of scientific clues by which the Yard men were able to reconstruct how Mrs Durand-Deacon died."[53]

To supplement this gripping narrative, the article carried a striking—and revealingly didactic—front page photograph: an annotated schematic of the Leopold Road crime scene, in which the key elements of the scene were indicated by superimposed captions (fig. 6.7). It set out an idealized space: crowds behind a conveniently positioned wooden fence, the interior

Figure 6.6. Plotting CSI—the Acid Bath crime scene. *Daily Mail*, March 2, 1949. Courtesy of the *Daily Mail* / Solo Syndication.

spaced labeled "sealed by police," the named pathologist departing from behind its gate. The *Daily Herald* ran a variation on this tableau that is equally compelling. Its image was of the activity taking place within the sealed crime scene, with captions identifying a prone Simpson faced by his secretary, the lead detective, and other police officers.[54] This is a compositional epitome of the pathologist's heroics at the newly articulated crime scene, an assertion, and celebration, both of his position as the focal point in the unfolding drama of murder investigation and of the active, engaged, and physically and emotionally demanding nature of the work he was bound to perform.

⁓ ↄ ↄ ⁓

Our account of the new, public face of the crime scene-pathology dyad has thus far focused on Keith Simpson, for the simple reason that his courting of a forensic "personality" was at once the most assiduous, and the most successful, of the postwar era. Crowned by his 1978 memoir, *Forty Years of Murder*, and by a BBC TV documentary of the same name, Simpson secured his place as (perhaps the last) English celebrity pathologist.[55]

By contrast, Francis Camps's efforts—though comparable in their ambitions—were less rewarding. From the late 1940s he also took to writing up a few of his major cases—notably "The Colchester Taxi Cab Murder" (1949) and "The Case of Stanley Setty" (1951)—both of which echoed ele-

Figure 6.7. Plotting CSI—the Acid Bath crime scene. *Daily Herald*, March 2, 1949. Courtesy of the *Daily Herald* Archive / National Media Museum / Science & Society Picture Library.

ments of Simpson's script of systematic crime scene investigation and the importance of trace evidence and teamwork.[56] But unlike Simpson, Camps did not manage to spin his case file into a compelling autobiographical memoir; his foray into the "true crime" book world was restricted to a slim 1966 volume that combined his reflections on notorious historical murder inquiries with chapters devoted to the need for reform of contemporary forensic practice. It disappeared without trace.[57]

But, in another respect, Camps's authorial self-fashioning is more central to our story, and in part this is due to the reasons for his failure as a best-selling raconteur. Simpson and Camps began their careers in a relationship of professed cooperation that, though later degenerating into bitter rivalry, was marked by a joint enterprise of shifting their profession onto firmer conceptual and institutional grounds. Of the two, however, Camps in his writings pursued the cause of reform more earnestly, arguably at a cost to his popularity as an author. Yet Camps succeeded in one aspect of authorship that eluded Simpson: the publication of a full monograph focused on a single case in which he was able to represent in exacting detail the powers of modern, multidisciplined, and team-driven forensic homicide investigation—featuring himself as the synoptic narrator.[58]

The next chapter will focus on Camps's labors—as investigator and author—at Rillington Place, using this analysis to illuminate the effects of the developments chronicled since the Crumbles on the landscape of English homicide investigation. As a preview, we now turn to a pair of *Police Journal* articles that Camps coauthored in 1951 and 1952. That his coauthor was Henry Holden, the former East Midlands regional lab director and, since 1946, head of the Metropolitan Police lab, is significant: the coming together of the personnel and conceptual apparatus of a forensics of bodies and a forensics of traces in this way signaled, and showcased, the synergies of pathology and the crime lab. The structure and content of these articles, which rejected the "celebrated case" formula of investigation—identification of suspect, arrest, trial, and verdict—in favor of the trappings of a scientific report, reflected this serious-minded purpose. Yet these were not entirely arid, bloodless accounts. Both were set in distinctive, and portentous, scenes of investigation, which function to confirm the pathologist's authorial repositioning in the post-Spilsbury landscape.

The first of these, unpromisingly entitled "Some Notes on the Examination of a Human Skeleton Found off the Essex Coast," opened with an atmospheric evocation of the topography and inhabitants of the Essex marshes, setting the scene for the discovery by a local fisherman of what appeared to be a human skull in tidal mudflats. The discovery went unreported for three weeks because the finder, "like many of his calling, was superstitious and, until brooding on his find had worried him sufficiently, had refrained from reporting his discovery to the local Police."[59] When finally called to the scene, police found a human skull lying "face partly uppermost and barnacled," seemingly "oozed out of the mud," and on further investigation they uncovered an almost complete human skeleton. Detailed search of the scene revealed "no trace of flesh, clothing or footwear, or any other means of identification."[60]

The barnacles were the key to unlocking the mystery (fig. 6.8). Holden and Camps identified two forms on the remains: the common British species (*Balanus balanoides*), the oldest of which was approximately two years old; and an invader from Australia (*Elminius modestus*), all of which were less than a year old, with many clustered on one side of the skull only a few weeks old. The earliest recorded sighting of the Australian species in British waters was from Chichester Harbour in 1943, after which they slowly spread, becoming abundant along the eastern coastline "sometime during 1945."[61] From this natural historical information, and the positioning of the skull in the mud and of the barnacles on it, Holden and Camps drew the following conclusions: parts of the skull must have been stripped of flesh and thus prepared for mollusk colonization not less than two years ago.

However, the silt in which the remains were discovered was too fine to cause the severe scouring and abrasion required to expose the side of the skull onto which the older barnacles had adhered. From this they surmised that there had been two distinct waves of colonization, the first taking place in an area where coarser material was present, after which the still-intact body partly denuded of flesh had drifted onshore to the site where it was discovered. "Here it was covered with fine marine silt and the partly encrusted parts of the skull and arm bones were again exposed about a year ago. That part of the skull showing a relatively light distribution of very immature barnacles had obviously been exposed only for a few weeks."[62]

Having reconstructed the temporal and spatial conditions to account for the remains as they had been found, Holden and Camps drew on further information to provide a partial resolution to the questions that the remains had initially posed. The skull showed no sign of injury, and the only surviving molar indicated crown wear suggestive of "African or, less probably, Asiatic origin although this can be little more than surmise." From this they deduced that the individual had died sometime prior to September 1947 and that the cause of death, though unknown, was not obviously violent. They concluded by thanking their team of police and lab workers, an acknowledgement that conveyed the collaborative aura that now surrounded modern investigations of suspicious death.[63]

The second report, "The Investigation of Some Human Remains Found at Fingringhoe," introduced another haunting story from Britain's southeastern coastal fringe (fig. 6.9). At the edge of a small, isolated community on the Colne estuary stood a dilapidated cottage, which along with its deaf, lame, secretive, and long-unseen elderly owner Ada Constance Kent had become the focal point of local interest: following her disappearance Kent had come to feature in the village children's ghost stories, while parents and local authorities considered the cottage a hazard to those drawn to its mysterious allure. In 1949, some ten years after the last confirmed sighting of Kent, a demolition order was drawn up, but with no one on whom the order could be served the police were called to survey the premises. In an

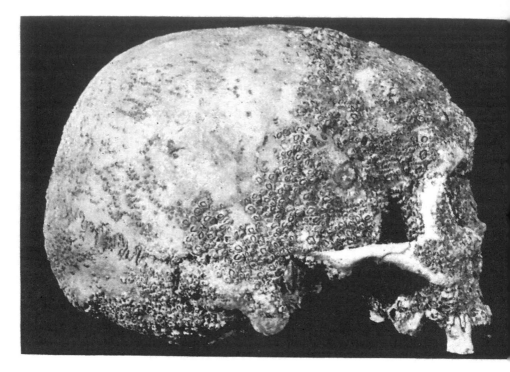

Figure 6.8. Barnacle clues. H. S. Holden and F. E. Camps, "Some Notes on the Examination of a Human Skeleton Found off the Essex Coast," *Police Journal*, 1951, face 104. Courtesy of Sage Publications.

upstairs bedroom they found a partly mummified body, its remaining flesh fused with rotted clothing, strands of dark hair adhering to flesh that had fused with the floor boards, and bones attacked by rodents.[64]

The bedroom was subjected to systematic scene investigation: a scale plan was drawn up (reproduced in the text), the debris sifted, collected, and packed for transport to two locations: "the garments and other debris, apart from the bones and the tissue associated with them, were removed to the Metropolitan Forensic Science Laboratory and the human remains were transferred to the Department of Anatomy of the London Hospital Medical School for detailed study."[65] At the latter location the skeleton was examined directly and through x-ray screening and photography, and subjected to Pearson correlation calculations to estimate stature. Examination of the skull revealed structural indications in the ear cavities of deafness and the presence in the right cavity only of old, empty blowfly pupa cases. This latter finding, coupled with the distribution of the remains of the liquefied brain,

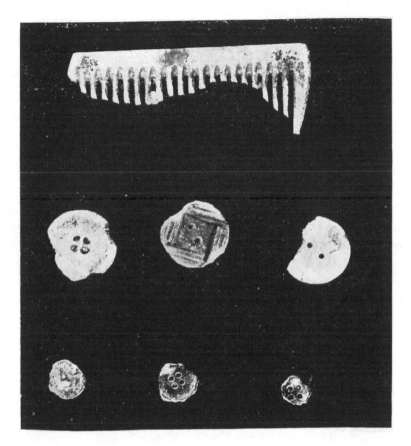

Figure 6.9. Fingringhoe relics. H. S. Holden and F. E. Camps, "The Investigation of Some Human Remains Found at Fingringhoe," *Police Journal,* 1952, face 179. Courtesy of Sage Publications.

which had settled on the left half of the skull, indicated that there had been little or no disturbance of the remains after death.

The examination of the partly rotted clothing and the assorted debris from the cottage yielded a further set of significant facts. The clothing (moccasins, hats, and a frock) was measured for correlation with the skeletal reconstruction, while hair removed from a brush was found to match that adhering to the mummified scalp. Pupae cases and dried, fungus-ridden rodent pellets on the clothing, moreover, testified to one wave of infestation, while the discovery that the rotting dress was "alive with the pupae and mature insects of the Brown Moth, *Monopis rusticella,*" indicated a subsequent and ongoing visitation.[66] Since *Monopis* fed on carrion and was a common inhabitant of bird nests, the active infestation suggested that it had resulted from a recent collapse of the roof and the consequent exposure of the clothing and tissue fragments to attack from an outside source.

Integrating the findings from the "relics"[67] from the body, the clothing, and the cottage, Camps and Holden developed a set of speculative correlations with the known movements and habits of Ada Kent. The condition of preservation of the flesh, for example, made it a "reasonable deduction that death had occurred during a period of low average temperature in dry surroundings."[68] Triangulating this with the last known sighting of Kent and the dates of a few unopened letters found in the house (both March 1939), and then checking the maximal and minimal temperatures and rainfall figures recorded for March–May 1939—which were found to be "wholly compatible with the above deductions"—they were able to take a step toward resolving the case.[69] The conclusion of the article used this and other evidentiary planks to reconstruct the (natural) circumstances of Kent's death, at the end of which acknowledgements were given to the staff at the lab and the hospital, and in particular to Chief Inspector Percy G. Law, of Scotland Yard's Photographic Department.

The two reports described above, with their evident synergy between the practices and personnel of crime scene investigation and the crime lab, were emblematic of a new genre for writing up the complex labor that was seen to characterize inquiries into possible cases of homicide. As we shall see in the next chapter, this genre would be extended to impose meaning and order upon one of the most notorious homicide cases in postwar England—the case of John Christie (1953). The investigation of the Christie ground-floor flat at number 10 Rillington Place called into play the new theatrics of team-driven forensics, with Francis Camps as its pathologist figurehead, deploying a network of differentiated expertise comparable to that which had underpinned his investigations on the Essex coast. As a result, Rillington Place emerged as a spectacular setting for articulating the reformed landscape of English CSI.

CHAPTER SEVEN

Interrogating "the House of Murder"

O n the afternoon of March 24, 1953, a crowd of spectators gathered in front of a rundown block of terraced houses in a West London cul-de-sac. They had been drawn by rumors of a body found in the ground-floor flat of number 10 Rillington Place. The flat had stood unoccupied following the departure of its tenant, John Christie, who had lived there for fifteen years with his wife Ethel. Ethel had not been seen since just before Christmas, and Christie himself had recently left the premises. The alarm had been raised by a neighbor who, when attempting to fit a shelf in the kitchen, discovered a hollow in the wall covered with wallpaper, which in turn concealed a darkened alcove. Peering in with the assistance of a torch he saw a bared and lifeless human back.

The police were immediately summoned, and a call was put through to the London Hospital's forensic pathologist Dr. Francis Camps. Camps arrived at the house by 7:30 p.m. and, together with police investigators, explored the alcove more fully. Removing the female body from the alcove revealed two more bodies, also wrapped in cloth and sacking and positioned on top of each another. Further searching of the property yielded a fourth body, enshrouded and buried under the floorboards of the front room. Journalists soon flocked to the scene and began to produce a steady stream of articles reporting on investigators entering the property and leaving with coffins or boxes of unspecified material. Within days the investigation had discovered six bodies, four inside the ground floor flat and two in its garden. Through this intensively public process, 10 Rillington Place was transfigured—no longer an inanimate structure, it became a "sentient" witness, perhaps even a guilty participant that needed to be questioned. It stood, in the *Daily Mirror*'s striking headline, as "The House of Murder"[1] (fig. 7.1).

Figure 7.1. The House of Murder. *Daily Mirror*, March 26, 1953, 1. Courtesy of Mirrorpix.

We are ending our account of the emergence of English CSI with one of the most notorious murder cases in British criminal history—the case of John Reginald Halliday Christie. The Christie case is best known to historians for its contribution to the abolition of capital punishment, and the epilogue will address this key historical legacy. But in this chapter, the focus is on the investigation, with the aim of demonstrating how it consolidated and put on public display the new, interdisciplinary regime of trace-centered homicide forensics that this book has been outlining.[2] What had started on the pages of Gross's *Handbook* and Freeman's Thorndyke mysteries was, in successive decades, transformed into a new forensic culture that, by the time of the Christie murders, was characterized by exacting protocols and procedures for trace hunting and retrieval at the crime scene and for analysis in forensic laboratories. This regime, moreover, was promoted by a generation of pathologists who had accommodated themselves to the drama and immediacy of a crime scene investigation.

The investigation of Christie's flat called into play this new theatrics of homicide forensics in which pathology and science were mutually dependent. This collaborative endeavor reflected an effort on the part of participants to forge a "team-driven" framework of investigation as a self-conscious corrective to the prior model based on individual "virtuosity" that was on display at the Crumbles. Led by the pathologist Francis Camps, the investigation transformed Rillington Place into a macabre excavation site, the stage for a prolonged, meticulous, and intensely public search for forensically actionable evidence of the murders committed within it. As it developed, moreover, the investigation reached back into the forensic past to determine whether Christie was responsible for a prior set of murders that had taken place in the same house and for which another individual, Timothy Evans, had in 1949 been convicted and executed. This dual investigation, and the questions it raised about the safety of British justice, assured the Christie case's standing as one of the most complex, public, and controversial homicide cases of the twentieth century.

REPORTING CSI AT THE HOUSE OF MURDER

The rundown streets of postwar London served as a fittingly austere backdrop to the House of Murder. Journalistic commentary also set the tone, reveling in the dinginess of "Murder Row," home to the "Rillington Ripper."[3] Number 10 was "the last house on the left" on a "short shabby street" ending with "a brick wall surmounted with some kind of furnace that looked like a sooty pyramid."[4] Newspaper observations on the progress of the forensic investigations carried out in and around the house were marked not just by abject horror but by absorbed interest. As with the Crumbles reportage a quarter of a century earlier, there was a striking attentiveness to the reporting of crime scene practice, but there was a discernible difference as well: accounts of Rillington Place included extensive detail on the mundane retrieval and packaging of trace material and on the day-to-day collaborative work and dialogues among police detectives, the pathologist Francis Camps, and lab scientists that promised to make the traces detected in the house "speak." Through a complex matrix of textual and photographic representations generated at and about the perimeters of the crime scene, the press laid out the visual architecture of the unfolding forensic investigation, communicating how investigators operated within an ordered and sequential process.

Homicide journalists positioned themselves (and their readers) in the midst of the scene, deploying the first-person voice to record the investigation's texture and to render it as suspenseful and action laden. A typical example of this was the *News of the World* correspondent's description of the discovery of the "remains of yet another woman buried in the garden of 'London's grisly House of Murder,'" in which he positioned himself as an intimate, firsthand observer: "I watch[ed] from [the rear] window" of a neighboring house.[5] The window served as a vantage point from which to bear witness to the methodical work carried out by officers with spades and garden sieves. Press photographs taken from the same vantage point enhanced the credibility of journalists' first-person narratives of the ongoing garden excavation (fig. 7.2). Their vertical composition and downward angle imbued the images with a dramatic sense of depth, ensuring that the most striking feature in the frame was the excavation itself.

Figure 7.2. Excavating at the House of Murder. Courtesy of Popperphoto /
Getty Images.

The stock of press photographs generated and publicly disseminated
during the course of the investigation also confirmed the crime scene as a
controlled space, visually and literally making evident the gap between the
public and investigators, the exterior and interior of the crime scene. Consider, for example, the *Daily Sketch* image of crowds gathering at the top of
Rillington Place. The image and the text that accompanies it show Scotland
Yard's use of crowd control measures to promote crime scene preservation

Figure 7.3. Securing Rillington Place. "Now a Sixth Body . . . a Seventh . . . Maybe an Eighth,"
Daily Sketch and Daily Graphic, March 30, 1953, 3.

and order at the site. The text describes how "sightseers on foot and in cars
[who had] poured into the cul-de-sac in the days following the discovery of
the body" were now being ejected by police investigators and kept out by the
establishment of a blockade to the street.[6] By foregrounding the expelled
crowds in its composition, the visual agenda of the photograph is to natural-
ize the investigators' claim to the scene, conveying their imposition of order
on a scene of purposeful forensic labor (fig. 7.3).

A further striking feature in the press coverage of the Rillington Place
investigation was the identification of Francis Camps as its indefatigable
figurehead. The *Evening Standard* provided a remarkably detailed description of the excavation work undertaken in the flat's back garden:

Two detectives in short sleeves began to dig. Within a few minutes they
stopped. A round blackened circular object [a bin] was lifted gently up. Dept.-
Inspector Kelly, of Notting Hill, stepped forward, and with Dr. Camps looked
at it. It was placed on newspaper spread out on top of a box. Dr. Camps examined it closely and then it was wrapped up carefully, placed in a crate and
nailed down by two policemen. The digging went on. Then all the men
stooped beneath the creeper-covered wall. When they rose they were lifting
a large rotted dustbin. It was bottomless, rusted with damp, and had a gash in

the side of it. It was put on one side. . . . Dr. Camps spoke hurriedly to Superintendent Barratt, who left and drove away. Another detective stepped
forward to the two digging men and they uprooted one of the forsythia
bushes. Its branches were tied with string and a larger paper bag covered the
roots. It was taken into the house. Pieces of bone, one more than a foot long,
were taken from the sieve and handed to Dr. Camps. He looked closely and
handed them to other detectives, who placed them in cardboard boxes with
newspaper. Other pieces were placed in shiny white paper bags. Then the digging stopped as two pieces of rotted cloth were found and placed in bags. . . .
After two and a half hours detectives were still digging and sifting. Police
made notes as the digging went on.[7]

In this account, the reporter creates a scene of immediacy and constant
activity by dwelling on seemingly mundane details, from the placement
of bones in designated cardboard boxes to the wrapping and nailing
down of the corroded bin in an appropriately sized crate. Camps cuts a
striking figure as a hands-on scene interrogator, working onsite and
alongside his team—a stark contrast to press projections of Spilsbury's
Holmesian distance from the physical scene work carried out by police at
the Crumbles.

As their initial excavation of the garden came to a close, investigators
turned their attention back to the interiors of Christie's flat, providing journalists with further occasion to document elements of collaborative crime
scene practice played out in and across the interrelating levels and sites of
the terraced house. The *Evening Standard* reported that Scotland Yard was
now conducting a new "big search" that might "last a week":

The House was split into four sections—the ground, first and second floors
and the garden. Mr Nickolls, with Superintendent Barratt, spent most of the
time in the garden. They pointed to the line of the chimney stack and also
drain pipes. Meanwhile, detectives climbed up and down the staircase, at
first in darkness. Then the gas light in the house was turned on. All the win-
dows were curtained. Two policemen stood guard at the doorway. Surveyors
began to trace the course of the chimney stack and the drains running beneath the house. Two of them came to the doorway and one of them pointed
to a manhole at the end of the roadway. Then they entered again. Inspector
Kelly took charge of the first floor. Here the sound of floorboards being prised
up could be heard. From here and the second floor came the sound of raking,

followed by the noise of hammer and chisel on the brick work of the chimney stack. Chief Inspector George Salter, of the Forensic Laboratory, and an assistant pushed the pole up the stack. This was done several times before the partial demolition began. In the kitchen outhouse, Chief Detective Griffin and Mr Nickolls concentrated on an old-fashioned iron copper joined to the wall by concrete surrounds. Beneath it was a small fire grate used for heating the copper. Cinders from it were raked out. Mr Nickolls examined them. Sieves were called for and taken into the house.[8]

As depicted in these journalistic reports, the search was highly organized and logical: duties had been divided, search patterns identified, personnel and equipment designated, and instruction given. Thorough and systematic searching was deemed indispensable to the efficient recovery of physical evidence, especially the less obvious traces left behind by the killer. The account dramatized and appraised investigators' search pattern, which began with the hunt for surface-level clues on walls, ceilings, and floors, before moving to the less accessible interiors of the house. As the passage makes clear, this involved the dismantling and destruction of the building's interiors to open up previously unseen and hidden spaces behind walls and underneath the floors. The reporter singles out the partial demolition of the chimney as a signal moment, praising the diligence, patience, and skills of the investigators tasked with penetrating the remaining secrets concealed within the bricks and mortar of 10 Rillington Place.

The same passage is also significant in the way it positions the crime lab and its personnel as integral features of CSI. The recently appointed director of the Metropolitan Police Laboratory, Lewis Nickolls, in particular, was cast as an individuated member of the forensic enterprise, whose trace-hunting powers, vividly displayed in the description of his raking and sieving of the cinders from a previously concealed fire grate, extends the investigation. In the days that followed, newspapers primed their readers for Nickolls's impending report of the results of his laboratory analysis of the fire grate samples. By weaving the activities and anticipated results of lab practitioners into the public narrative of the investigation, the press communicated how major breakthroughs in the case depended not only on the carefully conceived and labor-intensive search of a crime scene but also on subsequent lab analysis.

CSI AT THE HOUSE OF MURDER

Now let us move from the multiple ways in which journalistic coverage deployed CSI tropes to communicate the spectacle of an unfolding modern homicide investigation to the discourses generated through investigators' encounters with the physical space of the crime scene. It is only by carefully reconstituting the intricate sequence, features, and dynamics of the investigation that we can appreciate the forensic interrogations of the complex configurations of body, trace, and space that were accomplished at 10 Rillington Place. To do this, we return to where this chapter began: the discovery of a woman's body entombed in the alcove of John Christie's ground-floor flat on March 24. Shortly after the existence of the body had been confirmed by a police officer dispatched to the scene, investigators arrived, including Detectives Griffin and Kelly, who secured the scene, but also the Metropolitan Police photographer Chief Inspector Percy Law and the pathologist Francis Camps. As Camps stipulated in a later summary of the initial sequence of the investigation, he "had the opportunity of examining the scene in its original condition. The investigating officers had, of course, done no more than open the cupboard door."[9]

Several observations can be made on this remark. First, unlike at the Crumbles, where significant scene labor had been completed before Spilsbury arrived, Camps was present at Rillington Place from the outset. In immersing himself in the immediacy of the scene and its subsequent investigation, Camps reaffirmed the role of the forensic pathologist as an essential member of an integrated scene team. Second, police investigators waited for Camps to arrive before beginning their exploration of the alcove, thus displaying a collective recognition of the essential presence of the pathologist in the new forensic landscape. Moreover, we see that, on entering the alcove, investigators did not rush to strip it of its contents. Before the first body was touched, Law began to construct a choreographed photographic archive: first, of the cupboard with the door shut, concealing the body, and then again with the door open, showing the back of the woman—in effect, recreating the moment of discovery earlier that day.[10] At the entrance of the alcove, investigators observed that the head was bent forward and the trunk supported by a piece of blanket that was knotted to the victim's brassiere. Vertical scratch marks were visible on the skin of the back and buttocks, suggesting that the body had been dragged across a "rough surface." When Camps and the Scotland Yard detectives removed the body into the adjoining back room for closer examination, they noted that the victim's wrists had been tied together in front with a handkerchief and that both her brassiere and garter belt had been pulled up, indicating signs of sexual assault. There were also surface signs of injuries to the face and neck that were consistent with strangulation, including a ligature mark around the neck and significant facial hemorrhages.

Camps, Law, and the other detectives then returned to the alcove to examine a second body wrapped in a blanket, whose existence had become evident with the removal of the first body. As with the first body, Law photographed this one in situ before it was moved into the adjoining room, where the investigators established that the covering blanket had been secured around the ankles by a sock tied with a reef knot and that the head had been covered by a pillowcase, tied around the neck by a stocking. Once again the forensic ensemble returned to the alcove, where they photographed a third body, also wrapped in a blanket. Closer inspection revealed that the blanket around the body had been secured by a plastic-covered electric wire tied around the legs and that the head had been covered by a cloth.

On the completion of the alcove investigation, each body was photographed separately in the back room, before being removed to the Kensington Mortuary for post-mortem examination. After the removal of the alcove bodies, investigators conducted a search of the house and, noting that some floorboards in the sitting room appeared to be disturbed, lifted these up to reveal a fourth body. In a further exercise of restraint, they decided to leave this body untouched until the following day, when it was photographed and then removed to the mortuary for post-mortem examination.

For our immediate purposes, what is useful about the above sketch of the initial alcove investigation is how it demonstrated the enactment of a distinctive regime of photographic documentation and preservation, one that operated at two different levels of recording. Law's photographic inventory of the bodies and the interior of the alcove, at its most perfunctory level, functioned as a form of scene preservation, establishing a permanent and comprehensive record of each body in its undisturbed state (figs. 7.4–7.8). The photographic inventory served an additional, self-reflexive purpose: while documenting the bodies in their pristine state, it simultaneously catalogued the temporal sequence of the investigation, implicitly and explicitly communicating investigators' observance of systematic procedure.[11] In this sense Law's photographic practices established a documentary record of investigators' commitment to a complete, accurate, and orderly processing

Figures 7.4–7.8. Capturing the sequence of CSI
(*top, opposite page*). The National Archives, 1953.
Courtesy of The National Archives.

of the alcove. Echoing Gross's observations on the cognitive discipline stimulated by the practices of crime scene drawing, Law's sequential regime of forensic photographic recording also slowed down investigators' engagement with the scene and in so doing imposed restraint upon investigators, delaying their cognitive and physical engagement with the scene while at the same time capturing pristine details for future analysis at a distance.

MORTUARY, LAB, SCENE

At 9:30 on the night of March 27 and working through to the following day, Camps began his autopsies at Kensington Mortuary, all of which followed a common format. He surveyed the external appearance of the bodies, estimated the victims' ages, and noted surface ante- and post-mortem marks. In doing so he paid close attention to the state of the clothes of the bodies from the alcove, which he noted as "disarranged." He also identified what he described as "whitish soapy material" around their genital areas.[12] There were no signs of extensive trauma. He proceeded to open up the bodies for internal examination, assessing the appearance of the major organs, blood, and tissues and taking samples for further analysis.

On the basis of these preliminary inquiries, Camps classed the bodies into two groups. First, there were the bodies of three young women, aged between twenty and thirty, who had been found in the alcove and whom he estimated had been dead for between four and twelve weeks before discovery.

Early drafts of the post-mortem reports indicate that Camps provisionally concluded that these young women were victims of poisoning. They had been exposed to lethal doses of carbon monoxide, indicated by a "definite pink colouration of the skin of the whole body" and confirmed by a similar appearance of the blood and tissues.[13] He also found marks on their necks, suggesting manual or ligature pressure, but initially he did not consider these of sufficient severity to represent a primary cause of death. Body number 4 was different. This was a fifty-to-sixty-year-old woman, whom he believed had been asphyxiated twelve to fifteen weeks previously. Unlike the other bodies, the external appearance of this body did not suggest to Camps the presence of carbon monoxide, nor could he discern any of the "whitish soapy material." Within days police inquiries had established their identities: three local, single women in their midtwenties, Rita Nelson, Kathleen Maloney, and Hectorina MacLennan, and the fourth, Mrs. Ethel Christie, aged fifty-four.

The seeming solidity of Camps's mortuary findings, however, was in some respects illusory. Archival records show that he redrafted his reports several times over as the evidentiary elements of the case from outside the mortuary unfolded. This underlines the fact that Camps did not perform his autopsies in isolation—instead, he worked within a wider network of collaborative scientific and police expertise and locations. The meaning of his post-mortem findings thus shifted as the crime scene investigation intensified and as other experts and institutions reframed the evidence collected.

This process was enabled in part by the fact that the bodies in the mortuary not only were treated according to the protocols of forensic pathology but were, like a crime scene, closely inspected for trace evidence. Camps collected samples of clothing, hair, blood, nail cuttings, and stomach contents, and he took rectal and genital swabs. These he dispatched to Lewis Nickolls, who had taken over as director of the Metropolitan Police Laboratory in 1951. Nickolls's career trajectory was in many respects shaped by the significant shifts in the landscape of forensic investigation that took place in the 1930s. An analytical chemist by training, Nickolls had been one of the original members of staff at the first police laboratory at Hendon, established as a consequence of Lord Trenchard's attempts to create a medico-legal institute. Nickolls was then appointed as the first director of the North-Eastern Forensic Science Laboratory at Wakefield in 1940, one of the parallel labs whose conceptual and operational foundations were developed not by Trenchard but by the network of reformers that had formed around the Dixon committee. Nickolls assumed the directorship of the Metropolitan Police Lab following the retirement of the botanist Henry Holden, who had himself replaced the forensic pathologist James Davidson and had subsequently repositioned the Hendon lab as a disciplined space dedicated to processing, storing, and analyzing trace evidence.[14]

Nickolls proceeded to work upon the material generated by Camps at autopsy and the samples collected earlier at the crime scene. In some respects, lab analysis served to supplement the authority of the forensic pathologist, at times refining but not overturning the mortuary findings. In the case of body number 1, for example, Camps had initially estimated the age of the victim to be under twenty years, but subsequent x-ray examination of the humerus bone revealed a fusion of upper epiphyseal lines, suggesting that the victim was older.[15] However, evidentiary gaps emerged. Toxicological results on the blood and tissues from the three alcove bodies, most notably, indicated *nonlethal* carbon monoxide levels ranging from 34 to 40 percent saturation.

This led Camps to reconsider his initial elevation of poisoning over strangling as the cause of death for these victims.[16] To reconcile his autopsy findings with those generated by lab analysis, Camps was obliged to reengage with the crime scene. He was able to do this because, though physically removed from Rillington Place, the bodies in his mortuary had, in a sense, taken it with them: entombment in its alcove had marked them with signs that could only be properly deciphered by further analysis of the distinctive ecology of the House of Murder. Three examples of this synthesis of space, trace, and corpse in particular are worth exploring here: first, the determination of cause of death; second, the estimated duration of the bodies' interment in the alcove; and, last, the interpretation of the "whitish soapy material" discovered at autopsy.

To account for the discrepancy between his preliminary conclusion of carbon monoxide poisoning and the subsequent toxicology findings, Camps explained how the alcove atmospherics had generated an unusual set of surface signs: "In this particular instance the bodies were kept at an optimum cool temperature in dry surroundings with some air movement, almost perfect conditions [for preservation]. . . . Certainly they could not have been in a much better condition if they had been refrigerated."[17] To test this theory, Camps returned to Rillington Place with a minimum/maximum thermometer to take systematic measurements of the alcove over the course of a week. He found a constant temperature range approximating the conditions of modern cold storage. As the bodies had been stored in the cupboard during the winter months, Camps reasoned that the alcove had served as a "constant temperature cold room" that delayed the process of decomposition.

The interpretative value of Camps's equation of the alcove with refrigeration was also made explicit in his reevaluation of the pink coloration of the bodies' surfaces. By combining his experimentally derived knowledge of the alcove's atmospherics with the lab results that showed nonlethal saturations of carbon monoxide in the blood of the victims, Camps was able to advance an environmental explanation. The pink appearance had prevented Camps from properly evaluating the severity of the neck markings he had found on his initial inspections, which had in turn led him to his preliminary determination of carbon monoxide poisoning as the primary cause of death. But, as all morgue practitioners knew, pink discoloration is not uncommon for bodies stored in refrigerated conditions. Thus, his temperature readings allowed Camps to reconfigure the alcove of Number 10 as a surrogate morgue that had created the surface signs of death by carbon monoxide poisoning. The alcove bodies in question, in short, could only make sense in the context of the specific ambient atmospherics in which they had lain.

Camps's reinterrogation of the alcove also yielded evidence on the length of time that the three bodies had lain within it. Because the bodies were so well preserved, Camps had initially found this time difficult to estimate. However, they had been brought to the mortuary covered with surface mold. By taking into account his knowledge of the alcove atmospherics, he was able to draw on the expert opinion of Major H. A. Dade of the Commonwealth Mycological Institute at Kew regarding the expected rate of mold growth specific to that location. Dade analyzed and cultured molds derived from the coverings together with tissue samples, from which he determined that while the microfungi were all "common and ubiquitous moulds," only "one species had penetrated [the skin] to any depth"; this was *Mucar racemosus* Fresen.[18] Dade gave Camps estimated growth patterns of Fresen mold growth, and, with this information, Camps could reexamine the tissue slides to determine a differential pattern of mold penetration in the flesh of each of the bodies. His analysis identified a temporal pattern on the bodies that could be mapped onto the duration of their respective confinements in the alcove.[19] The longer the body had been in the alcove, the greater the penetration of the mold detected in the section of tissue taken from it. Thus, the appreciation of mold growth and its differential penetration of the alcove bodies provided Camps with an alternative, ecologically informed means of determining how long the bodies had lain in place.

Finally, the alcove's distinctive environmental conditions held the key to the interpretation of the "whitish soapy material," which in the lab Nickolls identified as intact semen. The analysis of the swabs and material exuding from the vulva from all three alcove bodies, he determined, contained numerous spermatozoa. In the case of body number 1, Christie's final victim, Nickolls declared that the sample "showed a remarkable state of preservation," "complete with tails" and looking "quite fresh."[20] The discovery of semen confirmed that the bodies entombed in the alcove had been sexually assaulted close to their deaths. However, it also raised clear tensions, as Nickolls noted: "the number and condition of the spermatozoa found in the vaginas of these bodies after such a long time was surprising."[21] According to conventional forensic wisdom, he explained, it was fruitless to attempt the detection of semen on and in bodies that had been dead for more than forty-eight hours.[22] This was because once semen was released it rapidly degenerated through contact with bodily or ambient temperature or was absorbed or drained away by the living body in which it had been deposited. The forensic interrogations of the alcove bodies of Rillington Place revised these previous understandings concerning the lifespan of deposited sperm, proving that under certain environmental and bodily circumstances, sperm could "remain identifiable in the dead body for periods of several months."[23]

In accounting for the surprising resilience of the alcove semen, environment once again held the key. The alcove chamber had served as a constant temperature cold room, which had not only delayed bodily decomposition but also "helped to preserve the spermatozoa."[24] But the fact that semen could also be discovered in its intact state from internal swabs suggested to Nickolls something more: that the murderer at Rillington Place was a disturbing sexual psychopath. Nickolls's reasoning was nuanced by two key considerations. The first one was sheer gravitational pull. Nickolls was struck by the volume of spermatozoa emission in each vagina, suggesting that little drainage had occurred. This led him to the view that the victims had probably died lying down on the floor, after which their attacker dragged their bodies into the alcove: for, if the victims had stood up after sexual intercourse, some drainage of the spermatozoa emission would be expected.

The second consideration was the ambient ecology of vaginal space. A cooling and nonphysiologically active ecology would, Nickolls speculated, be conducive to what he had found—a large pool of surprisingly intact spermatozoa.[25] Thus, if the receiving bodies were in a cooled or cooling state, sexual contact must have been made either immediately prior to or after death. The murderer at Rillington Place was a sexual psychopath—and a possible necrophile.

The mortuary-lab-scene nexus established in the investigation of the alcove bodies was subsequently consolidated and elaborated in the excavation of the Rillington Place's ill-kept garden. This proved another high-profile site of intensive forensic work, one in which Camps, in the words of an admiring assistant, adopted the role of "Commander-in-Chief," overseeing a "painstaking and meticulous" search through a "wilderness of rubbish and rubble" that included an astonishing variety of biomatter, including animal bones—fish (mainly cod), chickens, turkeys, rats, rabbits, cats, dogs, sheep, cattle—and human bones, many of which were charred and broken into small fragments.[26] The charnel ground that was Christie's garden posed a number of questions: How many human bodies did it contain; how long had they lain there; and were they connected to the events indoors? For answers the forensic team turned to a variety of practices, including archeological excavation, reconstructive paleontology, and ecological dating methods.

To begin this process, the garden was recast as a disciplined archeological site. The examination of the garden, in Nickolls's words, was a "gargantuan task" that involved "sieving the entire soil of the garden to a depth of two feet."[27] The excavation was methodical and ordered: the site was divided into numbered subplots, in which investigators were instructed to dig to a uniform depth.[28] Artifacts recovered from each plot were then placed in separate, numbered containers, which were sent to a sorting room. There the fragments were divided up and classified, with their place of discovery in the garden identified by a system of color-coding each fragment according to the preestablished digging plan. The sorting and subsequent reconstruction work involved an ensemble of medical, scientific, and police personnel who laboriously sifted the material using a combination of low- and high-tech equipment such as metal sieves of a uniform mesh and x-ray imaging. This arrangement, though time consuming, encouraged cooperation among participants and an efficient use of expertise, by allowing each object to be handed to the appropriate member of staff for further examination.

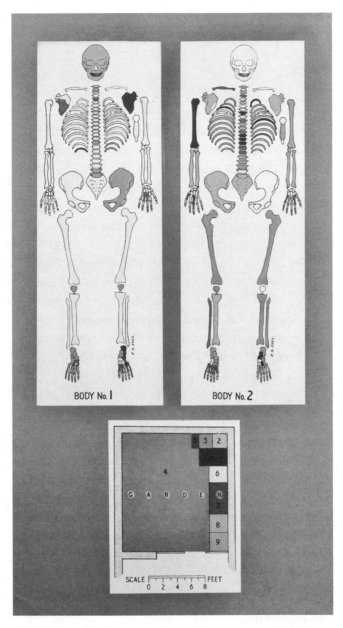

Figure 7.9. Garden Plots. The National Archives 1953. Courtesy of
The National Archives.

Lab personnel, for example, carried out tests on the soil to detect the presence of body fluids, in order to prevent the workers "from being overwhelmed with a mass of irrelevant material."[29]

The excavation was a complex, recursive process, involving the integration of new crime scene findings into the provisional schema being developed by the reconstruction team. "There was a continuous shifting of fragments," the investigation's medical artist recalled. "The discovery of one small fragment could mean major changes to the arrangement."[30] The reconstruction of a single human skull was, for example, repeated several times, as the finding of new fragments "almost always necessitated a readjustment of the pieces already placed."[31] Those assembling the skeletons also fed back their findings to the diggers and the sorters to guide them as they picked their way through the garden's cache of mortal remains. These interactions remind us how a range of distinct investigative practices were locked in a process of dynamic exchange—one that was dependent on enforcing an orderly flow of activity and matter across multiple sites. The patient and systematic search of the garden, as Nickolls recalled, was "fully justified because of the importance of the discovery of a bone which was found on the last day of digging in the last pile of soil. This was the fourth cervical vertebra which decided the final position of the fragmented skull."[32]

The end result of this process was the reconstruction of two skeletons, both identified as female, one in her early twenties, the other in her midthirties (fig. 7.9). To answer the question of when these women had died, and thus to discover how they might connect with the more recent deaths at the House of Murder, Camps's team again turned to the garden's ecology. Here soil analysis and entomology took their place, but the key finding stemmed from the examination of an ordinary-looking bush, the roots of which had grown through and around a buried vertebra, "a piece of a skull" and "a mass of decaying fabric."[33] Based on the root pattern, combined with a knowledge of the growth cycle specific to that plant, a botanist from Kew Gardens was able to estimate the number of years that the bone had lain in the ground, and thus to place the body chronologically within Christie's tenancy at Rillington Place.

⸻

On March 31, 1953, a week after the initial discovery of the bodies, and while the archeological investigations were still underway, Christie was spotted by a constable on the Embankment and taken to the Putney Police Station (fig. 7.10). There, over the course of a series of interviews, he admitted his involvement in the deaths of the four women discovered in his flat. Initially, Christie portrayed his part in Ethel's death as an act of mercy by a caring husband—he had assisted in her own suicide attempt. The other murders, he claimed, were committed in self-defense. He had been given no choice but to defend himself against aggressive and morally questionable women, who had taken advantage of his innocent interest in their well-being when he invited them back to his flat.

Christie's capture and confession, however, did not signal the end of Camps's efforts—quite the contrary, they opened up a new investigative front. This was because, in the days, weeks, and months that followed, Christie revised key parts of his statements, through which he emerged at best as an unreliable witness, at worst as a manipulative fantasist. Faced with a series of contradictory confessions, investigators turned once again to the material evidence. As a result, an extended and refocused crime scene analysis came to play a key role in making scientific sense of Christie's conflicting statements, an analysis that involved a continuous oscillation between the mind, the body, and the house of Christie.

This dynamic can be vividly illustrated in the hours following his arrest. As detectives took verbal testimony, the forensic gaze transformed Christie into a site from which telling trace evidence could be harvested. On arrest, Christie's clothes were taken from him and sent for lab analysis, yielding another set of useable signs in the pursuit of the truth of the man and his crimes—each item of his clothing bore traces that lab tests carried out by Nickolls determined to be seminal staining.[34]

I have examined Package No. 4 and found on the Trousers an area of seminal staining containing spermatozoa on the inside of the right fly opening near the bottom. I found a spot of seminal staining on the lining of the left pocket. On the front flap of the shirt there are extensive areas of staining: semen containing spermatozoa was identified in this staining. On the "Merridian" Vest there was found an area of old staining with semen; the other vest shows comparatively extensive areas of staining with semen containing spermatozoa, together with a number of small light blood smears. I have examined Package 6 and found that on the blue trousers there was staining with semen containing spermatozoa inside on both sides of the fly opening. On the Plimsolls there were found some spots and smears of seminal staining containing spermatozoa along the edge of the front of the left plimsoll.[35]

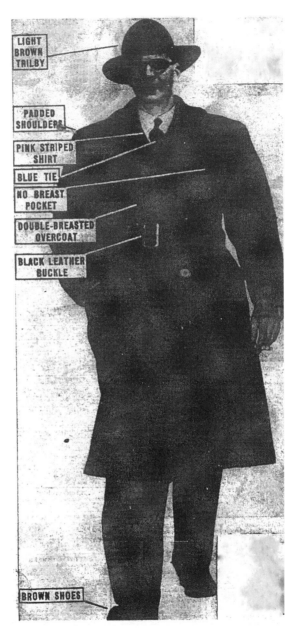

LIGHT BROWN TRILBY

PADDED SHOULDERS

PINK STRIPED SHIRT

BLUE TIE

NO BREAST POCKET

DOUBLE-BREASTED OVERCOAT

BLACK LEATHER BUCKLE

BROWN SHOES

Figure 7.10. "This Is How He Looks." *Daily Sketch and Daily Graphic*, March 31, 1953, 1.

This report emphasized again some of the core features of evidence preservation and the principles of lab-based trace recovery and analysis. The report captured detectives' systematic practices that had secured the clothes worn by Christie and turned them into material fit for examination. Each item had been individually separated and packaged to ensure its integrity before being forwarded on to the lab. There, Nickolls inspected one package at a time, subjecting each garment to a separate and systematic search. In hunting for traces, he examined the surfaces of the clothes but also spaces inside of pockets and behind the trouser zip and took scrapings of suspect stains, which he then subjected to a combination of microscopic and chemical investigation. Careful trace hunting and analysis had revealed that Christie's clothes were awash with semen stains.

Nickolls's trace findings on Christie's clothing, significantly, extended the investigation into the Rillington Place murders, revealing new connections and understandings of the relationships between Christie and his victims. Indeed, Nickolls's lab-based inquires transformed Christie himself into a trace-laden site, the analysis of which enabled conclusions that destabilized his initial account of the murders—which had contained no mention of any sexual element. Christie came to embody the sexual psychopath that had been suggested through prior forensic work, as the stains on his clothes were linked to the "soapy material" collected from the women's bodies in the alcove.

EXHUMING THE PAST OF RILLINGTON PLACE

On June 22, 1953, Christie's trial opened under intense public and media attention. Courtroom discussion of the forensic evidence, though relatively brief and uncontroversial, paid tribute to the scientific and medical investigations carried out at Rillington Place. The judge, referring in particular to the garden excavation, congratulated Camps on this "remarkable feat of investigation" that was an efficient product of "team work."[36] The painstaking work of forensic investigation, however, was largely overshadowed by psychiatric testimony debating the merits of an insanity plea that would spare Christie from the gallows.

But the work of Camps and his team did not evaporate with the shift in emphasis from the house to the mind of Christie. To the contrary, deliberations over Christie's mental state initiated a further reengagement with 10 Rillington Place. To follow this thread, we have to introduce an element of the case that, in the interest of clarity, we have withheld till now. That is, in the legal, political, and public mind, Christie was on trial not only for murder committed in the spring of 1953. He was widely suspected of an earlier crime that, in many respects, loomed even larger—the murder of Beryl and Geraldine Evans in 1949.

That year, the bodies of Beryl Evans and her baby daughter had been found lying together in the washhouse of 10 Rillington Place, where they had been tenants in a flat above Christie. They had been strangled, and Timothy Evans, the husband and father, had been convicted and executed for the death of his daughter, Geraldine.[37] The grim past of the House of Murder quickly became a prime feature of the newspaper coverage of the 1953 investigation, with reports repeatedly reminding readers that Christie had been the star prosecution witness at Evans's trial. In a statement to police from his prison cell just weeks before his trial, Christie set the lingering speculation alight by claiming responsibility for having gassed and strangled Beryl Evans in her kitchen, although he vehemently denied killing Geraldine.

At the center of Christie's latest confession was a tobacco tin containing four clumps of human pubic hair that had been discovered during the search of his garden. Christie's initial explanation of the hair was that it had come from the three women found in the alcove and from his wife, but now he claimed that one of the samples was from Beryl Evans. From the point of view of his defense, the more people Christie had murdered and could be included as evidence, the more likely the jury would waive the death penalty on the grounds of insanity. Thus, in May 1953, the Home Office granted their application to exhume Beryl and Geraldine's bodies—which had been buried together in a single coffin. News of the exhumation generated enormous public interest.[38] The exhumation shifted the status of Christie's tin of "trophies" from a material indicator of his sexual abnormality to a valuable evidentiary resource with which to interrogate the veracity of the extent of his self-professed murder spree. Thus, the Evans exhumation, by enabling the investigation to reach back into the forensic past, opened up a new discursive space in which representations about the past of Rillington Place could be made but also contested.

Newspapers presented the Evans exhumation not only as a sensational news story but also as a dramatic extension of the forensic investigation that had been carried out a few months earlier. An article published in the *News of the World* on the eve of the exhumation cast it as a highly anticipated event that would take place in the early hours of the morning; significantly, the article also detailed the work to be carried out by forensic pathologists "behind canvas screens":

> As the coffin is reached samples of the earth around it will be placed and sealed in glass jars already labelled. The undertaker will then examine the coffin nameplate and only when he is satisfied that is the right one will the coffin be brought to the surface and put on wooden trestles. The pathologists will take further samples of earth from the bottom and side of the grave. Then enclosed in a special shell the coffin will be taken to Kensington mortuary. . . . Behind locked and guarded doors the coffin will be opened. . . . Samples of hair, nails, skin and certain organs will be removed for detailed laboratory examination.[39]

What is interesting about this passage is its emphasis on the crucial role played by pathologists and, at the same time, its anticipation of a set of procedures that fused forensic pathology and CSI. In particular, it affirmed the image of the pathologist as a hybrid practitioner whose skills lay in not only in conducting and overseeing the exhumation and autopsy but also in collecting traces from the body. Emphasis is placed on how the pathologists were equipped with suitably labeled glass jars in which to place samples of earth and a range of tissue samples for laboratory analysis. Details such as these underscored the assumption that the laboratory would play a crucial role in confirming or refuting Christie's claim to have murdered Beryl Evans.

On May 18, "as dawn broke over the mist-enshrouded cemetery," the exhumation took place at the North Kensington Cemetery.[40] Journalists and members of the public vied for a view from the cemetery gates, where police officers were stationed. Reports called public attention to a familiar cast of experts moving in and out of view from behind the canvas screen, many of whom had played key roles in the investigation of 10 Rillington Place several months earlier. At one point, Chief Inspector Law could be identified on "a step ladder taking photographs of the grave," taking at least "a dozen pictures."[41] Francis Camps once again assumed his "commander-in-chief" role, but this time, journalists noted, he was accompanied by representatives from Christie's defense: the barrister Roy Arthur, the psychiatrist Jack Hobson, and the pathologist Keith Simpson. Also in attendance was the pathologist Donald Teare, who had performed the original 1949 autopsy on Beryl Evans and her daughter.[42]

Once the bodies had been removed from the coffin and placed upon the mortuary slab, Camps proceeded to retrieve a range of biomaterial, as he had done with Rillington Place bodies several months earlier. He took swabs of mold stalactites suspended from the top of the coffin, along with soil samples taken at the exhumation from the cemetery ground surrounding the coffin.[43] Camps then turned his attention to Beryl's remains. He cut away the surface of her abdominal wall, observing that the hair on the abdomen and pubis was "in its original state" and "suitable" for comparison with Christie's macabre collection of hair from his victims.[44] Camps also took vaginal swabs for possible seminal residue and retrieved samples of lung and muscle tissue to be analyzed for indications of carbon monoxide.

The records of the exhumation autopsy show that Nickolls was in attendance and took into his custody the assortment of labeled jars in which the bodily and soil samples were placed, after which he returned to his laboratory. On the basis of his chemical tests, Nickolls was "unable to detect any traces of carbon monoxide or semen."[45] But, as Nickolls explained in his subsequent report, this did not necessarily rule out the possibility that Christie had assaulted and killed Evans. The chances of detecting traces of semen or carbon monoxide in a body that had been buried for more than three years, he wrote, had never been great: "the presence of decomposition and other post-mortem changes precluded the possibility of finding these substances if they were present at death."[46]

Whereas these investigations had yielded no definitive findings, the collection and analysis of Beryl Evans's pubic hair proved more productive. Nickolls microscopically compared the hair from the exhumed body with the specimens in Christie's tin, first focusing on their gross morphological characteristics (fig. 7.11). On this basis he was able to rule out three of Christie's "trophies," but the fourth bore a resemblance in color, thickness, and general structure to the Evans sample. "The pubic hair from the exhumed woman," he declared, "is similar to one of the specimens of hair in the tin, and both samples of hair could be derived from the same person."[47]

However, as there was nothing unusual about the characteristics of the matching hair samples, Nickolls needed to extend his examination beyond the level of simple structure. To do this he turned his attention to the ends of the specimen hairs, finding that all the hair in Christie's collection had been cut at both ends. The root-end cuts were recent—obviously made by Christie when he took them from his victims—while the cuts at the free or "distal" ends were old. Nickolls's conclusion on this latter point was based

Figure 7.11. Split ends under the microscope. F. E. Camps, *Medical and Scientific Investigations in the Christie Case,* 1953, 52.

on the fact that they had frayed ends: as frayed hair ends were the consequence of growth after cutting, it followed that these older cuts must have been made by the women themselves while engaging in personal grooming. By contrast, the specimens taken from Evans's body proved to be "essentially uncut with its natural tips." Thus, despite superficial resemblance, Nickolls declared that the "sample in the tin could not have derived from Mrs. Beryl Evans." [48]

Nickolls extended the gap between the specimens taken at the exhumation and Christie's "trophies" by turning to the natural cycle of hair growth. If, as Christie claimed, one of the tin samples had been from Evans, it could only appear as it did if it had been trimmed at least eight months before her death. As the specimens from the tin showed post-cut fraying, if one of them had been Evans's, the hair would have had first to be trimmed and then allowed to grow "for approximately two or three months" in order to account for their frayed state. It would have to be at this point that they were taken as a trophy. However, for her hair to take on the "natural" uncut appearance found at exhumation, the purported trimmed hairs would have needed to fall out and be replaced by new ones of the same length as the tin specimens and with "natural" ends. This process, Nickolls estimated, would have taken approximately six months to complete.[49] Thus, by differentiating between the tips of the two samples of pubic hair, and understanding cycles of hair growth, Nickolls concluded that Christie had not taken a trophy from Beryl Evans at her death. Christie's confession was a lie.

During Christie's trial, the evidence from the Evans exhumation received only brief consideration.[50] The primary reason for this was that, for reasons of legal procedure, the charge facing Christie was the murder of his wife Ethel only. The trial judge, Mr. Justice Finnemore, made this narrow remit clear in his instructions to the jury: "though it is a matter of disturbing interest, you are not concerned in the least with what anybody thinks . . . about what happened in the Evans case—whether the result was right or wrong. I am going to ask you to put it entirely out of your minds."[51]

The jurors seem to have complied. After four days of testimony, they took little over an hour to find Christie guilty of Ethel's murder. However, outside the courtroom Finnemore's instructions went largely unheeded. Public and political concern over the possible miscarriage of justice in the Evans case grew, leading the home secretary to postpone Christie's execution pending the results of a special inquiry. Held in private and lasting barely a week, evidence from more than twenty witnesses was heard, including from Christie himself. Under questioning from the inquiry chairman John Scott Henderson, Christie explained that he could not remember his actions and motivations.[52] He vehemently denied strangling Geraldine—the crime for which Evans had been executed—and, more surprisingly, now declared that he was no longer sure that he had killed Beryl. On the basis of witnesses' testimonial evidence, Scott Henderson held that there was no convincing evidence implicating Christie in the death of either Beryl or Geraldine and, in his final report, dismissed outright Christie's statements claiming responsibility for killing Beryl: "I am satisfied that they are not only unreliable but that they are untrue."[53] As for Timothy Evans, Scott Henderson did not merely come to the conclusion that Evans was responsible for both the death of his wife and his daughter. He reported, "There was no ground for thinking that there may have been any miscarriage of justice in the conviction for the murder of Geraldine Evans."[54] This stark conclusion—that an innocent man had not been wrongfully hanged—was met with widespread outrage, and, as he went to the gallows on July 15, Christie had become an unlikely lightning rod for a gathering campaign to abolish the death penalty.

CLOSING THE DOOR ON THE HOUSE OF MURDER

It was in this highly charged atmosphere that in September 1953 Francis Camps published his *Medical and Scientific Investigations in the Christie Case*. The monograph, an impressively detailed exposition of the case, combines two functions: first, it aims to bring textual closure to the ongoing controversy by presenting a detailed synthesis of the multiple and complex scientific investigations that had been conducted, including those into the circumstances surrounding Beryl Evans's death; second, it asserts the legitimacy and interpretative powers of team-based forensic inquiry based on synergies and collaborations between crime lab and pathology over the singular and disruptive voice of Christie.

The book opens with a striking frontispiece image captioned "Rillington Place, Notting Hill, North Kensington, W.11, at dusk," which casts a haunting shadow over the otherwise restrained and scientific tone of the main text and the other scientific illustrations in the work (fig. 7.12). Indeed, the photograph echoes (and reworks) the sensational, journalistic image of the *Daily Mirror*'s "House of Murder," in drawing the viewers' attention to one focal point, to the farthest house of the row—Number 10. Its placement at the front of the book suggests that a physical entity, a house, stood at the center of the case and investigation, a point that is also made clear in the introduction's first sentence: "The case of John Reginald Halliday Christie was unusual in several respects, but especially because of the number of women who died from violence in one house, No. 10 Rillington Place."[55]

In a generously illustrated monograph spanning more than two hundred pages, Camps unveils the forensic secrets of Number 10 in exacting detail. In so doing he generates a complex account of the Rillington Place murder investigation, focusing on the challenging labor conducted in and across

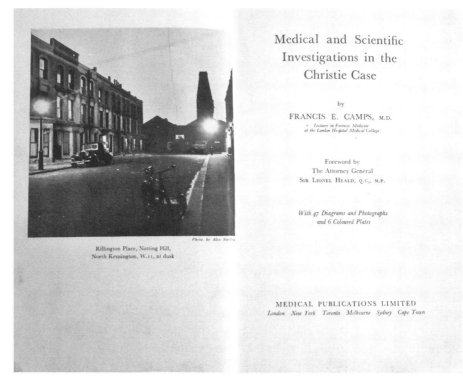

Medical and Scientific
Investigations in the
Christie Case

by

FRANCIS E. CAMPS, M.D.

Lecturer in Forensic Medicine
at the London Hospital Medical College

Foreword by
The Attorney General
SIR LIONEL HEALD, Q.C., M.P.

With 47 Diagrams and Photographs
and 6 Coloured Plates

MEDICAL PUBLICATIONS LIMITED
London   New York   Toronto   Melbourne   Sydney   Cape Town

Photo. by Alex Sterling

Rillington Place, Notting Hill,
North Kensington, W.11, at dusk

Figure 7.12. Camps's frontispiece: Rillington Place at dusk. F. E. Camps, *Medical and Scientific Investigations in the Christie Case*, 1953.

(and the synergies among) the crime scene, the laboratory, and the mortuary. He includes chapters on the multiple aspects of the investigation, including the mortuary investigations into the bodies, Nickolls's lab interventions, the painstaking reconstruction of the two skeletons from the human remains discovered in the garden, and the controversies surrounding the inquiries into the death of Beryl Evans. These chapters provide a synthesized account of how 10 Rillington Place had served as a spectacular demonstration of the reach of the interpretative powers of modern CSI.

Camps intended the book to serve as a beacon of multidisciplinary homicide forensics. The preface, written by Attorney General Sir Lionel Heald, lends legal support to this reading, paying a "tribute of sincere admiration to the skill, patience, and collaborative spirit of those responsible, at all levels and in all departments."[56] In his own introductory remarks Camps emphasizes that modern homicide investigation "requires a team of specialist workers." As a means of exemplifying these values, Camps provides a list of sixteen individuals involved in or consulted for their technical skills and support during the course of the investigation.[57] This acknowledgment was not simply a means to express his gratitude: it serves as a rhetorical device that conferred authority upon a forensic model conceived and practiced as an aggregate of sites and experts, each with their own identity and set of resources.

Another mark of the unequivocally collaborative spirit of the Rillington Place murder investigation conveyed by *Medical and Scientific Investigations in the Christie Case* was Camps's distinctive authorial positioning. Camps styles himself not so much as a single omniscient author but rather as a synthesizer and overseer of multiple inputs: "Four only of the ten chapters have been attributed to specific authors," he notes, "but all the others contain significant contributions from various sources representing a further example of the co-operation which was so evident throughout the course of the investigation."[58] In this textual space, then, Camps reifies his status as a hands-on commander-in-chief, underscoring in writing what he had done in the actual investigation. This authorial positioning is also evident in how Camps refers to himself in the third person in his account and explanation of his own knowledge-gathering activities. This mode of authorship in a sense mirrors the technical skills of a range of experts who had been given parity of esteem during the investigation, turning *Medical and Scientific Investigations* into a pluralist text, in which authority is dispersed among multiple actors but at the same time contained by a single dominant voice.

Camps's account serves as an elaborate and definitive reassertion of the facts created by the ambitious homicide investigation into the 10 Rillington Place murders. Yet it also serves another urgent purpose: to assert an authoritative narrative to contain the corrosive and destabilizing effects of Christie's multiple statements and thus to shield British justice from the charge of judicial murder. Christie's confession to killing Beryl Evans had shocked the nation, raised questions over the fairness of the death penalty, and, in the wake of the Scott Henderson verdict, cast a shadow over the British political establishment. Christie's statements, as Camps warns in his introductory remarks, were "both untrue and contradictory and necessitated extreme caution in accepting anything that he said until it had been fully corroborated."[59] To achieve this corroboration, Camps proposes recourse to his now-trusted objective touchstone: the material fabric of the House of Murder.

In opening the door to Rillington Place for one final time, Camps returns not to its ground floor but to the Evans upstairs flat. Here, Camps seeks to determine whether it was possible for the Evans front room to serve as an efficient gas chamber to render Beryl unconscious in the manner that Christie had described. Camps takes Christie's initial account of his gassing of Evans step by step, dismissing each element with observations such as "almost certainly not on this data" and "highly improbable if not impossible."[60] Camps bases these conclusions on a dense evidentiary network involving a full range of scientific and medical specialisms; here, once again, Rillington Place as a physical entity looms large.

The centerpiece of Camps's rebuttal is a detailed analysis of the volume of gas in the room required to create the toxicity level sufficient to render Beryl unconscious. To do this, Camps turns to F. C. Smith, a gas engineer who had "extensive knowledge of coal-gas poisoning."[61] Camps commissioned Smith to personally visit the House of Murder to calculate the rate at which gas filled the room and to "measure the concentration of this gas in the room after given intervals of time."[62] Smith at first established the room's spatial dimensions to determine its volumetric capacity, before attending to its architectural features, such as window positioning and dimensions, wall porosity, and the specific gravity and pressure flow of the flat's domestic gas flow. This included identifying "permanent air inlets and outlets" and the "orientation of [the] room in respect of wind direction," to determine and measure the concentration of gas in the room air after intervals of time.[63] Smith's measurements are then translated into tabulated graphic and mathematical representations, which lends additional solidity to Camps's written conclusion: that, in this precise space, Christie would have had to breathe a concentration of gas similar to that inhaled by his victims—and would thus have similarly succumbed.

By including these and numerous other detailed, physically engaged, and collaborative investigations, Camps's text presents an apt reflection of the key features of his interdisciplinary and consultative methodology. It also underscores his commitment to treating the crime scene not merely as a site for the recovery of trace evidence but as an environment that itself requires analytical engagement. As a pathologist, Camps is obviously interested in bodies, but he places them within a framework that emphasizes the reciprocities between body and trace. As a result, Camps recalls Rillington Place as a material witness to the ultimate truth of Christie—the evil fantasist whose claims of responsibility in the Evans murder was merely a perverse attempt to sully the reputation of British justice.

_⟶⟵_

At the center of *Medical and Scientific Investigations in the Christie Case* was a house. By detailing the synergies between crime lab and crime scene investigation, Camps creates an authoritative narrative of how collaborative scientific endeavor emptied 10 Rillington Place of its innermost secrets and thereby successfully contains the disruptive confessions of its notorious murdering resident. The book showcases the spectacular powers and possibilities of modern CSI, demonstrating how homicide forensics reconstructed the complex components of life and death that were scattered across the House of Murder as traces absorbed by its corpses or infused with its "atmosphere." And yet, as the epilogue will show, Camps's text was not able to bring closure to the public controversy surrounding the Christie case. Its meticulous narrative and interpretative command over 10 Rillington Place was not only challenged but ultimately eclipsed by a new version of events, one that was activated by a journalistically driven regime of inquiry into the context of the "permissive" political and sociocultural climate of the 1960s.

Revisiting Rillington Place

O ur main aim in writing this book was to illuminate the historical circumstances through which one of the most recognizable features of
the modern forensics of homicide—the crime scene as a highly choreographed space of investigation—came into being. The intent was not only to
present a compelling story on its own terms but to do what historians are
best placed to do: to put into historical perspective, and thus "denaturalize,"
ways of knowing and acting that are so familiar to modern eyes as to be
taken as given, as without a history.

This secondary aim was in part stimulated by current debates about the
relationship of the forensic past to its present, and future. The introduction
outlined two versions of this relationship: a dominant one that, taking the
post-DNA landscape of forensic investigation as its benchmark, engages in
retrospective criticism of prior regimes as founded upon "untested assumptions and semi-informed guesswork"; and a second, more recent, one that
seeks to use the forensic past—and in particular the origins of the concepts,
institutions, and practices that have been at the heart of our account—to recover a lost world of forensic "holism" lying before and beyond genomic
reductionism.[1]

Our objective in engaging, if only obliquely, with this contemporary set
of debates is not to use history to settle the issue. Instead, it is to provide
empirical evidence and analysis that might allow both sides to appreciate
the most useful contribution that history has to offer the present—that is,
to serve as a mirror through which to recognize, and reflect upon, the
complex and often surprising circumstances by which ways of knowing and
acting have come into being. Recognition enables an empathetic understanding of the past, while reflection can promote self-consciousness of the
inescapable historicity of the present moment. Nothing is learned from a

history flattened out for present purposes—in this case either as a primitive, or pristine, other. Neither is helpful as, irrespective of the intent, both are framed selectively and support partial purposes. No regime, past or present, is perfect—rather, perfection is attributed situationally and strategically.

Two related points about the attribution of perfection should make this contribution to both the historical and the contemporary forensic conversation more productive. First, this account should not be read as a story of the slow but inexorable ascent of an improved model of forensic investigation at the expense of an earlier flawed one. In straightforward terms, it bears repeating that this narrative is not about the rise of traces and the fall of bodies but rather the continuous shifting of the relationship between them. Second, we would like to undercut any suggestion that, even as we reach the apogee of this history of the making of modern CSI in the Rillington Place investigation, we are describing the ascendency of a seamless and transcendent model of forensic truth. Forensic regimes are always and inextricably tied to the historically contingent context of their production, and as such an exploration of their rise (or fall) tells us something about the specific moments that produce them.

Our unpacking of the processes through which, over the course of five decades, the crime scene was naturalized as an authoritative and essential starting point for a "modern" regime of homicide investigation provides a grounded case study of the struggles, processes, and negotiations that underpin forensic truth-making claims. More broadly, it reminds us that forensic regimes, no matter how sophisticated, are not conclusive in their own right. They are built, and, as complex and composite artifices, they are subject to fissure. Furthermore, as is plain from the range of sources we have used, they are built from materials that extend far beyond those fashioned by forensic practitioners. Consequently, however seemingly robust and elaborate, forensic regimes neither control the terms of their own production and composition nor command their terms of assent.

We will illustrate this, and in so doing conclude our account of both the making of English CSI and its spectacular staging at Rillington Place, by posing two questions. First, what do readers know about the Christie case? The answer may be just what was presented in the previous chapter. But if they have any prior knowledge of the case, it will be that John Christie killed Beryl Evans in a frenzied sexual assault under the guise of providing an abortion. This knowledge requires no awareness of alcove mold, the dynamics of domestic gas supply, or any of the other ways in which trace, space and body interacted in and around "the House of Murder." The second question is, how did they gain this knowledge? Not as the result of a cold case review—the well-trod route through which the errors of past regimes of forensic investigation are now retrospectively reconfigured. The regime of truth painstakingly assembled by Camps and his multidisciplinary team has not, to date, been successfully challenged. Rather than being revised, the Camps version has been displaced, and effaced, by another powerful truth-creating complex that repositioned Rillington Place within a different social, political, and moral landscape. There are two key anchor points of this new narrative: the 1961 book *Ten Rillington Place*, and, a decade later, the feature film *10 Rillington Place*. It is to this story of erasure that we now turn.

If any version of the Christie case is remembered today, it is the one portrayed in the 1971 Richard Fleischer film, *10 Rillington Place* (fig. 8.1). It was shot two doors down from the House of Murder, the sitting tenants having refused to open up Christie's former lair to the film crew. Set in 1949 and starring Richard Attenborough as the real-life serial killer John Christie, Fleischer's account focuses on the turbulent marriage of a young and gullible couple, Timothy and Beryl Evans. It reconstructs the events that took place when Beryl, played by Judy Geeson, reveals that she is pregnant with the couple's second child and tells her husband, played by John Hurt, that she wants to "get rid of it." Christie, their neighbor, presents himself as a man who could help. Boasting of his medical credentials, he convinces them to go ahead with the "operation," which takes place in their top-floor flat. Once Beryl lies down on a mattress on the floor, he approaches her and places a gas mask over her face, through which carbon monoxide flows to induce unconsciousness. When Beryl becomes distressed and starts to scream, Christie seizes the moment: climbing on top of her, he strangles and rapes her as she dies.

This horrific scene, and the film more generally, fundamentally reshaped how 10 Rillington Place was understood by future generations. It secured in the public consciousness that Christie was responsible for the deaths of both Beryl Evans and the Evans's baby daughter, Geraldine. This was all the more disturbing for an audience who knew that Timothy Evans, not John Christie, was convicted and hanged for his daughter's death in 1950.

The power of this cinematic version of events derived from its return to an initial line of investigation in the 1949 murders, one that had been mar-

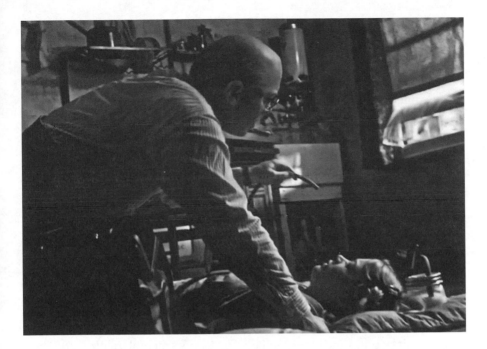

Figure 8.1. The moment of truth—*10 Rillington Place.* Directed by Richard Fleischer, 1971.

ginalized by police investigators and then effectively forgotten by the time of the forensic investigation that reopened the Evans case with the exhumation of Beryl and Geraldine's bodies in 1953. Under the stress of the 1949 police interrogations, Timothy Evans had declared in one of his statements that his wife was the victim of a botched abortion performed by Christie. The police dismissed this as a credible explanation for Beryl's death: the post-mortem investigation of her body carried out by the forensic pathologist Donald Teare had yielded none of the expected signs of criminal interference by an amateur abortionist. There were, for instance, no internal tears or infection, no traces of an air embolism, and no signs of sepsis. Most tellingly, Beryl's unpunctured uterus still carried her intact sixteen-week-old fetus. Her visible injuries, especially to her face and neck, combined with witness testimonies describing the turbulent nature of the Evans's marriage (including from John Christie himself), offered a more convincing interpretation of her death at the hands of a violent husband. Abortion was dropped from the script.[2]

Fleischer's reimagining of the House of Murder was itself based on the 1961 book *Ten Rillington Place*, written by the prominent liberal campaigner, broadcaster, and author Ludovic Kennedy.[3] Kennedy's exposé represents the culmination of public concerns that had been expressed in and around the Christie trial, first in the 1953 Scott Henderson inquiry and its skeptical reception, and then in a series of books and pamphlets on the case published in the mid- to late 1950s, which argue that Scott Henderson's assertion of the legitimacy of the Evans execution was flawed.[4] Kennedy not only expands these arguments but also sets them within a sophisticated and dramatized narrative schema that provides a compelling new account of what had happened to Beryl and Geraldine Evans. *Ten Rillington Place* also offered him an opportunity to promote his understanding of how the case fit within the broader judicial, political, and moral landscape of the 1950s: the true version of events had been deliberately suppressed in an attempt to prop up a regime of repressive institutions and values, symbolized by its illiberal embrace of capital punishment and its criminalization of abortion.

Kennedy's book, the result of a yearlong review of the Evans and Christie cases, presents in more than three hundred pages a detailed but highly readable reconsideration of the evidence. It discusses Christie's childhood and early adult traumas and illnesses, Timothy Evans's mental fragility, and the parlous state of the Evans's marriage, arguing unequivocally throughout that Evans had been the victim of a judicial murder. In piecing together fragments of various narratives and counterstories from the documentary record, Kennedy blends techniques of contemporary journalism, melodrama, horror, and dramatic reenactment to produce a compelling composite account. In contrast to Camps's dense, multivocal scientific monograph, *Ten Rillington Place* spins a plot that is developed through, and conveyed by, a detached third-person narrative, reimagining, incorporating, and synthesizing the viewpoints, desires, motivations, and fears of Christie and his victims, all set against the bleak backdrop that was Notting Hill.

In the opening paragraphs of the first chapter, Kennedy focuses readers' attention on the attempts to bury Number 10's terrible past:

> You will not find Rillington Place in any street map of London now, for as a result of the fearful things that happened there, it has changed its name to Ruston Close. It is a mean shabby cul-de-sac of ten houses on either side. Although the houses have three floors, they are small, almost miniature houses, and their most striking characteristic is peeling paint and rotting stucco. . . . No. 10 is the last house on the south side, . . . beneath the shadow of the foundry chimney. It differs from the other houses in that whereas

they are all grey and shabby, No. 10 is now bright with indigo paint. It is as if they were trying to shake off its hideous past, to become reformed and respectable.[5]

Like those who had preceded him, Kennedy puts Christie's house center stage. Indeed, this provocative passage recalls and reworks the initial 1953 newspaper tropes that had themselves found an (alternative) expression in Camps's haunting frontispiece. However, Kennedy's portrait sharply contrasts both to journalistic representations of Rillington Place as a grotesque site of urban decay and to Camps's version as a place of trace-centered revelation. For Kennedy, it was instead a house of cover-ups, the renaming and repainting of Number 10 Ruston Close portrayed as the emblematic work of a puritanical regime conspiring to conceal a multitude of inconvenient truths.

In Kennedy's account, then, the House of Murder stands as a literal and figurative blot on the judicial landscape that the nation could and should no longer ignore. Critical to his account of justice miscarried is his reworking of what took place in the top-floor flat on the morning of Beryl Evans's death into a narrative that fuses the initial 1949 suggestion that she had been a victim of a botched abortion with several key facts established about Christie's 1953 serial killings.[6] The evidentiary centerpiece for Kennedy's conclusion that Christie was responsible for Beryl and Geraldine's death is his discovery of a smoking gun buried in the reams of documents relating to the Evans and Christie cases. This is a paragraph written by Timothy Evans's solicitor in preparation for his 1950 trial, which, in reviewing the pathologist Donald Teare's pretrial testimony, referenced Teare's discovery during his autopsy on Beryl Evans of a "post-mortem" vaginal bruise. To Kennedy, this was evidence that Beryl Evans had been sexually assaulted after death and thus that she had suffered the identical form of violence that Christie had visited upon his three alcove victims. What was so shocking—and revealing—to Kennedy was that all mention of the bruise had been expunged from the courtroom record by lawyers seemingly motivated by prudery: "The case is sufficiently horrible," Evans's solicitor had written, "without disgusting surmises of this nature being introduced into the minds of the Jury."[7]

Kennedy draws attention to Teare's suppressed discovery throughout his book, underscoring its significance in stark terms:

Here was the vital, the missing link between Evans's claim that Christie had done it, and the reason why he had done it. Here, so to speak, were Christie's finger-prints. . . . But at the time Evans's guilt seemed so certain that it never occurred to anyone that this constituted a link. It never occurred to anyone that if there had been sexual penetration after death, it could have been done by anyone else than Evans. And if Evans had done it, then obviously the less said about it the better.[8]

In Kennedy's view, this stunning paper trail was vital on two counts. First, it linked Beryl Evans to what was the most sensational, and most singular, characteristic of the profile built up and projected by the Rillington Place forensic investigation led by Camps into Christie's modus operandi: "Not even those tortuous minds who believe that there were two stranglers living in the same house can believe that they were necrophiles too."[9] Second, it confirmed Kennedy's damning assessment of the Scott Henderson report as "one of the most extraordinary British legal documents of the twentieth century. It is, in its errors of omission and commission, little short of a shambles."[10] The inquiry had entered a portion of the Evans defense brief into evidence, which had been included in the inquiry's published report, but, crucially for Kennedy, the passage in which the defense counsel alluded to the "disgusting surmises" had been erased. This "extraordinary" omission, Kennedy continues, was compounded by the inquiry's "incomprehensible" failure to question Teare about the basis for his suggestion when he appeared at the hearing. By acting in this manner, Scott Henderson in his 1953 report had sacrificed truth to shore up a dying regime of Victorian puritanism.

Following the publication of *Ten Rillington Place* in early 1961, Kennedy's sensational claims to have discovered the "missing link" between Beryl Evans as murder victim and Christie as necrophile serial killer was, unsurprisingly, among the most highly publicized and discussed feature of his book. The claim was debated in the pages of the *Sunday Times* in a series of letters exchanged between Teare and Kennedy in which Teare attempted to explain the source of what he claimed was a mistake on Kennedy's part, one that had resulted in "the complete distortion of my evidence."[11] The suggestion of necrophilia, he explained, was the result of transcriptional error by the Evans's solicitor: "My own notes clearly read 'a small area of ante-mortem bruising in the vagina,' and there is no mention of any post-mortem injury."[12] His notes, moreover, were corroborated by medical common sense: "Post-mortem bruising is a contradiction in terms, as bruising does not occur after death."[13] The bruise, therefore, was not the "fingerprint" of Rillington Place's necrophilic psychopath.

Teare's explanation did not prevent Kennedy's revelation from reaching the House of Commons chamber, when on June 15, 1961, the Smethwick MP Patrick Gordon Walker opened an extended debate by invoking the bruise as a key point of evidence ignored in the Scott Henderson report. Though he acknowledged Teare's rebuttal, Walker insisted that there was no question about the simple fact of the bruise's existence and the possibility that it was caused by post mortem intercourse: "That," Walker observed in an echo of Kennedy, "was the horrible hallmark of all Christie's admitted murders, except that of his own wife."[14] Walker was joined in his call for a new inquiry into the legitimacy of the Evans conviction by numerous parliamentarians, including the Newport Labour MP Frank Soskice, but these calls were successfully resisted by the Conservative home secretary Rab Butler, who concluded the debate by stating, "There are no grounds for thinking, from Mr. Kennedy's book or elsewhere, that an inquiry would do any good."[15]

The Evans campaign, spearheaded by Kennedy, took the opportunity of the October 1964 Labour electoral victory to urge Soskice, as the incoming home secretary, to sanction an inquiry. Faced with initial resistance, a Timothy Evans Committee, with Kennedy as chair, was established in June 1965. To launch the committee's campaign, Kennedy organized a spectacular publicity stunt designed to catapult the House of Murder once again into public prominence. Accompanied by a party of committee members, reporters, and photographers, Kennedy visited Christie's former lodgings.[16] There they were confronted by a tenant who expressed little sympathy for their cause or the fate of the previous residents of the house, insisting its history was "no business of yours. That's all dead and buried."[17] Kennedy nonetheless successfully negotiated his way past the front door and escorted his audience around the notorious house, showing them the alcove where Christie had hidden three bodies, the tiny garden where the remains of two previous victims had been buried, and the washhouse where two more bodies—those of Beryl and Geraldine Evans—had been discovered.

In August 1965, after a short public lobbying campaign in which the Evans Committee garnered significant support among members of Parliament, Soskice appointed the High Court judge Sir Daniel Brabin to lead a public review of the Evans execution. The Brabin inquiry opened at a preliminary public hearing held at the Royal Courts of Justice on October 18,

1965, with its main sessions taking place, under the same conditions of publicity, over the course of thirty-two days between November 1965 and January 1966. The inquiry's early sessions coincided with the passage of the Murder (Abolition of Death Penalty) Act, whose provision for a five-year suspension of capital punishment was widely linked to the core question facing Brabin. A *Guardian* article, for example, greeted the act by reminding readers that the Evans case "looms reproachfully" as a "cloud of shame [that] still hangs over his memory—and over British justice."[18]

Given the highly publicized questions about post-mortem vaginal bruising, it is not surprising that this bruising featured as an important line of inquiry, at least in the first instance. But as it turned out the inquiry accepted Teare's explanation of the necrophilia angle as simple transcriptional error. When Kennedy was called to testify, he attempted to defend his "missing link," but under close questioning he eventually fell back on a kind of providentialist argument, asserting the value of his documentary discovery on the grounds that it was "such a rare thing to find . . . such a very odd thing."[19] The caustic reply of Geoffrey Lane, the counsel representing the interests of the Metropolitan Police, set the tone for the hearing's overall assessment of Kennedy's revelation: "Indeed it is so odd that everybody has been looking for the basis on which it was founded, and it transpires, does it not, . . . that there is no foundation for it except a mistake by [the Evans lawyers]?" Brabin himself was no more favorably inclined to what he regarded as a "simple factual mistake" to which even lawyers were liable: "to you it was tremendous point, and you built a pretty big house on it, did you not?"[20]

—◌ ◌—

In revisiting the forensic worlds of the House of Murder, Brabin did not commission a fresh set of investigations but rather examined the figures that had led the 1953 homicide investigation. During the course of this questioning, Camps and Nickolls in particular were invited to revisit and elaborate upon the ambitious, intricate, and multifaceted work that had transformed 10 Rillington Place into an exemplary locus of cutting-edge forensic achievement. In so doing they reminded the inquiry of the conclusion reached following their extensive investigation into the validity of Christie's confession to killing Beryl Evans: that they had found no evidence linking her death to Christie.[21]

The model of CSI represented by Camps and Nickolls emerged unscathed, but the same could not be said of the 1949 forensic regime that Teare represented. Even though he had been personally vindicated on the point of necrophilic penetration, through a series of close interrogations the Brabin inquiry recast Teare's work on Beryl and Geraldine Evans as, in significant respects, primitive. There are two, linked, aspects of this criticism that are worth briefly noting: first, Teare's limited engagement with the precepts of modern CSI; second, the consequent restriction of his horizon of investigation to the mortuary.

Teare's account of his involvement in the initial investigation of the bodies of Geraldine and Beryl when they were discovered in the washhouse of Rillington Place presented his activities as limited and somewhat vague, especially when contrasted with Camps's account of his own engagement four years later. When presented with photographs of the scene, for example, Teare positioned himself as a passive recipient of this documentary evidence generated through police practices in which he had taken no direct role. Asked whether the photograph of the bundled bodies as they were initially discovered depicted the scene that he witnessed when he first arrived, he was unsure. He could not, for instance, say whether the knot which secured the bundle containing Beryl's body had been altered prior to his arrival, nor did he take note of the kind of knot used. When asked about the condition of the wooden planks that had covered the bodies in the washhouse—whether they were split or "bruised," he replied, "I was not concerned with it."[22] On the state of the clothing, he could only give his "impression" that it was rumpled.[23]

Furthermore, in direct contrast to Camps's embrace of the hunting and harvesting of minute traces, Teare's evidence revealed his reliance on naked-eye appearances. Under cross-examination he explained that while he had taken specimens of stomach contents and blood, he had decided that "it was not necessary to take a vaginal swab." He was categorical in his justification for not doing so: there "was nothing to swab."[24] Asked by Brabin to clarify whether there had been any visual evidence of a seminal deposit, Teare responded that his deployment of "a magnifying glass" yielded negative findings. This answer prompted a second question from the Brabin team, in which they explicitly sought to criticize Teare for his reliance on macro-level evidence: "but visual examination is not always decisive, is it?"[25] By interrogating Teare's crime scene practices in such a manner, the inquiry simultaneously recast Teare as the embodiment of obsolete ways of knowing and working, and by implicit contrast elevated the practices and sensibilities of the Camps-led investigation as the gold standard for a modern forensics of homicide investigation.

_⌒ ⌒_

When Justice Daniel Brabin published his final report on October 12, 1966, neither defenders of British justice nor its crusading critics were fully vindicated. For reasons that lie beyond this account, his findings were at once surprising and confusing. On the one hand, Brabin agreed with Kennedy that there were errors in the conviction of Timothy Evans and that Christie had a part in the Evans murders. He wrote, "I am not satisfied that Evans himself killed Geraldine"—the crime for which Evans was hanged. "I think it is more probable than not that Christie did."[26] On the other hand, he concluded that it was "more probable than not that Evans killed Beryl Evans"— the charge held in reserve by the prosecution and for which he had therefore not been tried.[27] Two days later, the new home secretary Roy Jenkins made a statement to the House of Commons on the report. Thanking him for his "painstaking and thorough" work, Jenkins reprised Brabin's first conclusion. On these grounds Jenkins had recommended the granting of a Free Pardon, which he announced the queen had signed earlier in the day. Jenkins concluded his statement on a hopeful note: "This case has no precedent and will, I hope and believe, have no successor."[28]

The mood of the House was largely supportive of Jenkins's actions, and when one MP sought to open up a discussion of Brabin's second finding— that Evans was probably responsible for his wife's death—cries of "no" were noted by the session's recorder. Nonetheless, another member no doubt spoke for many when he professed that he was left with "an uncomfortable feeling" about the ambiguities of Brabin's findings, a sense expressed more strongly outside the chamber by those pressing for a clear resolution. Kennedy's sardonic reaction was typical: the inquiry's conclusion "certainly was an arresting theory, especially as there was virtually no evidence to support it."[29] For supporters of the Evans campaign, the repressive regime clung to the Brabin report, denying full access to and appreciation of the truth of what had transpired behind the closed doors of Number 10 Rillington Place.

It was this lingering odor of the past that Fleischer's 1971 film, by setting Kennedy's narrative free from both judicial murk and considerations of forensic detail, sought to dissipate. In doing so, the film highlighted two legislative symbols of liberation in a newly permissive era. First, by showing how the absence of a safe, legal, and medical abortion had driven a desperate Beryl Evans into the hands of an unorthodox practitioner with murderous motives, it confronted its audiences with an image of 1950s Britain as an unjust and repressed society from which they had been freed by the 1967 Abortion Act. Second, this cinematic distillation of Kennedy's narrative drew attention to the abolition of the death penalty, temporarily in 1965, and permanently four years later. The film projected an indelible portrait of the dangers of capital punishment, casting Timothy Evans as the innocent victim of an anachronistic judicial culture whose monstrous offspring—John Christie—hid in its repressive shadows, murdering behind the shabby Victorian façade of 10 Rillington Place.[30]

Its cinematic outing proved to be Rillington Place's final performance: shortly after the film crew dispersed, local officials summoned the wrecking crew (fig. 8.2). British Pathé Films captured the demolition, transforming the moment into a serial spectacle as it was replayed in newsreel previews

Figure 8.2. Curtain call on the House of Murder. Archives of the Royal Borough of Kensington and Chelsea. Courtesy of the Kensington and Chelsea Local Studies Collection at Kensington Central Library.

across the nation's cinema screens. Alongside Fleischer's film, it continuously relayed the same message: that the true story of what happened to Beryl Evans in the top floor flat had finally broken free from the confining walls of the House of Murder. The destruction of Rillington Place in this sense represents a final act of attempted closure on the Christie case by physically removing every trace of a location (and its past) that had simultaneously generated intense political, social, and legal controversy and served as the stage for spectacularly showcasing the powers and promise of a new regime of CSI.

Acknowledgments

Coauthoring a book is an intense experience, and at times it has seemed as if we've been involved in an endless conversation that, though fascinating to us, has been conducted to the exclusion of the rest of the world. Fortunately things are not always as they seem: our debts are many.

Our academic home, the University of Manchester's Centre for the History of Science, Technology and Medicine, has been a continuous source of creative inspiration for us, starting from its two former directors: the late and much missed John Pickstone engaged with our developing ideas with his trademark combination of playful curiosity and unstinting conceptual rigor, while Mick Worboys's generosity in support of this project has been manifold, necessary, and always deeply appreciated. We also thank our Centre colleagues Rob Kirk, Ray Macaulay, Carsten Timmermann, Elizabeth Toon, and Duncan Wilson, who at several stages along the way gave us their honest assessment of how we were getting on and how we might do better.

We have benefitted from comments and suggestions made by friends, colleagues, and attendees of the numerous academic and public events where we shared our provisional findings, of which we would like to single out Rima Apple, Dave Barclay, Mario Biagioli, Simon Cole, Jeremy Green, Fraser Joyce, Tom Laqueur, Chris Lawrence, Rachel O'Dowd, Jose Ramón Bertomeu Sánchez, Joan Scott, and James Vernon, all of whom followed up their initial thoughts with further and more sustained contributions to the cause. We owe a special debt to Michael Green, emeritus professor of forensic pathology at the University of Sheffield, who over the life of this project has been a constant source of advice, information, and encouragement.

Wellcome Trust grant 094353/Z/10/7 has provided crucial financial support, and we gratefully acknowledge it and those working in the Trust, past and present, to maintain and enhance opportunities for humanistic scholarship. It has been a pleasure to work with Jackie Wehmueller and her talented team at Johns Hopkins University Press to bring this book through to publication.

We've found our collaboration both enjoyable and exhilarating, and we hope readers have found this reflected in the preceding pages. However, much of the subject matter that we have dealt with is undeniably grim, and as we pursued it we were fortunate in our communities of family and friends that enabled us to reaffirm our ongoing place among the living. For Ian, his children, Cailin and Rohin, exemplify this reaffirmation: at the start of this project their dad's work was little more than an amusing oddity to them; as they and the project matured, they saw more in it of interest; now, as it has come to an end and they are both starting out on their own experience of the pleasures and pains of university learning, they have come to appreciate at least the spirit of the exercise. He dedicates his part of this book to them, with a father's enduring love. Neil dedicates his part to his mother, Janice. In many ways it was her trust in his curiosity that allowed him to discover a world of books and imaginative engagement that—although hardly anyone could have anticipated it—ultimately led him to the practice of writing history. He is deeply thankful to her for inspiring in him a passion for learning and for her unwavering support and love.

Notes

INTRODUCTION

1. For fingerprinting, see Simon A. Cole, *Suspect Identities: A History of Fingerprinting and Criminal Identification* (Cambridge, MA: Harvard University Press, 2002); for anthropometry in the British context, see Neil Davie, *Tracing the Criminal: The Rise of Scientific Criminology in Britain, 1860–1918* (Oxford: Bardwell Press, 2006); and, in other national contexts, see contributions to Peter Becker and Richard F. Wetzell, eds., *Criminals and Their Scientists: The History of Criminology in International Perspective* (Cambridge: Cambridge University Press, 2006). Our book is not a history of the emergence of a discrete set of forensic techniques or technologies. Consequently, it does not systematically chart or catalog the various technologies that were invented or used as aids to investigation, though the narrative does inevitably in places capture their use.

2. On forensics as a system, Anne Crowther and Brenda White, *On Soul and Conscience: The Medical Expert and Crime* (Aberdeen: Aberdeen University Press, 1988) provides an excellent analysis of Glasgow practice; Norman Ambage, "The Origins and Development of the Home Office Forensic Science Service, 1931–1967" (University of Lancaster Ph.D., 1987) gives a detailed and useful examination of institutional developments in English forensic services; and Katherine Watson's *Forensic Medicine in Western Society: A History* (London: Routledge, 2010), chapter 6, contains a useful outline of developments in twentieth-century forensic medicine and science. Also of interest is Claire Valier, "True Crime Stories: Scientific Methods of Criminal Investigation, Criminology and Historiography," *British Journal of Criminology* 38 (1998): 88–105. Alison Adams's *A History of Forensic Science: British Beginnings in the Twentieth Century* (Abingdon, UK: Routledge, 2016) was published after this manuscript had gone to press and could not therefore be properly considered. For an excellent account of the history of forensic expertise in the Anglo-American context, see Tal Golan, *Laws of Man and Laws of Nature: A History of Scientific Expert Testimony* (Cambridge, MA: Harvard University Press, 2004). We should note here that our focus on English forensics raises issues about the significant distinctions between the forensic contexts of England and Scotland. We do not propose a comprehensive British account, first because the Scottish story is comparatively well known and second in order to maintain manageable narrative parameters.

3. For practitioner accounts, see, e.g., Sydney Smith, *Mostly Murder* (London: Harrap, 1959); Keith Simpson, *Forty Years of Murder: An Autobiography* (London: Granada, 1981). For true crime biographies, see Douglas G. Browne and Tom Tullett, *Bernard Spilsbury: His Life and Cases* (London: Harrap, 1951); Colin Evans, *The Father of Forensics: How Sir Bernard*

Spilsbury Invented Modern CSI (London: Icon Books, 2007); Andrew Rose, *Lethal Witness: Sir Bernard Spilsbury Honorary Pathologist* (London: Sutton, 2007). For a useful overview of the history of crime in England, see Clive Emsley, *Crime and Society 1750–1900* (London: Routledge, 2009).

4. On the DNA wars generally, see Jay Aronson's historical account, *Genetic Witness: Science, Law, and Controversy in the Making of DNA Profiling* (New Brunswick, NJ: Rutgers University Press, 2007); on probability, see Michael Lynch and Ruth McNally, "'Science,' 'Common Sense,' and DNA Evidence," *Public Understanding of Science* 12 (2003): 83–100; on DNA scene and lab protocols, and other modes of DNA governance, see Sheila Jasanoff and Michael Lynch, eds., "Contested Identities: Science, Law and Forensic Practice," special issue, *Social Studies of Science* 28 (1998), on the O. J. Simpson trial; Michael Lynch et al., *Truth Machine: The Contentious History of DNA Fingerprinting* (Chicago: University of Chicago Press, 2008); and Robin Williams and Paul Johnson, *Genetic Policing: The Use of DNA in Criminal Investigations* (Cullompton, UK: Willan, 2008).

5. See, e.g., Michael Lynch, "Science, Truth, and Forensic Cultures: The Exceptional Legal Status of DNA Evidence," in Ian Burney, David Kirby, and Neil Pemberton, eds., "Forensic Cultures," special issue, *Studies in History and Philosophy of Science, Part C: Studies in History and Philosophy of Biology and Biomedical Science* 44 (2013): 60–70.

6. Michael J. Saks and David L. Faigman, "Failed Forensics: How Forensic Science Lost Its Way and How It Might Yet Find It," *Annual Review of Law and Social Science* 4 (2008): 149–71, 150.

7. These quotes are taken from the editorial written by the meeting's conveners, the forensic anthropologist Sue Black and the forensic biochemist Niamh Nic Daeid, and set the tone for the subsequent contributions. "Time to Think Differently: Catalysing a Paradigm Shift in Forensic Science," *Philosophical Transactions of the Royal Society B* 370 (2015): 1–4.

8. Claude Roux, Benjamin Talbot-Wright, James Robertson, Frank Crispino, and Olivier Ribaux, "The End of the (Forensic Science) World as We Know It? The Example of Trace Evidence," *Philosophical Transactions of the Royal Society B* 370 (2015): 1–8, 3.

9. Ibid., 2. These authors locate the origins of this broader conception of trace evidence in the writings of the key actors that will dominate our discussion of the making of CSI—especially Hans Gross and Edmond Locard. A similar historical lineage is developed in David A. Stoney and Paul L. Stoney, "Critical Review of Forensic Trace Evidence Analysis and the Need for a New Approach," *Forensic Science International* 251 (2015): 159–70. We are grateful to Simon Cole for drawing these articles to our attention.

10. Michael J. Saks and Jonathan J. Koehler, "The Coming Paradigm Shift in Forensic Identification Science," *Science*, 309 (2005): 892–95, 895.

11. The embrace of a (typically nostalgic) holism in the face of a turn toward a perceived reductionism is, of course, a long-running theme in the history of science and medicine. For a classic discussion, see Christopher Lawrence and George Weisz, eds., *Greater Than the Parts: Holism in Biomedicine, 1920–1950* (New York: Oxford University Press, 1998). The nostalgic tendency in this embrace of a lost forensic holism is noted by Simon Cole in his review of the turn from the lab to the crime scene in recent forensic literature. Simon A. Cole, "Response: Forensic Science Reform; Out of the Laboratory and into the Crime Scene," *Texas Law Review* 91 (2013): 123–36, 132–33.

12. "Crime Scene, n.," *OED Online* (Oxford: Oxford University Press, March 2015), accessed July 17, 2015, http://www.oed.com/view/Entry/276760?redirectedFrom=crime +scene+investigation.

13. For lab/field networks, see Bruno Latour, *Pasteurization of France* (Cambridge, MA: Harvard University Press, 1988); and Robert Kohler, *Labscapes and Landscapes* (Chicago: University of Chicago Press, 2002); for regimes of objectivity, see Lorraine Daston and Peter Galison, *Objectivity* (Cambridge, MA: Zone Books, 2007); for incommunicable knowledge, see Christopher Lawrence, "Incommunicable Knowledge: Science, Technology and the Clinical Art in Britain 1850–1914," *Journal of Contemporary History* 20 (1985): 503–520; for matter out of place, see Mary Douglas's foundational *Purity and Danger: An Analysis of the Concepts of Pollution and Taboo* (London: Routledge, 2000; first published 1966); for boundary objects, see Susan Leigh Star and James R. Griesemer, "Institutional Ecology, 'Translations' and Boundary Objects: Amateurs; and Professionals in Berkeley's Museum of Vertebrate Zoology, 1907/–39," *Social Studies of Science* 19 (1989): 387–420; for a recent discussion of the "spatial turn" in historical writing, Leif Jerram, "Space: A Useless Category for Historical Analysis?," *History and Theory* 52 (2013): 400–19. The classic scholarly text on space as a mode of analysis is Henri Lefebre, *The Production of Space* (Oxford: Blackwell, 1992; first published 1974).

14. Media scholars in particular have critiqued televisual spectacles of forensic science and criminal investigation, showing the ways in which a forensic gaze can create and mediate an abject gaze. Sue Tait, "Autoptic Vision and the Necrophilic Imaginary in CSI," *International Journal of Cultural Studies* 9, no. 1 (2006): 45–62; Tait, "Visualising Technologies and the Ethics and Aesthetics of Screening Death," *Science as Culture* 18, no. 3 (2009): 333–53; David P. Pierson, "Evidential Bodies: The Forensic and Abject Gazes in CSI: Crime Scene Investigation," *Journal of Communication Inquiry* 34, no. 2 (2010): 184–203.

15. For examples of different approaches to a gendered reading of the broad subject matter covered in our study, see Deborah Cameron and Elizabeth Frazer, *The Lust to Kill: A Feminist Investigation of Sexual Murder* (Cambridge: Polity Press, 1987); Jane Caputi, *The Age of Sex Crime* (Bowling Green, OH: Bowling Green State University Press, 1987); Judith R. Walkowitz, *City of Dreadful Delight, Narratives of Sexual Danger in Late-Victorian London* (Chicago: University of Chicago Press, 1992); Shani d'Cruz, *Crimes of Outrage: Sex, Violence and Victorian Working Women* (London: University College London Press, 1998); Martin Wiener, *Men of Blood: Violence, Manliness, and Criminal Justice in Victorian England* (Cambridge: Cambridge University Press, 2004); Lisa Dowling, *The Subject of Murder: Gender, Exceptionality, and the Modern Killer* (Chicago: University of Chicago Press, 2013).

CHAPTER 1: THE ORIGINS OF CRIME SCENE INVESTIGATION

1. Hans Gross, *Handbuch für untersuchungsrichter als system der kriminalistik* (Graz: Leuschner & Lubensky, 1893). Translated by John Adam and J. Collyer Adam as *Criminal Investigation: A Practical Handbook* (Egmore, Madras: Krishnamachari, 1906), 209.

2. Ibid.

3. In a series of articles the historian Peter Becker has provided a valuable framework locating Gross within a set of disciplinary and practical trends in continental criminology. Becker places Gross as part of a generation of German-speaking police and legal reformers in the second half of the nineteenth century whose main aim was to set the modern investigation and prosecution of crime on a systematic, standardized, objective footing. Peter Becker, "Objective Distance and Intimate Knowledge: On the Structure of Criminalistic Observation and Description," in P. Becker and W. Clark, eds., *Little Tools of Knowledge* (Ann Arbor: University of Michigan Press, 2001), 197–235; Becker, "Zwischen Tradition und Neubeginn: Hans

Gross und die Kriminologie und Kriminalistik der Jahrhundertwende," in G. Heuer and A. Götz von Olenhusen, eds., *Die Gesetze des Vaters* (Marburg/Lahn: LiteraturWissenschaft, 2004), 259–78; Becker, "The Criminologists' Gaze at the Underworld: Toward an Archaeology of Criminological Writing," in P. Becker and R. F. Wetzell, eds., *Criminals and Their Scientists* (Cambridge: Cambridge University Press, 2006), 105–33. For further biographical detail, see Roland Grassberger, "Pioneers in Criminology XIII—Hans Gross (1847–1915)," *Journal of Criminal Law and Police Science*, 47 (1957), 397–405.

4. The publication of Gross's text was a "watershed event" according to a recent assessment, "the first comprehensive textbook to systematically cover the integrated philosophy and practice of scientific criminal investigation, forensic analysis, and crime reconstruction. Its philosophies have not been diminished by the passage of time and should be required study for any student of these subjects." W. J. Chisum and B. E. Turvey, "A History of Crime Reconstruction," in Chisum and Turvey, eds., *Crime Reconstruction* (Waltham, MA: Elsevier Academic Press, 2011), 30, 32. The same authors regard Locard's "foundational research, publications, and the development of practice standards" as "nothing short of massive" (22–23).

5. Gross, *Handbook*, xxi.

6. Ibid., xxvi.

7. Ibid.

8. Gross's attention to the (interlinked) physical and mental aspects of investigator discipline is a recurrent theme in this chapter as well as in chapter 5. It is worth pointing out that his emphasis on mental discipline is a striking and thoroughly worked through precursor to the recent (re)discovery of the dangers of "cognitive contamination" in forensic practice in general, and in CSI in particular. In the words of Iteil Dror, a leading researcher in this emergent field, "Just as forensic examiners are well aware and take great steps to minimize physical contamination of the evidence, they also must be aware and take steps to minimize cognitive contamination." Presumably without having engaged extensively with Gross's writings, Dror asserts that, since the emergence of forensic science "about 100 years ago," this second source of contamination has been a matter of "systematic neglect." Iteil Dror, "Cognitive Neuroscience in Forensic Science: Understanding and Utilizing the Human Element," *Philosophical Transactions of the Royal Society B* 370 (2015): 1–8, 4, 1. For a magisterial analysis of distinct historical forms of objectivity, into which Gross's self-reflexive account fits as an interesting wrinkle on the interlaced cognitive, technical and emotional characteristics associated with the late-nineteenth- and early-twentieth-century regime of "mechanical objectivity," see Lorraine Daston and Peter Galison, *Objectivity* (Cambridge, MA: Zone Books, 2007).

9. Dror, "Cognitive Neuroscience," 1.

10. Ibid., 2–3.

11. For a nuanced historical account of fin-de-siècle legal and scientific discussions on the relative value of human and material testimony, see Tal Golan, *Laws of Man and Laws of Nature: A History of Scientific Expert Testimony* (Cambridge, MA: Harvard University Press, 2006), ch. 6.

12. Gross, *Handbook*, 16.

13. Ibid.

14. Ibid.

15. Ibid., 17.

16. Ibid.

17. Ibid., 123.

18. Ibid., 126.

19. Ibid., 126–7.

20. Ibid., 128.

21. Ibid., 130.

22. Ibid.

23. Ibid., emphasis original.

24. Ibid., 195–96.

25. Ibid., 132–33.

26. Ibid., 468.

27. Gross's graphic approach has affinities with those being developed in contemporaneous field sciences. Gavin Lucas, for example, notes the shift in late nineteenth-century archeological manuals away from artifact-based illustration to graphic representations of the site as a space of systematic excavation and investigation. Robert Kohler discussion of the introduction of the quadrat into ecological surveys is also relevant: the quadrat similarly functioned as a means of disciplining the surveyor by circumventing the human tendency to focus on (and thus to overestimate the numbers of) "attractive" plants. Gavin Lucas, *Critical Approaches to Fieldwork: Contemporary and Historical Archaeological Practice* (London: Routledge, 2001), 23, 24; Robert Kohler, *Landscapes and Labscapes: Exploring the Lab-Field Border in Biology* (Chicago: University of Chicago Press, 2002), ch. 4, esp. 100–108. Also of interest is Bruno Latour's analysis of the interactive field-sampling strategies of Amazonian pedology, geography, and botany in chapter 2 of *Pandora's Hope: Essays on the Reality of Science Studies* (Cambridge, MA: Harvard University Press, 1999).

28. For an excellent analysis of contemporary "chain of custody" practice, see Michael Lynch, Simon A. Cole, Ruth McNally, and Kathleen Jordan, *Truth Machine: The Contentious History of DNA Fingerprinting* (Chicago: University of Chicago Press, 2008), ch. 4.

29. Gross, *Handbook*, 49.

30. Ibid., 143–45.

31. Ibid., 553–54.

32. Ibid., 556.

33. Ibid., 555, 561.

34. Ibid., 556.

35. Ibid., 557.

36. Ibid., 578. Efforts made by perpetrators to remove blood stains may prove of evidential value in themselves: "it is possible to deduce from the manner in which a portion of wall has been removed, the spot where the largest part of the drop of blood has lain, the general bearing of the stains, the direction of the small splashes, and the instrument with which the wall has been scraped, etc." (578).

37. Ibid., 565.

38. Ibid., 567.

39. Ibid., 569. Gross provides similar level of material details for the handling of other crime scene surfaces, e.g. for walls: "To detach traces of blood from a wall its surface must be submitted to a preliminary inspection. If it has been several times whitewashed, it is best to attempt to raise the thin sheets of dried whitewash; but if the wall has never been whitewashed, or but once, it is necessary to raise at the same time a portion of the mortar" (570).

40. Ibid., 568.

41. Ibid., 572.

42. Ibid., 587. To illustrate poor practice, Gross cited a case in which a policeman took a blood-stained handkerchief round the neighborhood in a failed effort to identify its owner, after which it was submitted for analysis: "But in what a condition were now the stains of blood? Instead of the shining and thick crusts of before, there were only insignificant marks, the last traces of the blood absorbed by the cloth. And with what amount of certainty could it subsequently be stated that they were really original blood-stains?" (587).

43. Ibid., 589–90.

44. Ibid., 589.

45. Ibid., 155.

46. Ibid., 154–55.

47. Ibid., 151.

48. Ibid., xxi.

49. Ibid., 187.

50. Ibid., 149.

51. Ibid., 188.

52. The only discussion of the morphological significance of hair was an extended case narrative involving an expert's erroneous declaration of identity between two samples, thereby illustrating the dangers of such evidence: "We learn from this case that even the fact that distinctive signs of quite exceptional character are to be found in both the specimens examined, does not always prove that the hair under comparison is indeed hair coming from the same head." Gross, *Handbook*, 202–3.

53. Ibid., 194.

54. Ibid., 195.

55. Johann Ludwig Casper, *Practical Handbook of Forensic Medicine* (London: New Sydenham Society, 1861), 1:87, emphasis added.

56. Ibid., 1:195. This is not to say that Casper's text is devoid of exhortations for investigative rigor. However, for him this is directed at the medical encounter with the corpse—both in the need for a systematic approach to the post-mortem examination and for a corresponding emotional discipline.

57. Gross, *Handbook*, 211.

58. Ibid.

59. Ibid., 212.

60. Ibid., 163, 213.

61. Edmond Locard, *L'enquête criminelle et les méthods scientifiques* (Paris: Flammarion, 1920). Locard's biography is sketched in Michel Mazévet, *Edmond Locard: Le Sherlock Holmes français* (Brignais: Editions des Traboules, 2006). Douglas Starr's *The Killer of Little Shepherds: The case of the French Ripper and the Birth of Forensic Science* (London: Simon and Schuster, 2011) provides an excellent and accessible outline of late nineteenth-century French criminalistics.

62. Locard, "The Analysis of Dust Traces: Part I," *American Journal of Police Science* 1 (1930): 276–98, 276.

63. Ibid., 277. We discuss the interplay between criminalistics manuals and detective fiction in chapter 2.

64. Ibid., 278.

65. Ibid., 279–80.

66. Ibid., 279.

67. Both Locard and before him Gross cited Liebig's maxim that "dirt is an object found in a place where it does not belong." Locard, "Analysis of Dust Traces: Part I," 278; Gross, *Handbook*, 211. For them, however, Liebig's observation was only the start of an analytical regime that sought to make sense of misplaced matter. The resonance with Mary Douglas's classic discussion is evident.

68. Locard, "Analysis of Dust Traces: Part I," 287–88.

69. Ibid., 282–83.

70. Ibid., 282.

71. Ibid., 284.

72. Useful background for this model of scientific excavation can be found in Stephen Dyson, *In Pursuit of Ancient Pasts: A History of Classical Archaeology in the Nineteenth and Twentieth Centuries* (New Haven: Yale University Press, 2006); Philippa Levine, *The Amateur and the Professional: Antiquarians, Historians and Archaeologists in Victorian England, 1838–1886* (Cambridge: Cambridge University Press, 1986); Lucas, *Critical Approaches*; Bruce Trigger, *A History of Archaeological Thought* (Cambridge: Cambridge University Press, 1989); and Richard Morris, *Time's Anvil: England, Archaeology and the Imagination* (London: Weidenfeld & Nicolson, 2012).

73. Augustus Henry Lane-Fox Pitt-Rivers, *Excavations in Cranborne Chase, Near Rushmore, on the Borders of Dorset and Wiltshire*, 4 vols. (London, 1887–98), 1:xvi–xvii. We are indebted to Boris Santander Pizarro for suggesting Pitt-Rivers as a point of reference for the argument developed here.

74. Ibid. As Lucas has observed, recording every detail required a new set of graphic tools as well as a new attitude. In contrast to traditional archeological texts that were illustrated by artifacts—signifying their value as objects in themselves—*Excavations* was filled with plans and sections that plotted the site as a space of excavation and investigation. Lucas, *Critical Approaches*, 19–27. As we argue elsewhere, a similar graphic discipline is discernible in Gross's plan of systematic crime scene investigation. Ian Burney and Neil Pemberton, "Making Space for Criminalistics: Hans Gross and *fin-de-siècle* CSI," *Studies in History and Philosophy of Science Part C: Studies in History and Philosophy of Biological and Biomedical Sciences* 44, no. 1 (2013): 16–25.

75. Pitt-Rivers, *Excavations*, 3:9, cited in Levine, *Amateur*, 34.

76. W. M. Flinders Petrie, *Methods and Aims in Archaeology* (New York: Macmillan, 1904), vii.

77. Ibid., 5.

78. Ibid., 48. "The unpardonable crime in archaeology," Petrie continues, "is destroying evidence which can never be recovered and every discovery does destroy evidence unless it is intelligently recorded. Our museums are ghastly charnel-houses of murdered evidence; the dry bones of objects are there, bare of all the facts of grouping, locality, and dating which would give them historical life and value."

79. For a suggestive outline of this argument, see Gavin Lucas, *Understanding the Archaeological Record* (Cambridge: Cambridge University Press 2012), 20–29.

80. Locard, *L'enquête criminelle*, 258.

81. Locard, "The Analysis of Dust Traces: Part III," *American Journal of Police Science* 1 (1930): 496–514, 506–7. Locard's second article engaged in an extended technical survey of

the characteristic macro- and microscopical appearances of a range of dust traces, detailing for example sixteen varieties of flour, twenty-one constituents of mud, and an analytical table of seed and textile traces.

82. Ibid., 498.

83. Ibid., 506–7.

84. Ibid., 506.

CHAPTER 2: CRIME SCENES BEFORE CSI

1. For background, see Haia Shpayer-Makov, *The Ascent of the Detective: Police Sleuths in Victorian and Edwardian England* (Oxford: Oxford University Press, 2011). In her analysis, even Scotland Yard, as the vanguard of national criminal investigation methods, was well behind its Continental counterparts in the provision of training and equipment that foregrounded investigative technique (50, 94–100).

2. The CID was itself formed to increase force discipline in the wake of a series of corruption scandals involving Met detectives. Shpayer-Makov discusses this context in *Ascent of the Detective*, 38–40.

3. Howard Vincent, *The Police Code, and General Manual of the Criminal Law*, 8th ed. (London: Francis Edwards, 1893).

4. Ibid., 72.

5. Ibid., 57.

6. Ibid., 109.

7. Act to Provide for the Attendance and Remuneration of Medical Witnesses at Coroners Inquests (6 & 7 Will. 4, c. 89). For a fuller discussion of the context for this act, see Ian Burney, *Bodies of Evidence: Medicine and the Politics of the English Inquest, 1830–1926* (Baltimore: Johns Hopkins University Press, 2000), ch. 4.

8. William A. Guy, *Principles of Forensic Medicine* (London: Henshaw, 1844), 274.

9. Ibid., 275.

10. Ibid., 278.

11. The classic formulation of this argument, for the nineteenth and early twentieth centuries, is in Christopher Lawrence, "Incommunicable Knowledge: Science, Technology and the Clinical Art in Britain 1850–1914," *Journal of Contemporary History* 20, no. 4 (1985): 503–20. Also highly relevant is his extension of the analysis to the interwar period, in his *Rockefeller Money, the Laboratory and Medicine in Edinburgh, 1919–1930* (Rochester, NY: University of Rochester Press, 2005), esp. ch. 2. For a recent attempt to link this clinical tradition to the figure of the detective, see Nicki Buscemi, "The Case of the Case History: Detecting the Medical Report in Sherlock Holmes," *Journal of Victorian Culture* 19, no. 2 (2014): 216–31.

12. Alfred Swaine Taylor, *The Principles and Practice of Medical Jurisprudence* (London: John Churchill & Sons, 1865), xxii.

13. Ibid., xxiii. For simplicity, the first edition of Taylor's *Principles* is used as a guide to the conventional advice provided to would-be medico-legal witnesses over the course of the nineteenth century. A review of editions of Taylor's treatises for the remainder of the century has not identified any changes of significance that would affect this analysis.

14. Ibid., 423, emphasis added.

15. Ibid., 435.

16. Ibid., 427.

17. Ibid., 435–39, 452.

18. Ibid., 439, emphasis added.

19. Hans Gross, *Handbuch für untersuchungsrichter als system der kriminalistik* (Graz: Leuschner & Lubensky, 1893). Translated by John Adam and J. Collyer Adam as *Criminal Investigation: A Practical Handbook* (Egmore, Madras: Krishnamachari, 1906), 563–64.

20. Taylor, *Principles*, 424. Though blood featured as Taylor's primary example of trace evidence, he does provide brief consideration of other forms of more direct resonance with those at the center of Grossian and Locardian CSI—hair, fiber, and even "dust." His treatment of dust stems from commentary on three English cases that, despite the absence of the supporting framework found in the work of later Continental practitioners, nevertheless share an analytical sensibility. The case of *R v. Snipe* (York, 1852) provides a striking example; microscopic analysis of mud spots on a suspect's boots and clothes yielded "infusorial shells, and some rare aquatic vegetables, particles of soap, confervae and hairs from the seeds of groundsel." The analyst—a grammar school headmaster with an interest in local botany—testified that the mud of a ditch close to where the corpse was discovered "presented the same microscopic appearances as the mud from the prisoner's boots" and that his subsequent examination of "all the other ditches in the locality" yielded no other mud of comparable composition. Taylor, *Principles*, 441.

21. Andrew Wilson, Science Jottings, *Illustrated London News*, August 17, 1907, 236.

22. Basil Home Thomson, "A Manual for Detectives," *Times Literary Supplement*, May 31, 1907, 170.

23. For more on the distinction between Continental and Anglo-American evidentiary models, see Catherine Crawford, "Legalizing Medicine: Early Modern Legal Systems and the Growth of Medico-legal Knowledge," in Michael Clark and Catherine Crawford, eds., *Legal Medicine in History* (Cambridge: Cambridge University Press, 1994), 89–116; and Katherine Watson, *Forensic Medicine in Western Society: A History* (Abingdon, UK: Routledge, 2011), ch. 3.

24. For English preference for "information" over "detection," see Shpayer-Makov, *Ascent of the Detective*, 149. This concern about the potential of Gross's work to unrealistically raise public expectation about the declarative powers of modern investigation foreshadows contemporary debates about the deleterious consequences of the so-called CSI effect. For a review and balanced analysis, see Simon A. Cole and Rachel Dioso-Villa, "Investigating the 'CSI Effect': Media and Litigation Crisis in Criminal Law," *Stanford Law Review* 61 (2009): 1335–73.

25. Charles Tempest Clarkson and J. Hall Richardson, *Police!* (London: Leadenhall Press, 1889), 272–73.

26. Arthur Griffiths, *Mysteries of Police and Crime: A General Survey of Wrongdoing and Its Pursuit* (London: Cassel & Co., 1899), 1:445.

27. *Daily Mail*, August 26, 1908, 5.

28. *Daily Mail*, August 31, 1908, 5.

29. "A Bad System," *Daily Mail*, September 3, 1908, 4.

30. F.B., "Crime Detection," *Daily Mail*, September 3, 1908, 5.

31. G. R. Sims, "Crime Detection: Defence of the Old System," *Daily Mail*, September 4, 1908, 5.

32. "Crime Detection: Blunders Committed in a Famous Case," *Daily Mail*, September 12, 1908, 6.

33. C. Ainsworth Mitchell, *Science and the Criminal* (Boston: Little, Brown, 1911), 2.

34. Raymond Fosdick, *European Police Systems* (New York: Century, 1915), 366–67.

35. Edmond Locard, *Policiers de roman et policiers de laboratoire* (Paris: Payot, 1924), 15. Here and elsewhere translations are our own.

36. Ibid., 12, 14–15.

37. By drawing together techniques that were previously only articulated as separate domains of knowledge and practice (and indeed at times inventing new ones), Holmes created an integrated language of police science, a feat rivaled in Locard's estimation only by Gross himself. In his exploration of Holmes's genius, Locard devotes particular attention to the elements of CSI that we have outlined thus far. This distinguished Holmes from Dupin, whom Locard views as an armchair logician content to work with information gathered secondhand. Gaboriau's Lecoq improves on Poe's creation, in that his adventures feature an added dimension—"the study of the technique of traces, the analysis of the crime conducted at the scene." Locard, *Policiers*, 63.

38. Ibid., 113.

39. Ian Burney, "Our Environment in Miniature: Dust and the Early Twentieth-Century Forensic Imagination," *Representations* 121 (2013): 31–59; discusses, among others, Ronald Thomas, *Detective Fiction and the Rise of Forensic Science* (Cambridge: Cambridge University Press, 1999), 75; and Melissa Littlefield, "Historicizing *CSI* and Its Effect(s): The Real and the Representational in American Scientific Detective Fiction and Print News Media, 1902–1935," *Crime Media Culture* 7 (2011): 133–48, 134.

40. Frank suggests, furthermore, that it was the function of the detective story to explore this new model of "conjectural" meaning production and the contingent world that it called into being, and in particular to highlight the fragility of the trace record, in which fragmentary remains preserved by chance were processed from an equally arbitrary, hypothetical, and imaginative interpretive position. This level of reflexivity is absent from the vision of CSI that we are analyzing here. Lawrence Frank, *Victorian Detective Fiction and the Nature of Evidence* (Basingstoke, UK: Palgrave, 2003). Historicizing the epistemic status of minor, and unintentional, trace evidence, of course, resonates with Carlo Ginzburg's classic articulation of the "conjectural paradigm" in his "Morelli, Freud and Sherlock Holmes: Clues and Scientific Method," *History Workshop Journal* 9 (1980): 5–36.

41. R. Austin Freeman trained as an apothecary and then studied medicine at Middlesex Hospital, qualifying in 1887. He then entered the Colonial Service and was sent to West Africa. In 1891 he returned to England suffering from blackwater fever and, unable to find a permanent medical position, turned to writing. His first detective stories, *The Adventures of Romney Pringle*, appeared under the pseudonym of Clifford Ashdown in 1902. These were followed by *The Red Thumb Mark* (1907), written under his own name, in which Thorndyke makes his debut. For more on Freeman, see Norman Donaldson, *In Search of Dr. Thorndyke: The Story of R. Austin Freeman's Great Scientific Investigator and His Creator* (Bowling Green, OH: Bowling Green University Press, 1971). Shorter accounts of Freeman and his creation include J. K. Van Dover, "From Sherlock Holmes to Dr. Thorndyke: Arguments for the Morality of Science," *Clues: A Journal of Detection* 16, no. 1 (1995): 1–12; Charles Rzepka, *Detective Fiction* (Cambridge: Polity, 2005), 139–40; Joseph Kestner, *The Edwardian Detective, 1901–1915* (Aldershot, UK: Ashgate, 2000), 149–57; and Martin A. Kayman, "The Short Story from Poe to Chesterton," in Martin Priestman, ed., *Cambridge Companion to Crime Fiction* (Cambridge: Cambridge University Press, 2003), 47–48.

42. Kayman, "Short Story," 47. Dorothy Sayers, in a contemporary assessment, paid tribute to Freeman's "unique position in the history of detective fiction," crediting him above all others with shifting interest from casual thrill to the rigors of science: "In taking the scientific stuff seriously, Dr Freeman opened up a new field of interest which nobody has ever explored so thoroughly as he. He can get as much excitement out of the melting-point of platinum as a lesser man can get out of a whole bushel of death-rays." He was, however, in her view "becoming a little too much addicted to the analysis of dust." *Sunday Times*, October 22, 1933, 7.

43. Littlefield's "Historicizing *CSI*" makes this point, as does Eyal Segal's "Closure in Detective Fiction," *Poetics Today* 31 (2010): 153–215, 184–89. We are grateful to Simon Stern for pointing out the relevance of Freeman's narrative innovation to this overarching argument.

44. For a parallel argument on the use of visualizing techniques in the *CSI* series, see Corinna Kruse, "Producing Absolute Truth: *CSI* Science as Wishful Thinking," *American Anthropologist* 112 (2010): 79–91.

45. R. Austin Freeman, *John Thorndyke's Cases* (London, 1909), http://www.feedbooks.com/book/2062/john-thorndyke-s-cases, preface, 4.

46. Freeman, "The Stranger's Latchkey," in *Thorndyke's Cases*, 62.

47. Ibid., 63. "Sermons in Dust" was the chapter title for the 1937 Thorndyke novel *Felo-de-Se*.

48. Freeman, "The Anthropologist at Large," in *Thorndyke's Cases*, 76–77.

49. Freeman, "A Message from the Deep Sea," in *Thorndyke's Cases*, 175.

50. Ibid., 180.

51. Ibid., 183.

52. Ibid., 194.

53. Ibid., 196.

54. The original book-length biography is Douglas G. Browne and E. V. Tullett, *Bernard Spilsbury: His Life and Cases* (London: Companion Book Club, 1952). See also Colin Evans, *The Father of Forensics: How Sir Bernard Spilsbury Invented Modern CSI* (London: Icon Books, 2007); Andrew Rose, *Lethal Witness: Sir Bernard Spilsbury, Honorary Pathologist* (London: Stroud, 2007); and Jane Robins, *The Magnificent Spilsbury and the Case of the Brides in the Bath* (London: John Murray, 2011).

55. For a fuller discussion of the debates over specialist pathologists, see Burney, *Bodies of Evidence*, ch. 4, esp. 122–36; see also Jennifer Ward, "Origins and Development of Forensic Medicine and Forensic Science in England, 1823–1946" (PhD diss., Open University, 1993), ch. 5. For mortuaries, see Burney, *Bodies of Evidence*, ch. 3, esp. 86–92.

56. Norman Ambage and Michael Clark, "Unbuilt Bloomsbury: Medico-Legal Institutes and Forensic Science Laboratories in England between the Wars," in Michael Clark and Catherine Crawford, eds., *Legal Medicine in History* (Cambridge: Cambridge University Press, 1994), 293–313, 301.

CHAPTER 3: MURDER AT "THE CRUMBLES"

1. Colin Evans, *The Father of Forensics: How Sir Bernard Spilsbury Invented Modern CSI* (London: Icon Books, 2009), 136–37.

2. We have outlined our notion of "celebrity pathology" in earlier work: Ian Burney and Neil Pemberton, "Bruised Witnesses: Bernard Spilsbury and the Performance of Early

Twentieth-Century English Forensic Pathology," *Medical History* 55 (2011): 41–60; and Ian Burney and Neil Pemberton, "The Rise and Fall of Celebrity Pathology," *British Medical Journal* 341 (2010): 1319–21.

3. This discussion of the Crumbles case is based on investigative and trial documents at the National Archives, Kew (hereafter, TNA); and Edgar Wallace, *The Trial of Patrick Mahon* (London: Geoffrey Bles, 1928).

4. TNA, DPP 1/78, letter reviewing police contributions to the case written by Chief Inspector Savage to Superintendent Wensley, August 5, 1924, 2.

5. To detectives Mahon gave a detailed and graphic account of the dismemberment of Kaye's body: "I boiled some of the flesh in a pot. I burnt the head in an ordinary fire, it was finished in three hours. The poker went through the head when I poked it. The next day I broke the skull and put the pieces in the dust bin. The thigh bone I burned. It is surprising what a room fire will burn. There is one in the back sitting room, and one in the front sitting room. You will find some bones there. Her clothes are still there. The reason for going for the bag was because I was returning to the bungalow that night to get some more flesh." TNA, DPP 1/78, further statement of Patrick Herbert Mahon, May 2, 1924, 1.

6. Mahon described the struggle in these words:

> At this time we were in the front sitting-room, the coal cauldron was at the side of the fireplace in the sitting-room where we were. My body of course being on top when she fell, her hold relaxed a bit and she lay apparently stunned or dead. The events of the next few seconds I cannot remember except as a nightmare of horror, for I saw blood beginning to ooze from Miss Kaye's head where she had struck the cauldron. I did my best to revive her, and I simply could not at the time say whether I strangled her or whether she died of the fall, but from the moment she fell and struck her head she did not move.

TNA, DPP 1/78, further statement of Patrick Mahon, May 5, 1924, Scotland Yard.

7. The house acquired this name when it was used as an officer's residence for the coast guard.

8. TNA, DPP 1/78, Superintendent David Sinclair's evidence to the inquest on Emily Kaye, June 4, 1924.

9. TNA, DPP 1/78, letter reviewing police contributions to the case written by Chief Inspector Savage to Superintendent Wensley, August 5, 1924, 2.

10. Using police, Home Office, and court files at the National Archives, we conducted a survey of just under eighty murder cases in which Spilsbury was involved over the course of his career, to determine how many times he actually visited the crime scene. He did so in only one out of every ten instances. There was no immediately obvious pattern of circumstances to explain the cases where he did make a visit, though, as with our examination of the Crumbles, careful scrutiny of each instance would no doubt yield a set of case-specific reasons.

11. TNA, DPP 1/78, Bernard Spilsbury's evidence, Committal Court, June 6, 1924.

12. TNA, DPP 1/78, Bernard Spilsbury's evidence to the inquest on Emily Kaye, June 4, 1924.

13. Ibid.

14. Ibid.

15. Ibid.

NOTES TO PAGES 69–75   211

16. TNA, DPP 1/78, letter reviewing police contributions to the case written by Chief In-spector Savage to Superintendent Wensley, August 5, 1924, 5. For a historical account of dogs and homicide investigation, see Neil Pemberton, "'Bloodhounds as Detectives': Dogs, Slum Stench and Late-Victorian Murder Investigation," *Cultural and Social History* 10 (2013), 68–91.

17. Though, according to medico-legal literature, it was possible to identify signs of strangulation in bodily organs, the putrid and decomposed state of the organs prevented "the [pathological] signs of death from strangulation being detected." TNA, DPP 1/78, Ber-nard Spilsbury's evidence to the inquest on Emily Kaye, June 4, 1924.

18. Ibid.

19. E.g., "I was shown many articles of clothing that were blood stained and greasy"; "in the dining room was a two gallon saucepan." TNA, DPP 1/78, Bernard Spilsbury's evidence, Committal Court, June 6, 1924.

20. TNA, DPP 1/78, Superintendent David Sinclair's evidence to the inquest on Emily Kaye, June 4, 1924.

21. Spilsbury's blood work is customarily seen as evidence of his embrace of CSI-style trace hunting. Indeed, Evans goes as far as expunging the CSI labors of police investigators from the historical record, insisting that Spilsbury was solely responsible for detecting the pool of blood in the living room. According to Evans, in the lounge where Mahon said the fight had occurred, Spilsbury detected "some rubbing where the paint had flaked off, but nothing, no mark or indentation to support Mahon's claim that the axe had struck with suf-ficient force to snap its handle. What he did find were bloodstains on the bottom right corner of the door, which had spread onto the adjoining floor." Evans, *Father of Forensics*, 137–38.

22. For an account of this work see, TNA, DPP 1/78, Superintendent David Sinclair's evi-dence to the inquest on Emily Kaye, June 4, 1924, 12; and TNA, DPP 1/78, Superintendent David Sinclair's evidence to the Committal Court, June 8, 1924.

23. Traces of blood were also detected on the door's underside edge. These stains, it fol-lowed, must have been caused by the door swinging over a pool of blood sitting on top of the carpet, before the carpet had been scrubbed to remove the stain. TNA, DPP 1/78, Superinten-dent David Sinclair's evidence to the Committal Court, June 8, 1924.

24. TNA, DPP 1/78, John Webster's evidence to the Committal Court, June 8, 1924.

25. TNA, DPP 1/78, "*R v. Patrick Herbert Mahon*: Trial Transcripts of Shorthand Notes of the Trial," 134.

26. Ibid., 139.

27. Ibid., 133.

28. Ibid., 111–16.

29. Ibid., 140.

30. Ibid., 135–36.

31. Ibid., 140.

32. Ibid., 136.

33. Ibid., 137.

34. Ibid., 261.

35. Ibid., 262.

36. Ibid.

37. Ibid., 25.

38. Ibid., 26.

39. Ibid.

40. TNA, DPP 1/78, letter reviewing police contributions to the case written by Chief Inspector Savage to Superintendent Wensley, August 5, 1924, 6–7.

41. *"Mahon:* Trial Transcripts," 26.

42. TNA, DPP 1/78, letter reviewing police contributions to the case written by Chief Inspector Savage to Superintendent Wensley, August 5, 1924, 4–5.

43. TNA, MEPO 3/1605, murder bag correspondence, August 8, 1924.

44. Evans, *Father of Forensics,* 148.

45. Andy Williams, *Forensic Criminology* (London: Routledge, 2014), 171.

46. A recent crime procedural novel written by Tony Parson entitled *The Murder Bag* draws upon the mythology surrounding Spilsbury and the eponymous case: "Murder bags were where modern detective work began. . . . They had two of them in the Yard from 1925. Always packed and ready to go. . . . The Murder bags came in when Sir Bernard Spilsbury saw a detective handling a dismembered body with his bare hands. They were the start of modern homicide investigation." Tony Parsons, *The Murder Bag* (London: Century, 2014), 61.

47. TNA, MEPO 3/1605, Metropolitan Police chief commissioner to home secretary, October 29, 1924.

48. TNA, MEPO 3/1605, C.I.D. New murder bag, c. September 1934.

CHAPTER 4: CELEBRITY PATHOLOGY AND THE SPECTACLE OF MURDER INVESTIGATION

1. For skillful analyses of murder, popular culture and crime reporting, see Shani d'Cruz, "Intimacy, Professionalism and Domestic Homicide in Interwar Britain: the Case of Buck Ruxton," *Women's History Review* 16, no. 5 (2007): 701–22; and, more recently, Rosalind Cronin, *Victorian Victorians: Popular Entertainment in Nineteenth-Century London* (Manchester: Manchester University Press, 2012). For a broad historical account of the politics and changing practices of crime journalism across nineteenth- and twentieth-century Britain, see Judith Rowbotham, Kim Stevenson, and Samantha Pegg, *Crime News in Modern Britain: Press Reporting and Responsibility 1820–2010* (Basingstoke: Palgrave 2013).

2. Martin Conboy, *The Press and Popular Culture* (London: Sage, 2002), 101–7, 118–33.

3. It was the *London Evening Standard* that gave the Crumbles holiday cottage the horrific title, the "bungalow of death." "Woman's Identity Solved," *London Evening Standard,* May 5, 1924, 1. The gothic and melodramatic framings of the Mahon case are beyond the scope and ambition of this study. For a historical approach to reading of the complex configuration of melodrama, Gothicism, and homicide journalism, see Judith Walkowitz's sophisticated and pathbreaking account of the Jack the Ripper murders. Judith Walkowitz, *City of Dreadful Delight: Narratives of Sexual Danger in Late-Victorian London* (Chicago: Chicago University Press, 1992).

4. For an exemplary account of the boundary blurring between reality and fiction in the context of nineteenth-century detective stories, see Ronald Thomas, *Detective Fiction and the Rise of Forensic Science* (Cambridge: Cambridge University Press, 1999).

5. "The Art of Detection," *Detective Magazine,* August 3, 1923, 307.

6. "Fearful Crime in Bungalow," *Western Morning News and Mercury,* May 9, 1924, 5.

7. The press reinforced the image of a guilty landscape with the information that several years earlier the beach had served as a shallow grave. In 1920, less than a hundred yards from the bungalow, the decomposing body of a woman named Irene Munro, a victim of violent

sexual assault, had been discovered. The discovery of a second body appeared to be more than a morbid coincidence, Crumbles beach resembling if not a perpetrator, then a silent witness. In the words of the *Western Morning News* commentator, "The Crumbles bungalow is situated at the by-gone edge of the desolate Crumbles, made notorious by the Munro murder." "Fearful Crime in Bungalow."

8. "The Bungalow Crime," *Western Daily Press*, May 5, 1924, 10. For an in-depth discussion of driving and public discourses, see Sean O'Connell, *The Car in British Society: Class, Gender and Motoring, 1896–1939* (Manchester: Manchester University Press, 1998).

9. "Bungalow's Grim Secret," *Dundee Courier*, May 5, 1924, 5.

10. "Scenes at Bungalow Trial," *Hull Daily Mail*, July 19, 1924, 5.

11. "Bungalow Crime," 10.

12. One newspaper correspondent reported that at the end of the first day of the investigation "[the] keys were turned and the doors heavily sealed until" the morning. "The Lonely Cottage," *Daily Mail*, May 5, 1924, 9.

13. For instance, as the special correspondent for the London *Evening Standard* explained:

Hundreds of sight-seers visited to-day the lonely bungalow on the Crumbles where were found the mutilated remains of Miss Emily Kaye. "Early this morning," said a constable to me—today, "fourteen people arrived in a charabanc. They offered £1 each if I would allow them to go over the cottage." In order that access to the garden and bungalow shall be prevented there has been placed behind the little late-gate a hurdle which would have to be forced by someone going in. During the day the officer on duty stands outside the gate.

"Crumbles Crowds: Trippers Willing to Pay £1 to See Bungalow!," *London Evening Standard*, May 10, 1924, 2.

14. "Grim Bungalow Scene," *Daily Mirror*, May 9, 1924, 2.

15. "New Clues," *Daily Mail*, May 12, 1924, 9.

16. For an analytical account of poison and its scientific hunter the toxicologist, see Ian Burney, *Poison, Detection and the Victorian Imagination* (Manchester: University of Manchester, 2006). For a broad overview of poison in Victorian social and cultural life, see James C. Whorton, *The Arsenic Century: How Victorian Britain Was Poisoned at Home, Work, and Play* (Oxford: Oxford University Press, 2010). For a social history of the poisoner, see Katherine Watson, *Poisoned Lives: English Poisoners and Their Victims* (London: Continuum, 2004).

17. "New Clues," *Daily Mail*, May 12, 1924, 9.

18. "Crumbles Trial: Sir Bernard Spilsbury Tells of His Find at Bungalow," *Daily Mirror*, July 18, 1924, 15; "Mahon's Story of the Bungalow: What Dr Spilsbury Found," *Daily Express*, May 23, 1924, 1.

19. "Spilsbury of the Home Office," *Dundee Courier*, July 8, 1924, 3.

20. "Sir Bernard Spilsbury: Our Most Brilliant Solver of Complex Crimes," *Nottingham Evening Post*, May 24, 1924, 5

21. Ibid. Emphasis added.

22. In the literary tradition of Victorian and Edwardian crime fiction, as Haia Shpayer-Makov has most recently observed, Scotland Yard detectives were typically characterized "as not very discerning, often inept, unimaginative and devoid of the mental acuity that characterised the likes of Sherlock Holmes." Haia Shpayer-Makov, *The Ascent of the Detective:*

Police Sleuths in Victorian and Edwardian England (Oxford: Oxford University Press, 2011), ch. 6, 249.

23. It could be argued that the belief in Spilsbury as England's superdetective, single-handedly solving complex and demanding murder mysteries, indulged what Michael Saler has called the "ironic imagination," in which people were willing to believe that Sherlock Holmes was a real person. As Saler argues, the emergence of a polymorphous mass media by the turn of the twentieth century allowed its participants to immerse themselves in fantastical worlds. As a consequence, he argues, consciously pretending came to be a more and more socially acceptable and common experience. This phenomenon, he insists, is best seen in regard to the emergent fandom culture that formed around Holmes from the late nineteenth century onward. Michael Saler, " 'Clap If You Believe in Sherlock Holmes': Mass Culture and the Re-enchantment of Modernity, c.1890–1940," *Historical Journal* 46 (2003): 599–622.

24. "Dismembered Body in Locked Bungalow on Lonely Beach," *Daily Mirror,* May 5, 1924, 2.

25. "Lonely Cottage," 9.

26. "Gruesome Discovery in Lonely Bungalow," *Eastbourne Gazette,* May 7, 1924, 1.

27. "Lonely Cottage," 9.

28. Ibid.

29. "Bungalow Secret of Murdered Girl," *Daily Mirror,* May 6, 1924, 19.

30. For historical discussions of the historical emergence and formation of distinct cultures of celebrity and fame, see Leo Braudy, *The Frenzy of Renown: Fame and Its History* (Oxford: Oxford University Press, 1986); Fred Inglis, *A Short History of Celebrity* (Princeton: Princeton University Press, 2010); Gail Collins, *Scorpion Politics: Gossip, Celebrity and American Publics* (New York: Morrow, 1998); Richard de Cordova, *Picture Personalities: The Emergence of the Star System in America* (Urbana: University of Illinois Press, 1990); Frank Donoghue, *The Fame Machine: Book Reviewing and Eighteenth Century Literary Careers* (Stanford: Stanford University Press, 1996); Neal Garbler, *Life: The Movie; How Entertainment Conquered Reality* (New York: Knopf, 1990). For recent and useful critical reflections on celebrity as a historical category, see a cluster of interrelated commentaries in *Cultural and Social History* 8, no. 1 (2011): Simon Morgan, "Celebrity: Academic 'Pseudo Event' or a Useful Concept of Historians," 95–114; Ellis Cashmore, "Celebrity in the Twenty-First Century Imagination," 405–13; Rublack Ulinka, "Celebrity as Concept: An Early Modern Perspective," 399–403.

31. Scholars of cinematic celebrity argue that curiosity about actors outside of their film work is how the celebrity culture endemic to Hollywood commenced and flourished. See Cordova, *Picture Personalities*; Peter D. Marshall, *Celebrity and Power: Fame in Contemporary Culture* (Minneapolis: University of Minnesota Press, 2004); Edgar Morin, *The Stars* (Minneapolis: University of Minnesota Press, 2005)

32. It is worth quoting at length Judith Brown's description of the model of celebrity fame that emerged around and was embodied by Greta Garbo:

> The celebrity would not provide access to the lumpen detail that might mar the effect of her gorgeous surface; rather, she would fascinate through the absence of those details. . . . [Greta] Garbo was all-personality and at the same time none, (her most quoted line: "I want to be alone"). . . . Garbo's celebrity tells us something about the desiring structure through which we produce the category of star: her ambition for

celebrity was countered always by her resistance to it, her on-screen persona resolutely negated the qualities that suggest "personality."

J. Judith Brown, "Garbo's Glamour," in Aron Jaffe and Jonathan E. Goldman, eds., *Modernist Stars: Celebrity, Modernity and Culture* (Farnham, UK: Ashgate, 2010), 107–22, 108.

33. "London Letter: Real-Life Mr. Holmes," *Hull Daily Mail*, May 17, 1924, 2.

34. "Sir Bernard Spilsbury: Our Most Brilliant Solver of Complex Crimes," *Nottingham Evening Post*, May 24, 1924, 5.

35. "Scenes at Bungalow Trial," 5. During the trial of Mahon the press projected Spilsbury as medical hero, his actions and gestures part of the drama and of his performance in it. Given the disturbing nature of the evidence, Mr. Justice Avory ordered that no woman should serve on the jury, but on hearing the grisly details an elderly juryman collapsed during Curtis Bennett's opening speech, and at the judge's invitation, Spilsbury attended him, bringing him back to consciousness. "Mahon Trial Begins Afresh after the Collapse of a Juror," *Daily Mirror*, July 17, 1924, 2.

36. Spilsbury's celebrity and attractive surface represented a triumph over an older regime of expert personae and fame. Arguably, this prior model had been firmly anchored in the science of physiognomy, the intricacies and dictates of which the Victorian reading public was well versed. The underlying premise of physiognomy was that character and ability could be read scientifically in the physical morphology of the face. In public discourse Spilsbury's predecessors like Alfred Swaine Taylor were subjected to physiognomic readings and imaginings, in which his acumen as a keen observer of medico-legal and toxicological detail was evident in his penetrating eyes, clear brow, and resolute jawline. For an account of nineteenth-century physiognomy, see Sharrona Pearl, *About Faces: Physiognomy in Nineteenth-Century Britain* (Cambridge, MA: Harvard University Press, 2010).

37. Hans Gross, *Handbuch für untersuchungsrichter als system der kriminalistik* (Graz: Leuschner & Lubensky, 1893). Translated by John Adam and J. Collyer Adam as *Criminal Investigation: A Practical Handbook* (Egmore, Madras: Krishnamachari, 1906), 291.

38. Ibid.

39. Ibid., 292.

40. Ibid., emphasis original.

41. 173 Parl. Deb. H.C. (5th ser.) (May 15, 1924) col. 1529.

42. Ibid., col. 1530.

43. "Fresh Move by Police in Bungalow Murder Inquiries," *Dundee Courier and Argus*, May 12, 1924, 4.

44. See, for example, the description offered by a *Daily Sketch* news correspondent: "A number of amateur detectives searching near the bungalow have found among the shingle bones, which they have brought to police attention. In no case have these bones proved to be human." "Bungalow Search Ends," *Daily Sketch*, May 14, 1924, 2.

45. "Murder tourism" is a variant of the phenomena described by scholars as "dark tourism"—that is, travel to (or the exploration of) places associated with tragedy, suffering, or death. On Ripper murder tourism, see David Cunningham, "Living in the Slashing Grounds: Jack the Ripper, Monopoly Rent and the New Heritage," in Alexandra Warwick and Martin Willis, eds., *Jack the Ripper: Media, Culture and History* (Manchester: University of Manchester Press, 2007), 159–78. For analytical commentators on the modern-day phenomenon of dark tourism, see Leanne White and Elspeth Frew, eds., *Dark Tourism and Place*

Identity: Managing and Interpreting Dark Places (London: Routledge, 2013); Derek Dalton, *Dark Tourism and Crime* (London: Routledge, 2015); John Lennon and Malcolm Foley, eds., *Dark Tourism: The Attraction of Death and Disaster* (London: Continuum, 2000).

46. "Accused Man Attends Bungalow Inquest," *Daily Mirror*, May 8, 1924, 1.

47. Widely cited as evidence of the depravity of the crowd was the sight one entrepreneur selling bananas and chocolate from a large basket from within the crowd. "Morbid Curiosity: Disgraceful Scenes after Crumbles Inquest," *Nottingham Evening Post*, May 8, 1924, 1.

48. Ibid. For alternative accounts, see "Scandalous Crumbles Inquest Scene," *Daily Sketch*, May 8, 1924, 2; and "Bungalow of Horror," *News of the World*, May 11, 1924, 4.

49. "Horrid Women," *Hull Daily Mail*, May 19, 1924, 4.

50. The press sought to capture and document the full range of morbid behavior of the Crumbles crowds. One budding entrepreneur, it was reported, offered to buy all the wall flowers in the garden, explaining that he would cultivate them for sale and rename them "Miss Kaye." "Fresh Move by Police on Bungalow Crime Inquiries," *Dundee Courier and Argus*, May 12, 1924, 5.

51. "Another Discovery at Crumbles: Spectator Finds Bone under Boulder," *Manchester Guardian*, May 13, 1924, 9. In other newspaper reports the boy was named: "A little boy, named Hugget . . . , who, with his little sister Ellen, was among the crowd of people visiting the cottage, stumbled over a stone, knocking it out of the ground. Looking around, his sister noticed a small piece of bone about 6 inches long and about a 1/2 inch thick. Her brother picked it up and gave it to the police. It has since been forwarded to Sir Bernard Spilsbury." "New Miss Kaye Clue," *Daily Mail*, May 13, 1924, 7.

52. "Another Discovery," 9.

53. "Seeing the Bungalow," *Hull Daily Mail*, July 26, 1924, 1.

54. "Shilling Chamber of Horror," *News of the World*, July 27, 1924, 1. Newspapers went into graphic detail about the business practices behind the "shilling chamber of horror," exposing the attempts of the owner to legitimate the decision to open the bungalow for and charge tourists. According to the owner of the Crumbles bungalow, the fee covered the entertainment tax, and profits were meant to go to local charity—split between the Police Orphanage and the Eastbourne Hospital. When confronted with the allegation of being recipients of money raised through dark tourism, the Eastbourne Hospital stressed that that it would not accept any charitable donation raised in such circumstances, agreeing with media reports that the Bungalow murder tourism was crudely voyeuristic. "Seeing the Bungalow," *Hull Daily Mail*, July 26, 1924, 1.

55. "Shilling Chamber of Horror," 1.

56. "Bungalow of Death as a 'Fairground': Owner Bows to Public Opinion and Closes It to Sightseers," *Sunday News*, July 27, 1924, 1. Sightseers' fetishist sensibilities extended to a wash basin in which Mahon was supposed to have washed his blood-stained hands and an iron saucepan, still containing sediments of human fat. Emily Kaye's final box of chocolates was also reported to be a highlight.

CHAPTER 5: CSI IN ENGLISH TRANSLATION

1. W. Singleton, "Dust as a Clue," *Daily Mail*, June 27, 1924, 8.

2. "Sir Bernard Spilsbury and His Methods," *Sunday News*, February 8, 1925. Other descriptions of his prowess include "the prince of observers" ("How Scotland Yard Ob-

serves," *Daily Mail*, September 10, 1928) and "the scientific expert of the novelists come to life" ("A Man of the Moment," *Daily Telegraph*, November 28, 1928).

3. See ch. 3, n10.

4. Ian Burney and Neil Pemberton, "Bruised Witnesses: Bernard Spilsbury and the Performance of Early Twentieth-Century English Forensic Pathology," *Medical History* 55 (2011): 41–60. In this article we developed a detailed analysis of Spilsbury's role in the Thorne investigation. There we made no mention of Spilsbury as a crime scene investigator but instead devoted our attention to articulating his engagement with the evidentiary elements of the case arising from his encounters with the victim's body.

5. Helena Normanton, ed., *The Trial of Norman Thorne* (London: Geoffrey Bles, 1929), 120–37.

6. Ibid., 148–49.

7. We have two further observations to make on Spilsbury's relationship to CSI as a practice, both stemming from material deposited in the Wellcome Archives. The first provides additional confirmation of his disassociation from the crime scene. The Spilsbury collection is dominated by a series of index cards, running from 1905 to 1946, on which Spilsbury recorded findings from nearly seven thousand post-mortem investigations. Only a fraction of these examinations, of course, involved cases of suspected homicide, but nonetheless a hand search of the entire collection revealed just one card featuring a crime scene sketch. The second complicates this disassociation, in that it captures him directly engaging with the emergent discourse of CSI. In a lecture delivered to a conference of detectives held in Birmingham in January 1934, Spilsbury freely adopts discernibly Grossian language to urge a "complementary" relationship between forensic experts and police investigators—including the need for physical and cognitive restraint, and for systematic recording of trace matter found at the crime scene—no matter how seemingly trivial—prior to the scene being disturbed. Wellcome Archives: PP/SPI/D.7, Chief Constables' Conference no. 4, lecture by Spilsbury on "Medico-legal Principles and Police Investigations," 1934.

8. For a comprehensive discussion of Dixon's reformist agenda, see Norman Ambage, "The Origins and Development of the Home Office Forensic Science Service, 1931–1967" (PhD diss., University of Lancaster, 1987), ch. 1.

9. National Archives, Kew (hereafter, TNA), MEPO 2/4980, 1–2, 1.

10. *Yorkshire Post and Leeds Intelligencer*, November 21, 1935; *Daily Mirror*, November 21, 1935.

11. *Hull Daily Mail*, October 7, 1936.

12. TNA, MEPO 2/4971, Arthur Dixon to S. J. Baker, October 28, 1933.

13. TNA, HO 45/17085, Dixon memo, August 23, 1934, 1.

14. The terms of Symons appointment were, at an annual salary of £800, to advise on the development of local police laboratories and training arrangements, to maintain contact by correspondence and visits with, to record work undertaken in extant labs, to keep abreast of relevant technical literature, and to prepare Home Office bulletins on scientific aids to criminal investigation. TNA, HO 45/17085.

15. TNA, HO 45/16215, Arthur Dixon to F. G. Tryhorn, August 2, 1935. The course had originally been capped at twenty, but at Dixon's request Tryhorn agreed to an increased size. He had been delivering lectures to police officers since at least 1932–33, and in March 1934 had sent a course outline to R. M. Howe, assistant commissioner of the Metropolitan Police

and chair of subcommittee D. TNA, MEPO 2/4971. However, the 1935 outline provides the most detailed information on the course's structure and content.

16. TNA, HO 45/16215, chief constable to Arthur Dixon, Birmingham, July 22, 1935.

17. TNA, HO 45/16215, Detective-Sergeant Frederick Carter, "Report: 'Scientific Aids in the Detection of Crime,'" September 30, 1935, 1.

18. Ibid., 2–5.

19. TNA, HO 45/16215, Detective-Sergeant Frederick Carter, "Report: 'Scientific Aids in the Detection of Crime,'" October 24, 1935, 1.

20. Ibid., 2.

21. "Introduction," *Police Journal* 1 (1928): 1.

22. Ibid., 2. Five years later, the journal reaffirmed this practical commitment to the advancement of what was increasingly being identified as the Dixon committee's agenda. Though the journal was not directly tied to government departments, the editors embraced the interest taken in its progress by the Home Office and positioned it as a sanctioned ally in the reform project: the *Journal*'s work met with "warm appreciation in official quarters and is earnestly commended to all Police Forces as worthy of their generous and practical support." A. L. Dixon, "The New Series of the Police Journal," *Police Journal* 6 (1933): 1–3, 3.

23. Sgt. James Healy, "Qualifications of a Detective," *Police Journal* 7 (1934): 216–18, 217.

24. John J. Duncan, "The Investigation of a Murder Case," *Police Journal* 12 (1939): 218–41, 218–19.

25. Ibid., 220.

26. Ibid.

27. Ibid., 221.

28. Ibid., 225.

29. Arthur Cain, "Obtaining Information," *Police Journal* 9 (1936): 54–62, 58.

30. Ibid., 60.

31. Walter Martyn Else and James Main Garrow, *The Detection of Crime: An Introduction to Some Methods of Scientific Aid in Criminal Investigation, with Some Illustrations of the Methods Employed in the Preservation and Examination of Matter Relevant to the Investigation, Compiled Principally for the Use of Police Officers and Members of the Detective Branch* (London: Office of the Police Journal, 1934).

32. Ibid., 3.

33. Ibid., 137.

34. Ibid., 139.

35. F. G. Tryhorn, "The Assessment of Circumstantial Scientific Evidence," *Police Journal* 8 (1935): 404.

36. Ibid., 406–7.

37. F. G. Tryhorn, "Scientific Aids in Criminal Investigation, Part 1," *Police Journal* 9 (1936): 33–41, 38.

38. Ibid., 38–39.

39. F. G. Tryhorn, "Scientific Aids in Criminal Investigation, Part 2, Searching at the Scene of Crime," *Police Journal* 9 (1936): 152–64, 154, 155.

40. F. G. Tryhorn, "Scientific Aids in Criminal Investigation, Part 3, Searching and Packing," *Police Journal* 9 (1936): 303–17, 303.

41. Ibid., 304.

42. Ibid., 306.

43. Ibid., 305. The searching board's function as an instrumental aid to systematic spatial identification and recording of trace matter is reminiscent of innovations like the quadrat discussed in ch. 1, n27.

44. Ibid., 314.

45. Ibid., 315.

46. F. G. Tryhorn, "The Packing of Exhibits," *Police Journal* 8 (1935): 19–26, 20.

47. Tryhorn, "Searching and Packing," 316–17.

48. For an excellent analysis of the significance of chains of custody from a contemporary sociological position, see Michael Lynch, Simon A. Cole, Ruth McNally, and Kathleen Jordan, *Truth Machine: The Contentious History of DNA Fingerprinting* (Chicago: University of Chicago Press, 2008), especially ch. 4.

49. Regional laboratories were officially under the wing of the Home Office—and were the end result of a process through which local, highly individual initiatives were subsumed under its administrative oversight. By 1940, there were five laboratories providing coverage of the main regions of England and Wales: East Midlands (Nottingham), West Midlands (Birmingham); South Wales (Cardiff); Northwest (Preston); and Northeast (Wakefield). However, these labs had been recognized earlier as Home Office-sanctioned prototypes, beginning with Nottingham in June 1936. Readers seeking a full administrative account of the development of the network of regional forensic laboratories should consult Ambage's admirably detailed dissertation, "The Origins." Alison Adam's recently published monograph, *A History of Forensic Science: British Beginnings in the Twentieth Century* (Abingdon: Routledge, 2016), updates Ambage's account.

50. This is a reversal of the classic approach to lab-field relations, in which it is the gestures and protocols generated within the laboratory that are extended outward into the field such that, in Bruno Latour's phrasing, the lab is "brought to bear on an 'outside' situation and that situation is transformed so that it fits laboratory prescriptions." Bruno Latour, "Give Me a Laboratory and I Will Raise the World," in Karin Knorr-Cetina and Michael Mulkay, eds., *Science Observed: Perspectives on the Social Study of Science* (London: Sage, 1983), 141–70, 166. Our emphasis on how the requirements of the field configures laboratory practice echoes more recent work in reconceptualizing lab-field boundaries, including Robert Koehler's *Labscapes and Landscapes: Exploring the Lab-Field Border in Biology* (Chicago: University of Chicago Press, 2002); and Vanessa Heggie's "Why Isn't Exploration a Science?," *Isis* 105 (2014): 318–34.

51. TNA, HO 45/17710, C. T. Symons, "Some Notes on the Starting of Regional and Police Laboratories for Forensic Science," c. February 1936, 1–7, 3.

52. Ibid., 4. A set of draft rules based on Symons's notes and issued by Dixon's office in February 1936 provides still greater specificity on this fundamental "gatekeeping" stage, with instructions on how to treat parcels received by post and those received by messenger; how to handle damaged parcels; how, where, and by whom parcels should be opened—each stage accompanied by exhortations to formally note both adherence to and deviations from standard practice, to preserve all material associated with the processing of objects for possible future interrogation, and, in general, to exercise "the greatest caution." TNA, HO 45/17110, "Rules for the Safeguarding of Materials Submitted for Examination," 1–5, 2.

53. Symons, "Some Notes," 4.

54. Ibid., 3.

55. Ibid., 3–4.

56. Ibid., 5.

57. "Police of this City Can Teach the Yard—and the World," *Daily Express*, March 27, 1934.

58. Athelstan Popkess, "Pursuit by Science," *Police Journal* 8 (1935): 199–214, 205.

59. TNA, HO 45/18103, C. T. Symons, Nottingham: attempted murder by James Rowlson, present position of evidence, as given in court. April 1935, 1–3, 1.

60. TNA, HO 45/18103, Arthur Dixon memorandum, April 1935, 1–6, 4.

61. Ibid., 2–3.

62. TNA, HO 45/18103, C. T. Symons, note on visit to Nottingham, August 16, 1935, 1–3, 2.

63. Ibid., 3.

64. Dixon memorandum, 4.

65. TNA, HO 45/18103, Athelstan Popkess to Arthur Dixon, November 26, 1935

66. Symons, note on visit to Nottingham, 1.

67. TNA, HO 45/18103, Holden-Symons correspondence, December 1936.

68. Ibid.

69. TNA, HO 45/18103, brief particulars of cases dealt with in the laboratory, quarter ending December 31, 1936, 5.

70. TNA, HO 45/18103, case notes accompanying letter Holden to Symons, March 22, 1937.

71. Home Office, *Scientific Aids to Criminal Investigation: Instructional Pamphlet for the Use of Police Officers* (London: HMSO, 1936), 5–6.

CHAPTER 6: FORENSIC PATHOLOGY IN THE LANDSCAPE OF CSI

1. Norman Ambage and Michael Clark, "Unbuilt Bloomsbury: Medico-legal Institutes and Forensic Science Laboratories in England between the Wars," in Michael Clark and Catherine Crawford, eds., *Legal Medicine in History* (Cambridge: Cambridge University Press, 1994), 293–313.

2. "The Proposed Formation of a Medico-Legal Institute," *Transactions of the Medico-Legal Society* 19 (1925): 128–62, 137, 138.

3. Thomas Blench, "Crime Investigation in Paris," *Transactions of the Medico-Legal Society* 25 (1930–1931): 167–91, 182–83.

4. Ibid., 183–84.

5. For more on Trenchard's reformist enterprise, see Norman Ambage, "The Origins and Development of the Home Office Forensic Science Service, 1931–1967" (PhD diss., University of Lancaster, 1987), ch. 3; also Keith Laybourn and David Taylor, *Policing in England and Wales, 1918–39* (Basingstoke: Palgrave Macmillan, 2011), esp. ch. 4.

6. National Archives, Kew (hereafter, TNA), HO 45/20546, Maurice Drummond to Arthur Dixon, March 16, 1934.

7. TNA, MEPO 3/2540, Hugh Trenchard, "Note on Medico-Legal Department for the Metropolitan Police Force," October 1934, 2.

8. "Scotland Yard Will Soon Have a Crime Laboratory," *Daily Herald*, November 21, 1934.

9. Ibid. The *Times'* coverage of Hendon's opening was more focused on the lab's promise to develop a center of English excellence in trace investigation.

10. TNA, MEPO 3/2540, Hugh Trenchard to Lord Dixon, November 16, 1934, 5.

11. TNA, MEPO 3/2540, R. R. Scott to Hugh Trenchard, November 13, 1934, 2, 3, emphasis added. Another early indication of this divide is that, before deciding on Davidson, Trenchard explicitly rejected a Home Office suggestion of Symons as a suitable director for Hendon: "I

have satisfied myself," he wrote in a letter to Scott, "that Mr. C.T. Symons, who was mentioned to me and who did scientific criminal investigation work in Ceylon, would not be as suitable for the appointment as Dr. Davidson." TNA, MEPO 3/2540, October 26, 1934, 4.

12. TNA, HO 45/20547, docket minute, Metropolitan Police Laboratory, return for 1937.

13. TNA, HO 45/20547, Henry Holden memo, December 15, 1941, 1.

14. Ibid.

15. TNA, MEPO 2/9177, docket minute, November 2, 1936, 13.

16. TNA, MEPO 2/9177, undated memo addressed to assistant chief constable, 2.

17. TNA, HO 45/20547, Metropolitan Police Laboratory, note of conversation with Mr. Symons [n.d., c. 1937].

18. TNA, HO 45/18103, Forensic Science Laboratory (East Midlands Area), Nottingham, November 1936, 1–7, 1.

19. Ibid., 2. In a short article written for his regional police magazine, the lab director-designate Henry Holden stressed the need for a liberal regime of scene-lab interaction, encouraging each officer "to make the fullest use of the facilities provided by the Laboratory. The material he submits may prove unsuitable for further investigation but it may, on the other hand, prove to be the keystone of the case." TNA, HO 45/18103, Holden typescript, "The Laboratory and the Police Officer," December 1936, 1–3, 3.

20. TNA, HO 45/18104, Dixon remarks to a conference of chief constables of East Midlands October 1936, 2.

21. C. T. Symons, "Scientific Aids in Prospect," *Metropolitan Police College Journal* 1 (1935): 30–34, 31.

22. TNA, HO 45/20547, Phillip Game to Alexander Maxwell, October 20, 1938, 4.

23. Home Office, *Report of the Departmental Committee on Detective Work and Procedure*, 5 vols. (London: HMSO, 1938), 5:12.

24. Game to Maxwell, 5.

25. TNA, HO 45/20547. Phillip Game to Alexander Maxwell, January 16, 1939, 1–2.

26. TNA, HO 45/20547, Home Office memo, March 30, 1939, 1. The experience of the regional laboratories, the memo continued, "has demonstrated conclusively that, given full collaboration between the scientific staffs and Chief Officers of Police, the system can make an invaluable contribution to the efficiency of the detective work of the forces" (2).

27. TNA, HO 45/20547, Alexander Maxwell to Phillip Game, April 5, 1939, 2. In a response dated April 11, 1939, Game wrote, "It is not that we place a small value on the help science can give us but that we feel we can get a good deal of it just as well or better and certainly cheaper, from other sources than a laboratory of our own. . . . The picture you draw of a team of scientific workers developing their scientific knowledge along lines which are specially valuable for police purposes is very pleasing in theory but I confess to very great doubt as to how far it can become a fact in a police laboratory" (1).

28. TNA, HO 45/20547, Home Office memo, May 10, 1939, 2.

29. TNA, HO 45/20547, Home Office memo, March 4, 1941, 1–3, 2.

30. Ibid., 3. It is worth noting here that one of the forensic laboratories that developed under Dixon's regime had a medical director: Birmingham's James Webster. Webster, however, was cut from a different cloth than was Spilsbury. A police surgeon used to working with and for police, Webster did not seek to extend the primacy of pathology within the laboratory. When consulted in late 1937 on the desirable professional qualifications for the director of the proposed Preston lab, Webster compared the value of a pathologist to that of a

biologist and came out in favor of the latter: "So far as routine laboratory examination went, the only thing a biologist could not do which a pathologist could do was post-mortem work and examination of pathological sections. On the other hand, a competent biologist can carry out all the routine tests for semen, blood, etc., and in addition can give to a laboratory, expert knowledge in such matters as woods, fibres, etc.—all matters completely out with the ken of a pathologist." Webster bolstered his argument by recourse to the relative infrequency of murder cases: "It is obvious that the sensational types of crime such as murder upon which a pathologist has to work to justify his existence and his appointment are few indeed compared with the vast number of other types of crime where the biologist is of use." Pathologists, he concluded, were "ornamental passengers" and "entirely to be deprecated." TNA, HO 45/18112, James Webster to Arthur Dixon, November 3, 1937, 1–2, 1, 2.

31. By 1932, Simpson was senior demonstrator in Guy's Hospital's pathology department; from 1934 he was its supervisor of medico-legal post-mortems, and in 1937 he was appointed medico-legal adviser to Surrey Constabulary. For a biographical summary, see Elisabeth A. Cawthon, "Simpson, Cedric Keith (1907–1985)," *Oxford Dictionary of National Biography* (Oxford University Press, 2004), http://www.oxforddnb.com/view/article/31688.

32. Keith Simpson, *Forty Years of Murder* (London: Granada, 1980), 30. Simpson made critical comments about other notable predecessors: Roche Lynch, he wrote, was a fine chemist but was "persuaded disastrously to undertake glass, hair, fibres, dust and blood-grouping work of which he had no experience whatever"; the pathologist Davidson was a failure at Hendon—it was only when the botanist Holden took over that it had a director able to "put the laboratory on its feet" (33).

33. Keith Simpson, "The Changing Face of Forensic Medicine, 1930–1960," *Guy's Hospital Reports* 122, no. 3 (1963): 338–44, 338–39.

34. Ibid., 341.

35. Keith Simpson, *Forensic Medicine* (London: Edward Arnold, 1947), 2.

36. Alfred Swaine Taylor, *The Principles and Practice of Medical Jurisprudence* (London: John Churchill & Sons, 1865), xxiii.

37. Simpson, *Forensic Medicine*, 204. In his 1961 edition Simpson draws a still clearer contrast between the modern medical observer and Spilsbury's "detective" image: "He is not called as a sleuth and should not interfere with the police in their search for evidence—in rifled desks, jemmy marks, finger-prints, even the more sensational colour that marks some crimes. . . . During his examination of the body and its immediate surroundings the doctor must be careful to avoid disturbing things" (210–11).

38. A. K. Mant, "The Pathologist's Role and Modern Scientific Techniques at the Scene of the Crime," in Mant, ed., *Modern Trends in Forensic Medicine*, 3rd ed. (London: Butterworths, 1973), 93. Mant's reference to "sacred space" of the crime scene was taken from a 1960 article in the *Journal of Forensic Medicine*.

39. Ibid., 95.

40. Ibid., 95, 98–99.

41. Ibid., 98–99.

42. Francis Camps, *Recent Advances in Forensic Pathology* (London: J & A Churchill, 1969), 1.

43. Keith Simpson, "Autopsy Procedure," *Police Journal* 40 (1967): 263–66, 266.

44. Francis Camps and Richard Barber, *The Investigation of Murder* (London: Scientific Book Club, 1966), 75, emphasis original.

45. Francis Camps, ed., *Gradwohl's Legal Medicine*, 2nd ed. (Bristol: John Wright & Sons, 1968), ix. Camps's preface singles out the importance of trace evidence as an example of the extended remit for the forensic pathologist and his need to engage in a multidisciplinary and team-driven approach: "In order to show the potential breadth of the subject, I have deliberately introduced short annotations on the identification of fibres, inks, and other physical examinations which may be associated with trace evidence, to underline, thereby, the importance of team-work" (ix). The increased significance and technical demands of trace evidence is also acknowledged by Simpson in his 1953 edited volume entitled *Modern Trends in Forensic Medicine*, which contains a forty-page, highly technical review of "physical aids in criminal science" written by the Guy's medical physicist C. B. Allsopp.

46. Keith Simpson, "Developments in the Practice of Forensic Medicine," *Police Journal* 43 (1970): 267–70, 270.

47. Some of Spilsbury's cases had been written up during his lifetime, but not by him. In the 1920s, a newspaper's attempts to serialize his exploits were thwarted by a successful legal challenge by Spilsbury. In the next decade Spilsbury appears to have relented: in 1933–34, the *Sunday Pictorial* ran a series, "Death in the Lens: The Cases of Sir Bernard Spilsbury, as Told to Harold Dearden." Following Spilsbury's suicide, the Dearden series was published as *Death under the Microscope: Some Cases of Sir Bernard Spilsbury and Others* (London: Hutchinson, 1948).

48. Many of these would later form Simpson's core repertoire of "classic" cases, which he would then retread for other media purposes—notably for his best-selling 1980 autobiography *Forty Years of Murder*.

49. Keith Simpson, "*R v. Dobkin*: The Baptist Church Cellar Murder," *Police Journal* 16 (1943): 270–80, 270.

50. Keith Simpson and Eric Gardner, "The Godalming Wigwam Girl Murder," *Police Journal* 17 (1944): 212–20, 212.

51. Simpson's collection of scene drawings of course also stands out in stark contrast to its absence in the equivalent Spilsbury archive, as noted in ch. 5, n7. We are grateful to Bill Edwards, curator of the Gordon Museum of Pathology at Guy's Hospital, for allowing us to consult and reproduce material contained in the Simpson archive, and for sharing with us his considerable knowledge of Simpson's life and career and of Simpson's place in forensic medicine and science more generally.

52. Haigh, quoted in Keith Simpson, "The Acid-Bath Murder(s): *Rex v. John George Haigh*," *Police Journal* 23 (1950): 190–202, 194.

53. "Six 'Acid' Murders," *Daily Mail*, March 2, 1949, 1–2.

54. In an echo of Mrs. Bainbridge's cameo role at the Crumbles as Spilsbury's shrouded shadow, press accounts of Simpson's and Camps's visits to crime scenes at times featured them accompanied by female secretaries. But in contrast to Bainbridge, their role as members of the pathologist's "team" who actively engage with the rigors of crime scene work is clear. Simpson's first secretary, Molly Lefebure, will be recognizable to some readers as the author of a memoir that served as the basis for the 2013 ITV series *Murder on the Home Front*. As far as we have been able to discern, however, it was Simpson's second secretary (and future wife) Jean Scott Dunn who received the most contemporary comment. Under the headline "Jean, 27, Goes to Murders: It's Her Job," for example, the July 1, 1947, edition of the *Daily Mirror* carried a photograph of Dunn, five steps behind Simpson and carrying a notebook, leaving a house in Forrest Gate that had been the scene of an axe murder: "For twenty

minutes yesterday an attractive auburn-haired girl of twenty-six in a smart green suit stood beside the mutilated body of a woman, taking notes. . . . Whenever Dr. Simpson is called in by the police to make on-the-spot inquiries at a suspected murder or suicide the girl—his secretary Miss Jean Dunn—goes with him. . . . Her coolness has surprised hardened detectives; often she has to be present after gruesome killings" (1).

55. "40 Years of Murder," *Horizon*, September 16, 1977.

56. These were published in the *Medico-Legal Journal* in its 1949 and 1951 volumes. On completing his studies at Guy's Hospital in 1928, Camps initially joined an Essex-based general practice, but in 1935 he took a position as pathologist at the Chelmsford and Essex Hospital, and it was in this position that he began his forensic work. After the war, Camps began to lecture in the subject at the London Hospital, where he was eventually appointed as a lecturer in 1953 and a professor ten years later. For biographical background, see J. M. Cameron, "Camps, Francis Edward (1905–1972)," rev. K. D. Watson, *Oxford Dictionary of National Biography* (Oxford University Press, 2004), May 2010, http://www.oxforddnb.com/view/article/30896; and Robert Jackson, *Francis Camps: Famous Cases of the Most Celebrated Pathologist of Our Time* (London: Granada, 1975).

57. The Camps archive at the London Hospital contains documents relating to this publication, including a pointed refusal on the part of the US publisher Walker and Company to consider an American imprint despite Camps's promise to make it more interesting by including additional celebrated cases. London Hospital Archives, PP/CAM/2, letter from Edward L. Burlingame, October 16, 1965. His attempt to interest the BBC in his account of the notorious Setty case (*R v. Hume*) was similarly unsuccessful. Nevertheless, his efforts were not wholly unrewarded, as he made occasional appearances on radio and television and as a newspaper columnist in the 1960s and 1970s.

58. This was a genre with precedent: the celebrated Ruxton case (1936) had been written up by its lead forensic investigators, the Scottish pair of John Glaister and J. C. Brash. John Glaister and J. C. Brash, *The Medico-legal Aspects of the Ruxton Case* (Edinburgh: E. & S. Livingstone, 1937)

59. H. S. Holden and F. E. Camps, "Some Notes on the Examination of a Human Skeleton Found off the Essex Coast," *Police Journal* 24 (1951): 104–6, 104.

60. Ibid.

61. Ibid., 105.

62. Ibid., 106.

63. Ibid.

64. H. S. Holden and F. E. Camps, "The Investigation of Some Human Remains Found at Fingringhoe," *Police Journal* 25 (1952): 173–80.

65. Ibid., 175.

66. Ibid., 179.

67. Ibid.

68. Ibid., 180.

69. Ibid.

CHAPTER 7: INTERROGATING "THE HOUSE OF MURDER"

1. "The House of Murder," *Daily Mirror*, March 26, 1953, 1.

2. The John Christie murders have a very threadbare historiography, which is dominated by sensationalism. See, for example, J. Eddowes, *Two Killers of Rillington Place*

(London: Little, Brown, 1994); E. F. Gammon, *A Place to Remember: 10 Rillington Place* (Ciren-cester, UK: Memoirs, 2012); E. Marsten, *John Christie* (London: Bloomsbury, 2007); J. Oates, *John Christie of Rillington Place: Biography of a Serial Killer* (Barnsley: Wharncliffe Books, 2012); and N. Root, *Frenzy! How the Tabloid Press Turned Three Evil Serial Killers into Celebrities* (London: Preface, 2012). The best analysis of the Rillington Place murders to date has been produced by Frank Mort, who uses the Christie case to examine cultural, moral, racial, and class concerns and the social geography of postwar London. Frank Mort, *Capital Affairs: London and the Making of the Permissive Society* (New Haven: Yale University Press, 2010). Emma Jones and Neil Pemberton have used the Christie case to explore the social, cultural, and political history of backstreet abortion in modern Britain. In particular, they focus on how and why representations of Christie as backstreet abortionist gained traction in the 1960s, rather than in the period of the discovery of his victims' bodies and his subsequent conviction. Emma L. Jones and Neil Pemberton, "Ten Rillington Place and the Changing Politics of Abortion in Modern Britain," *Historical Journal* 57 (2014): 1085–109.

3. "Now a Sixth Body . . . a Seventh . . . Maybe an Eighth," *Daily Sketch and Daily Graphic*, March 30, 1953, 3.

4. "The Murder Belt," *Evening Standard*, April 13, 1953, 11. References to the furnace evoked the horrors of the Second World War, as did reports that Christie had turned his flat into an efficient "death house," converting its kitchen into a gas chamber and its garden into a sinister makeshift crematorium.

5. "Notting Hill: Fifth Woman Found," *News of the World*, March 28, 1953.

6. "Now a Sixth Body," 3.

7. "Notting Hill: Fifth Woman Found," *Evening Standard*, March 28, 1953, 1.

8. "Police Break Up Chimney of Death House," *Evening Standard*, April 7, 1953, 7.

9. Francis E. Camps, *Medical and Scientific Investigations in the Christie Case* (London: Medical Publications, 1953), 3.

10. For more detail on Percy Law's crime scene photography, see the National Archives, Kew (hereafter, TNA), CAB 143/13, "R v. John Reginald Halliday Christie: Trial Transcripts from Shorthand Notes," vol. 1, 14–19.

11. The history of forensic photography has been dominated by accounts of Alphonse Bertillon's application of photography to criminal identification and its role and integration into his larger bureaucratic-statistical apparatus, which note how the camera represented only one part of the archival practices underpinning his system of anthropometric identification. See Alan Sekula, "The Body and the Archive," *October* 39 (1986), 3–64. Teresa Castro has expertly analyzed Bertillon's extension of this methodology to crime scene photography, which was designed to situate persons and objects of evidence within a metric screen that preserved critical information about the contours of the space (depth, scale) and its contents. Teresa Castro, "Scènes du crime: La mobilisation de la photographie métrique par Alphonse Bertillon," in Pierre Piazza, ed., *Aux origines de la police scientifique: Alphone Bertillon, précurseur de la science du crime* (Paris: Karthala, 2011). In our earlier published work on Hans Gross, we explore how his observations on photography dovetailed with his overall vision of CSI and, taking his lead from psychological and philosophical discussions about the nature of perception, refused a simple equation of photograph and truthful reproduction. For Gross, in photography, as in all matters of crime scene investigation, seeing effectively required disciplined self-awareness that cannot be achieved through mechanical means alone. Ian Burney and Neil Pemberton, "Making Space for Criminalistics: Hans Gross and

Fin-de-Siècle CSI," *Studies in History and Philosophy of Science Part C: Studies in History and Philosophy of Biological and Biomedical Sciences* 44, no. 1 (2013): 23–24.

12. Camps, *Medical and Scientific Investigations*, 25.

13. Ibid., 24.

14. Nickolls sets out his views on the role of the forensic laboratory in the detection of crime in his textbook, Lewis Nickolls, *The Scientific Investigation of Crime* (London: Butterworth, 1956).

15. Camps, *Medical and Scientific Investigations*, 25. Camps uses the point concerning the consultation with a radiologist to emphasize the importance of consultative expertise: the discrepancy "underlined the importance of radiological facilities and the opinion of an expert radiologist" (33).

16. Ibid., 35.

17. Ibid., 38.

18. A copy of H. A. Dade's report can be found in the appendix of Camps's *Medical and Scientific Investigations*, 222–24, 222.

19. Here Camps drew upon histological work carried out by Dr. A. C. Hunt, a summary of which is included in the appendix of *Medical and Scientific Investigations*, 217–22.

20. Lewis Nickolls, "The Laboratory Investigations," in Camps, *Medical and Scientific Investigations*, 43.

21. Ibid., 44–45.

22. Nickolls summarizes this previous line of reasoning: "It is obvious, however, that the comparatively rapid degeneration and loss of spermatozoa from the vagina of the living female, which is found in investigations of cases of rape and unlawful carnal knowledge, is influenced by natural secretions and drainage, together with the more rapid bacterial action due to temperature." Nickolls, "Laboratory Investigations," in Camps, *Medical and Scientific Investigations*, 45.

23. Ibid.

24. Ibid.

25. Ibid.

26. Peter Cull, "The Murders in Rillington Place—a Personal Recollection," *Journal of Audiovisual Media in Medicine* 16, no. 4 (1993): 149–57, 157, 153.

27. Nickolls, "Laboratory Investigations," in Camps, *Medical and Scientific Investigations*, 46.

28. Our description and analysis of the garden excavation draws upon a range of documentary evidence. TNA, MEPO 2/9535, Francis Camps, "Report upon Bones and Material Recovered from Garden of 10 Rillington Place" (undated); TNA, MEPO 2/9535, Lewis Nickolls, "Report on the Bones in the Garden of 10 Rillington Place Excavation."

29. Cull, "Murders in Rillington Place," 155.

30. Ibid.

31. Richard J. Harrison, "Examination of the Bones from the Garden," in Camps, *Medical and Scientific Investigations*, 66.

32. Nickolls, "Laboratory Investigations," in Camps, *Medical and Scientific Investigations*, 46.

33. Ibid., 2.

34. TNA, MEPO 2/9535, Nickolls, "Continued Report on the Examination of Articles in Connection with Woman No. 4 and the Property of Christie," April 15, 1953, 3.

35. Ibid.

36. "*R v. Christie*: Trial Transcripts," vol. 2, 82.

37. For strategic reasons, the prosecution had decided to proceed with the charge of murder of Geraldine rather than with that of Beryl. If the prosecution had proceeded with the murder of Beryl, no evidence would have been allowed in respect to the death of Geraldine. This situation would have created the opportunity for Timothy Evans's defense lawyers to enter a plea of provocation and seek a manslaughter verdict. To thwart this, the prosecution instead proceeded on the murder of Geraldine: her death, they argued, could not be understood without exploring the circumstances of her mother's death and, fortunately for them, the judge agreed that the two murders were part of the same transaction. TNA, CAB 143/11, "*R v. John Timothy Evans*": Trial Transcripts from Shorthand Notes.

38. "Christie's Advisors Stand by for Exhumation," *News of the World*, May 17, 1953, 1.

39. Ibid.

40. "Behind a Canvas Screen a Woman Is Exhumed," *Evening Standard*, May 18, 1953, 2.

41. Ibid.

42. For a list of all the attendance of the exhumation and the post-mortem, see TNA, MEPO 2/9535, Francis Camps, "Report upon Exhumation and Examination of the Body of Beryl Evans," 1.

43. TNA, MEPO 2/9535, samples taken at Kensington Mortuary on 18th May, 1953, and handed to Mr. Nickolls, director of the Metropolitan Police Laboratory in the presence of Detective Chief Inspector Griffin, and Dr. Keith Simpson.

44. Camps, "Exhumation of Beryl Evans," in Camps, *Medical and Scientific Examinations*, 139.

45. TNA, MEPO 2/9535, statement of Lewis Charles Nickolls, director of Metropolitan Police Laboratory on exhumation, May 27, 1953, 2. In his exhumation report, Francis Camps made a similar point: "Material which might offer the possibility of showing the presence of carbon monoxide was also taken as requested by defense representatives but post-mortem change is so [extensive that] the possibility of any such identification [is] unlikely." TNA, MEPO 2/9535, Francis Camps, "Report upon Exhumation and Examination of the Body of Beryl Evans," 4.

46. TNA, MEPO 2/9535, statement of Lewis Charles Nickolls, director of Metropolitan Police Laboratory on exhumation, May 27, 1953, 2.

47. Ibid.

48. TNA, MEPO 2/9535, "Further Report—*R v. Christie*: Statement of Lewis Charles Nickolls, Director of Metropolitan Police Laboratory on Exhumation," June 5, 1953, 1.

49. Ibid.

50. Under cross-examination by the defense attorney during his trial, Christie described his killing spree in Rillington Place but also his role in Beryl Evans's death, explaining to the courtroom that he had helped her to commit suicide. He recalled how he had discovered Evans lying unconscious on a mattress in front of the fireplace and, detecting a "terrible smell of gas," opened the window in an attempt to avoid an explosion. According to Christie, when she had come around, she asked him to help her and, in return, "she offered intimacy," though he did not pursue this because of his back pain. He then took a piece of gas tubing, which he held to her face, and when she was unconscious, he strangled her. "*R v. Christie*: Trial Transcripts," vol. 2, 106.

51. Ibid., 205.

52. TNA TS 58/851, evidence of John Christie, transcripts of evidence of witnesses to the private inquiry to Scott Henderson, QC into the deaths of Beryl Evans and Geraldine Evans, 5.

53. Home Office, *Report of an Inquiry into Certain Matters arising out of the Deaths of Mrs. Beryl Evans of Geraldine Evans and out of the Conviction of Timothy John Evans of the Murder of Geraldine Evans*, Cmnd. 8896 (London: HMSO, 1952–53), 18.

54. Ibid., 19.

55. Camps, *Medical and Scientific Investigations*, xix.

56. The attorney general continued, "This remarkable story provides a concrete example of the part which modern science can play in the detection, and thus, it may be hoped, in the prevention of crime." Camps, *Medical and Scientific Investigations*, xv.

57. See list under "The Investigators," Camps, *Medical and Scientific Investigations*, xxii–xxiii.

58. Camps, *Medical and Scientific Investigations*, xx. Camps's volume includes chapters written by Nickolls (ch. 3, "The Laboratory Investigation"), Dr. Richard J. Harrison (ch. 4, "Examination of the Bones from the Garden"), Dr. Richard J. Harrison (ch. 5, "Examination of the Skeletons in respect of Sex, Age and Stature"), and Professor A. E. W. Miles and R. W. Fearnhead (ch. 6, "Examination of the Jaws and Teeth").

59. Camps, *Medical and Scientific Investigations*, xx.

60. Ibid., 164.

61. Ibid., 165–66.

62. Ibid., 166.

63. Ibid.

EPILOGUE

1. Michael J. Saks and Jonathan J. Koehler, "The Coming Paradigm Shift in Forensic Identification Science," *Science*, 309 (2005): 892–95, 895; Claude Roux, Benjamin Talbot-Wright, James Robertson, Frank Crispino, and Olivier Ribaux, "The End of the (Forensic Science) World as We Know It? The Example of Trace Evidence," *Philosophical Transactions of the Royal Society B* 370 (2015): 1–8, 3.

2. For a more detailed account of the complex interweaving of abortion and the Christie and Evans cases, see Emma L. Jones and Neil Pemberton, "Ten Rillington Place and the Changing Politics of Abortion in Modern Britain," *Historical Journal*, 57 (2014): 1085–109.

3. Ludovic Kennedy, *Ten Rillington Place* (London: Victor Gollancz, 1961). Kennedy had already engaged the issue of wrongful conviction by writing a play, performed in London's West End, that questioned the legitimacy of the execution of nineteen-year-old Derek Bentley for the 1952 murder of a policeman. He subsequently took his crusading credentials to the electorate, standing as Liberal candidate in 1958 and again in 1959. For an outline of Kennedy's life and work, see Will Wyatt, "Kennedy, Sir Ludovic Henry Coverley (1919–2009)," *Oxford Dictionary of National Biography* (Oxford University Press, January 2013), accessed August 13, 2015, http://www.oxforddnb.com/view/article/101900. See also his autobiography, *On My Way to the Club* (London: Argo, 1994).

4. In 1955 the lawyer Michael Eddows published the first influential book on the Evans-Christie cases, *A Man on Your Conscience: An Investigation of the Evans Murder Trial* (London: Cassell, 1955).

5. Kennedy, *Ten Rillington Place*, 21.

6. Ibid., 65.

7. Ibid., 137.

8. Ibid., 137.

9. Ibid., 138.

10. Ibid., 240.

11. The quotes in this paragraph are all taken from Teare's evidence before the 1965 Brabin inquiry, where he recounted his *Sunday Times* exchange with Kennedy. National Archives, Kew (hereafter, TNA), CAB 143/32, 469–73.

12. Ibid.

13. Ibid.

14. 642 Parl. Deb., H.C. (5th ser.) (June 15, 1961) col. 656.

15. Ibid., col. 708.

16. "SHUT IN at no. 10 Rillington Place," *Daily Mail*, July 29, 1965, 9.

17. Ibid.

18. John Grigg, "Legacy of Shame," *Guardian*, November 11, 1965, 18. The death penalty was permanently abolished in 1969. James B. Christophe's *Capital Punishment and British Politics: The British Movement to Abolish the Death Penalty 1947–57* (Chicago: University of Chicago Press, 1962) provides a brief discussion of the impact of the Evans and Christie cases for the ongoing abolitionist campaign. Lizzie Seal's *Capital Punishment in Twentieth Century Britain: Audience, Justice, Memory* (London: Routledge, 2014) provides a more recent analysis. See also Victor Bailey, "The Shadow of the Gallows: The Death Penalty and the British Labour Government, 1945–51," *Law and History Review* 18, no. 2 (2000): 305–49; and Bernard Carpenter, "A Punishment in Search of a Crime: Murder and the Death Penalty in Post-war Britain, 1945–1970" (PhD diss., Boston College, 2000).

19. TNA, CAB 143/47, Brabin inquiry, evidence of Ludovic Kennedy, 1439.

20. Ibid., 1440.

21. In light of its mandate to consider the possibility of Christie's culpability in the Evans murders, the Brabin inquiry questioned Camps and Nickolls closely on the full range of medical and scientific evidence that might establish a forensic link between Christie and Beryl Evans—evidence of carbon monoxide poisoning, semen traces and sexual assault, and pubic hair. In the process Camps and Nickolls shed fascinating new light on the nature of their investigations, but for our purposes what is crucial is that their original conclusions emerged intact.

22. TNA, CAB 143/37, Brabin inquiry, evidence of Donald Teare, 441.

23. Ibid., 443.

24. Ibid., 487.

25. Ibid., 488.

26. Home Office, *The Case of Timothy John Evans: Report of an Inquiry by the Hon. Mr. Justice Brabin*, Cmnd. 3101 (London: HMSO, 1966–67), 155.

27. Ibid., 153.

28. 734 Parl. Deb., H.C. (5th ser.) (October 18, 1966) col. 38.

29. Cited in Harold Evans, *My Paper Chase: True Stories of Vanished Times: An Autobiography* (London: Little, Brown, 2009), 297.

30. In a 2007 National Film Theatre interview, Richard Attenborough pointed to the threat to this newfound liberation as the primary motivation for those involved in making the film. Declaring himself and other key figures—including Kennedy, the agent and producer

Leslie Linder, and the *Sunday Times* editor Harry Evans—"passionately opposed to capital punishment," he recalled that the urgency of bringing this story about the execution of an innocent man stemmed from the need to thwart the plans of a conservative MP to introduce a bill to reinstate capital punishment. He went on to describe his repulsion at playing the part of Christie, recalling that when he went home to his family he "almost felt unclean." Still, he concluded it was worth it, as the film "did have an impact. It did add to the anti-capital punishment lobby and to that extent I feel proud to have done it." The interview transcript is reproduced as a BFI blog, http://bfi-features.blogspot.co.uk/2007/01/richard-attenborough-richard.html, accessed August 17, 2015.

Index

media (cont.)
  93–94; and the Rillington Place murders, 153,
    155–59
Medical and Scientific Investigations in the Christie
  Case (Camps), 179–83
medical experts, 27–31; Guy's model of, 42–43;
  Spilsbury's model of, 60–62, 70–75; Taylor's
  model of, 44–45. See also forensic pathologists
Medical Witnesses Act (1836), 41–42
Medico-Legal Society, 127, 128–29, 130,
  135
medico-legal textbooks, and crime scene
  investigation, 41–48, 53
Methods and Aims in Archaeology (Petrie), 36
microscopy: in detective fiction, 58; importance
  of, 28–29, 31. See also dust; hair analysis
Mitchell, C. Ainsworth, 52, 108
mold growth, and the Rillington Place murders,
  166–67
Mort, Frank, 225n2
Munro, Irene, 212–13n7
Münsterberg, Hugo, 15
murder bag, 8, 212n46; origins of, 76–79. See also
  crime scene kit bag
murder tourism, 215–16n45; at the Crumbles
  bungalow, 95–97, 213n13, 216n54

National Medico-Legal Institute, 126–30
Nelson, Rita, 164
Nickolls, Lewis, 136; as investigator in the
  murder of Beryl Evans, 176–77; and the
  Rillington Place murders, 158–59, 164–65,
  167–70, 171–73, 176–78, 179, 192, 229n21
Nottingham Police Laboratory, 121–25

Parisot, Pierre, 37–38
Parson, Tony, 212n46
pathologists. See forensic pathologists
Pepper, Augustus, 60, 61
perception, psychophysiology of, 14–17
Petrie, Flinders, 35, 36, 205n78
photography, as used in crime scene investiga-
  tion, 160–63, 225n11
Pitt-Rivers, Augustus, 35
Poe, Edgar Allan, 53, 208n37
Police Code and Manual of the Criminal Law
  (Vincent), 39–40
Police Journal, 107–10, 142

Policiers de roman et policiers de laboratoire
  (Locard), 53
Popkess, Athelstan, 121–23
Popp, Georg, 37, 106
post-mortems, 61; in the Crumbles investigation, 66–70; in the Rillington Place
  investigation, 162–70
preconceived theories, dangers of, 15–17, 18
press coverage. See media
Principles and Practice of Medical Jurisprudence
  (Taylor), 43–48

Recent Advances in Forensic Pathology, 138–39
Richardson, J. Hall, 50
Rillington Place murders: abortion as issue in,
  185–89, 195, 225n2; botanical evidence relating
  to, 170; Camps as investigator of, 148, 153, 154,
  157–58, 160–61, 165–67, 170, 179–83, 192–94,
  229n21; and Camps's autopsy findings, 162–64,
  165–67; carbon monoxide evidence relating to,
  165–66, 176, 181–82; crime scene security at,
  156–57; death penalty as issue in, 179, 181, 192;
  demolition of site of, 195–96; as depicted in
  book and film, 186–91, 194–96; forensic
  archeology involved in, 168–70; forensic
  teamwork in, 152–54, 158, 160, 173, 180; hair as
  evidence in, 174, 176–78; mold as evidence in,
  166–67; necrophilia as issue in, 168, 189–93;
  photographic documentation of, 160–63;
  post-mortem investigation relating to, 162–64;
  press coverage of, 153, 155–59; and renaming
  of street, 189; semen as evidence in, 167–68,
  171, 173
Roux, Claude, 5
R v. Brittle, 141
R v. Christie, 3
R v. Mahon. See Crumbles, murder investigation
  at the

Saler, Michael, 214n23
Salter, George, 159
Savage, Chief Inspector, 65–66, 71, 75–76, 77, 84,
  85
Sayers, Dorothy, 209n42
Scientific Aids to Criminal Investigation, 125
Scott, Sir Robert, 129, 131
Scott Henderson, John, inquiry conducted by,
  178–79, 181, 188